Edited by Thomas K. Johnson and William S. Barker

The Decalogue Project

World of Theology Series

Published by the Theological Commission of the World Evangelical Alliance

Volume 24

Vol 1   Thomas K. Johnson: The First Step in Missions Training: How our Neighbors are Wrestling with God's General Revelation
Vol 2   Thomas K. Johnson: Christian Ethics in Secular Cultures, Vol. 1
Vol 3   David Parker: Discerning the Obedience of Faith: A Short History of the World Evangelical Alliance Theological Commission
Vol 4   Thomas Schirrmacher (Ed.): William Carey: Theologian – Linguist – Social Reformer
Vol 5   Thomas Schirrmacher: Advocate of Love – Martin Bucer as Theologian and Pastor
Vol 6   Thomas Schirrmacher: Culture of Shame / Culture of Guilt
Vol 7   Thomas Schirrmacher: The Koran and the Bible
Vol 8   Thomas Schirrmacher (Ed.): The Humanisation of Slavery in the Old Testament
Vol 9   Jim Harries: New Foundations for Appreciating Africa: Beyond Religious and Secular Deceptions
Vol 10 Thomas Schirrmacher: Missio Dei – God's Missional Nature
Vol 11 Thomas Schirrmacher: Biblical Foundations for 21st Century World Mission
Vol 12 William Wagner, Mark Wagner: Can Evangelicals Truly Change the World? How Seven Philosophical and Religious Movements Are Growing
Vol 13 Thomas Schirrmacher: Modern Fathers
Vol 14 Jim Harries: Jarida juu ya Maisha ya MwAfrika katika huduma ya Ukristo
Vol 15 Peter Lawrence: Fellow Travellers – A Comparative Study on the Identity Formation of Jesus Followers from Jewish, Christian and Muslim Backgrounds in The Holy Land
Vol 16 William Wagner: From Classroom Dummy to University President – Serving God in the Land of Sound of Music
Vol 17 Thomas K. Johnson, David Parker, Thomas Schirrmacher (ed.): In the Name of the Father, Son, and Holy Spirit – Teaching the Trinity from the Creeds to Modern Discussion
Vol 18 Mark Wagner and William Wagner (Ed.): Halfway Up the Mountain
Vol 19 Thomas K. Johnson: The Protester, the Dissident, and the Christian – Essays on Human Rights and Religion
Vol 20 Thomas K. Johnson: Humanitarian Islam, Evangelical Christianity, and the Clash of Civilizations
Vol 21 Thomas K. Johnson: Christian Ethics in Secular Cultures, Vol. 2
Vol 22 Reuben van Rensburg, Thomas Schirrmacher (Ed.): "Be Focused ... Use Common Sense ... Overcome Excuses and Stupidity ..." Festschrift in Honor of Dr. Manfred Waldemar Kohl
Vol 23 John W. Ewing. Goodly Fellowship – A Centenary Tribute to the Life and Work of the World's Evangelical Alliance 1846–1946
Vol 24 Thomas K. Johnson, William S. Barker (Ed.): The Decalogue Project – Disciples from Six Continents Engage God's Ten Commandments
Vol 25 Hannes Wiher: Holistic Mission – An Historical and Theological Study of Its Development, 1966–2011

Edited by Thomas K. Johnson
and William S. Barker

The Decalogue Project
Disciples from Six Continents
Engage God's Ten Commandments

WIPF & STOCK · Eugene, Oregon

Wipf and Stock Publishers
199 W 8th Ave, Suite 3
Eugene, OR 97401

The Decalogue Project
Disciples from Six Continents Engage God's Ten Commandments
By Johnson, Thomas K.
Copyright © 2022 Verlag für Kultur und Wissenschaft All rights reserved.
Softcover ISBN-13: 978-1-6667-8000-0
Hardcover ISBN-13: 978-1-6667-8001-7
Publication date 5/9/2023
Previously published by Verlag für Kultur und Wissenschaft, 2022

Contents

The Decalogue Project
Discipleship and the Blessing of Meditating on God's Law 7
   Thomas K. Johnson, United States and Czech Republic

Written in Stone 11
   Thomas K. Johnson, United States and Czech Republic

The Ten Commandments: Given by God? 23
   Pierre Berthoud, France

Are the Ten Commandments Still Valid? 45
   Risimati S. Hobyane, Republic of South Africa

The Relation between Biblical Law and Christian Faith 53
   Glenn N. Davies, Australia

God's Commandments Require Us to Read and Think Carefully 65
   Thomas Schirrmacher, Germany

The First Commandment:
You Shall Have No Other Gods before Me 75
   David Zadok, Israel

The Second Commandment:
You Shall Not Make for Yourself a Carved Image 87
   Robert Norris, United States

The Third Commandment:
You Shall Not Misuse the Name of God 99
   Kin Yip Louie, Hong Kong

The Fourth Commandment:
Sabbath and Shalom 113
   Fergus MacDonald, Scotland

The Fifth Commandment:
"Parents Are Valleys for Quenching the Fires of Life" 131
   John P. Wilson, Australia

The Sixth Commandment:
You Shall Not Murder – Crying Out for the Outcast 145
   Leah Farish, United States

God Hates Murder More Than You Hate Murder 167
   Thomas K. Johnson, United States and Czech Republic

The Seventh Commandment:
You Shall Not Commit Adultery 177
    Diane Langberg, United States

The Eighth Commandment:
You Shall Not Steal 191
    Andrew McGowan, Scotland

The Ninth Commandment:
You Shall Not Bear False Witness against Your Neighbor 203
    Samuel Logan, United States

The Tenth Commandment:
You Shall Not Set Your Desire 219
    Davi Charles Gomes, Brazil

Afterword
Our Obedience Praises and Delights the Lord 231
    Samuel Logan, United States

Appendices 235
Sign and Countersign: The Battle against Pornography in the Church .. 237
    Daniel Weiss, United States

Abortion in the United States after June 24, 2022 247
    Leah Farish, United States

Homosexuality and the Commandments 251
    The Editors

Scripture Index 255
Contributors 261
    Listed Alphabetically by Surname

The Decalogue Project

Discipleship and the Blessing of Meditating on God's Law

Thomas K. Johnson, United States and Czech Republic

Psalm 1 begins:

> Blessed is the man
> who walks not in the counsel of the wicked,
> nor stands in the way of sinners,
> nor sits in the seat of scoffers;
> but his delight is in the law of the Lord,
> and on his law he meditates day and night.[1]

Our team of scholars from six continents has invested thousands of hours meditating on God's law on behalf of the millions of members of the body of Christ. We have not done this instead of your efforts but rather to stir you up to join us in our meditation. Our meditation on God's law is an organic component of our discipleship to Jesus Christ, to whom we belong.

The Hebrew word translated "law" in this Psalm is *Torah*, which sometimes refers to the five books of Moses (Genesis, Exodus, Leviticus, Numbers, and Deuteronomy), sometimes refers to the comprehensive teaching found in the Old Testament, and sometimes refers especially to the Ten Commandments as a focal point of Old Testament teaching. In this book we are especially meditating on God's law as the Ten Commandments, though keeping in mind the comprehensive teaching about God, humanity, and salvation found in the entire Bible.

When Jesus was about to ascend to the Father, He told His disciples, "All authority in heaven and on earth has been given to me. Go therefore and make disciples of all nations, baptizing them in the name of the Father and of the Son and of the Holy Spirit, teaching them to observe all that I have commanded you. And behold, I am with you always, to the end of the age" (Matthew 28:18-20). This commission is comprehensive in multiple ways, not only in our destination, "*all* nations," or in the mention of *all* three Persons of God our Sender, "Father, Son, and Holy Spirit," but also in the

---

[1] Psalm 1:1-2. The Holy Bible, English Standard Version (ESV), (Wheaton, IL: Crossway Bibles, 2001). Throughout this book, Scripture is quoted from the ESV unless otherwise indicated.

command to "teach them to observe *all* that I have commanded you." The comprehensive way of faith and life into which Jesus wants us to disciple all nations builds on the Old Testament Torah, the comprehensive teaching about God, humanity, and life. Discipleship requires meditating on God's law, delighting in God's law.

Biblically informed meditation is, I believe, quite different from the types of meditation that expect people to empty their minds. It is true that, while meditating before God, our hearts may be emptied of fear and anxiety, but then our hearts should not be left emptied; our hearts may be filled with "the peace of God that surpasses all understanding" (Philippians 4:7). And in the next verse the apostle tells believers to think about or consider certain things. The peace of God does not lead to empty minds; it leads to thoughtfulness.

Biblical meditation or thoughtfulness includes three primary aspects: 1. The normative aspect, which includes a careful consideration of God-given norms (such as the Ten Commandments), along with the assumptions and expectations of those norms; 2. The situational aspect, which includes a careful consideration of the consequences of our choices (for which the book of Proverbs gives many illustrations); and 3. The existential aspect, which carefully considers the hearts of the people involved, questions about guilt and gratitude, faith or unbelief (for which biblical history gives many examples).[2]

Our authors who contributed to this volume have very naturally addressed these aspects of biblical thoughtfulness, according to their diverse spiritual gifts, without me asking them to do so. For example, Glenn Davies has provided a profound assessment of the relation between faith (in grace) and God's law, on the intersection of what I have called the normative and the existential aspects of biblical thoughtfulness. Robert Norris has very thoughtfully exposed the organic ties between idolatry and ideology, taking the normative commandment as a critique of our political situation, which is shaped by competing idolatrous ideologies. Diane Langberg has heard the heart-rending trauma of sexual abuse, too often at the hands of church leaders, from many clients in her office, driving into our minds the deep existential consequences of disobeying God's law.

As mentioned, our contributors come from different continents; they also have different callings (pastors, theology professors, church leaders,

---

[2] For more on this theme, see Thomas Schirrmacher, *Leadership and Ethical Responsibility: The Three Aspects of Every Decision*, The WEA Global Issues Series Volume 13 (Bonn: VKW, 2013); https://iirf.eu/site/assets/files/92916/wea_gis_13_-_thomas_schirrmacher_-_three_aspects_of_every_decision.pdf.

lawyer, clinical psychologist) and belong to different churches. I do not know the church memberships of them all, but I know they represent Presbyterian, Anglican, and Reformed churches (and perhaps other churches). What they have in common is truly believing orthodox Protestant beliefs, participating in churches that use historic Protestant confessions or catechisms, and see the Ten Commandments as crucial for Christians in our era. They were brought together by Samuel Logan, who has long served the World Reformed Fellowship.

The introductory essays in the first part of the book, and the expositions of each of the Ten Commandments in the later part of the book, along with the appendices at the end of the book develop (among many other things) these four principles regarding God's law:

1. The commandments relating to God (the first four) and the commandments relating to our fellow humans (the latter six), though distinguished, belong together. Our Lord Jesus, when asked which is the greatest commandment, said, "You shall love the LORD your God with all your heart and with all your soul and with all your mind. This is the great and first commandment. And a second is like it: You shall love your neighbor as yourself. On these two commandments depend all the Law and the Prophets" (Matthew 22:37-40).
2. The Ten Commandments represent a covenant relationship. They are introduced by God's statement: "I am the LORD your God, who brought you out of the land of Egypt, out of the house of slavery" (Exodus 20:2). Salvation by God's grace is the condition for keeping the laws, not the other way around. God never said: If you keep all the commandments, you will be My people.
3. Sinful actions come from the heart. This is why there are commandments forbidding invisible sin in our hearts as well as the acts coming from it – for example, "You shall not covet" – and as Jesus said about "You shall not commit adultery," "I say to you that everyone who looks at a woman with lustful intent has already committed adultery with her in his heart" (Matthew 5:28).
4. Negative language ("You shall not") is needed in all but two (the fourth and the fifth) of the Ten Commandments, because otherwise each commandment would have to state, in total, what we must do. Freedom is protected by declaring the boundaries but not spelling out detailed instructions. Each of us must actively consider, meditate on, what we should do in each area of responsibility. This is freedom within form.

I would invite you, as disciples and students who belong to Jesus, to join in the process of lifelong learning from our covenant God. Blessed are those who meditate on God's law!

Written in Stone

Thomas K. Johnson, United States and Czech Republic

> This is a revised version of a sermon based on Deuteronomy 5:1-33 (the Ten Commandments), preached on May 27, 2018, at the International Church of Prague, in the Czech Republic. The scripture reading follows the sermon introduction.

I first preached a long series of sermons on the Ten Commandments some thirty years ago when I was a young church-planting pastor, serving a new congregation. Then the Lord opened a special door for me to spend almost twenty years teaching philosophy, ethics, and religious history in secular universities, partly in the U.S., partly in the former Soviet Union, and then more than a decade in universities in Prague. Many of my classes were small, almost all fewer than 25 students, many fewer than 15 students, so I included a lot of discussion in my classrooms. I did not generally identify myself as a Christian at the beginning of the semester, but that was not necessary. I might be teaching about ancient Greek philosophy and see on their desks that students had printed sermons I had preached or my articles on Christian ethics and apologetics. Only a few of my students identified themselves as Christians; many regarded themselves as agnostic, atheist, or undecided, while a few identified themselves as Muslims.

I always tried to challenge my students to think very deeply, but I tried to be very gentle and to show respect as they wrestled with humanity's ultimate questions and talked openly about their concerns, convictions, and fears. One of the deepest compliments I received from students was that I, the Christian philosopher, was the one who taught them *how* to think, whereas their atheist professors taught them *what* to think. Part of what I received from hundreds of such gentle, respectful discussions was the privilege of looking inside their minds to see what they thought about the Christian faith and about Christian ethics. And I noticed some clear **patterns** of how my students thought about the matters that I hold dear. Some of these patterns had to do with the Ten Commandments, even if many students had never read the Bible. I will mention three such patterns.

1. Many students thought that biblical commandments are arbitrary and irrational, having no connection with human nature or human well-being, so that they do not contribute to human happiness. Though it was

seldom stated directly, many seemed to think that if one wants to be self-destructive and have a miserable life, one should simply follow these old-fashioned, irrational rules.

2. The second misinterpretation was that the main purpose of the Ten Commandments is to teach people how to earn God's favor. If you want to go to heaven, if you want to be sure you are accepted by God, you must keep the Commandments.

3. Many students would claim to be moral relativists, saying either that there are no universal moral rules or that we cannot know universal moral rules, but then be passionately committed to a few moral principles that were similar to some of the Ten Commandments. Once I taught a class on ancient texts on ethics and included the Ten Commandments in class discussion. I then told the students to look at only the last six, and I asked if they learned anything new by reading them. Most of the class of religiously agnostic moral relativists said they really did not learn much, because they already knew these moral principles. This is not what some Christians would expect. I then explained that many Christians have thought some of these principles were built into the human mind in creation, so it is impossible not to know some of them.

I would like us to try, together, to take a new look at the Ten Commandments to see what we will see. It is good, so far as possible, for us to read the Bible in community with other people who are reading the Bible; we always come to the Bible with expectations and assumptions that may be partly wrong, so we need input from each other. That is also why it is good, so far as possible, to learn how Christians in the past have understood key texts in the Bible; if we listen to them, our predecessors may prevent us from some misunderstandings.

The Ten Commandments[1]

Deuteronomy 5

And Moses summoned all Israel and said to them, "Hear, O Israel, the statutes and the rules that I speak in your hearing today, and you shall learn them and be careful to do them. ² The LORD our God made a covenant with us in Horeb. ³ Not with our fathers did the LORD make this covenant, but with us, who are all of us here alive today. ⁴ The LORD spoke with you face to face at the mountain, out of the midst of the fire, ⁵ while I stood between the LORD

---

[1] The report of the first official proclamation of the Ten Commandments is in Exodus 20. Earlier portions of Scripture show that God-fearing people were aware of most of these principles before they were written in stone.

and you at that time, to declare to you the word of the Lord. For you were afraid because of the fire, and you did not go up into the mountain. He said:

⁶ "'I am the Lord your God, who brought you out of the land of Egypt, out of the house of slavery.

⁷ "'You shall have no other gods before me.

⁸ "'You shall not make for yourself a carved image, or any likeness of anything that is in heaven above, or that is on the earth beneath, or that is in the water under the earth. ⁹ You shall not bow down to them or serve them; for I the Lord your God am a jealous God, visiting the iniquity of the fathers on the children to the third and fourth generation of those who hate me, ¹⁰ but showing steadfast love to thousands of those who love me and keep my commandments.

¹¹ "'You shall not take the name of the Lord your God in vain, for the Lord will not hold him guiltless who takes his name in vain.

¹² "'Observe the Sabbath day, to keep it holy, as the Lord your God commanded you. ¹³ Six days you shall labor and do all your work, ¹⁴ but the seventh day is a Sabbath to the Lord your God. On it you shall not do any work, you or your son or your daughter or your male servant or your female servant, or your ox or your donkey or any of your livestock, or the sojourner who is within your gates, that your male servant and your female servant may rest as well as you. ¹⁵ You shall remember that you were a slave in the land of Egypt, and the Lord your God brought you out from there with a mighty hand and an outstretched arm. Therefore, the Lord your God commanded you to keep the Sabbath day.

¹⁶ "'Honor your father and your mother, as the Lord your God commanded you, that your days may be long, and that it may go well with you in the land that the Lord your God is giving you.

¹⁷ "'You shall not murder.

¹⁸ "'And you shall not commit adultery.

¹⁹ "'And you shall not steal.

²⁰ "'And you shall not bear false witness against your neighbor.

²¹ "'And you shall not covet your neighbor's wife. And you shall not desire your neighbor's house, his field, or his male servant, or his female servant, his ox, or his donkey, or anything that is your neighbor's.'

²² "These words the Lord spoke to all your assembly at the mountain out of the midst of the fire, the cloud, and the thick darkness, with a loud voice; and he added no more. And he wrote them on two tablets of stone and gave them to me. ²³ And as soon as you heard the voice out of the midst of the darkness, while the mountain was burning with fire, you came near to me, all the heads of your tribes, and your elders. ²⁴ And you said, 'Behold, the Lord our God has shown us his glory and greatness, and we have heard his voice out of the midst of the fire. This day we have seen God speak with man, and man still live. ²⁵ Now therefore why should we die? For this great fire will consume us. If we hear the voice of the Lord our God any more, we shall

die. ²⁶ For who is there of all flesh, that has heard the voice of the living God speaking out of the midst of fire as we have, and has still lived? ²⁷ Go near and hear all that the Lord our God will say, and speak to us all that the Lord our God will speak to you, and we will hear and do it.'

²⁸ "And the LORD heard your words, when you spoke to me. And the LORD said to me, 'I have heard the words of this people, which they have spoken to you. They are right in all that they have spoken. ²⁹ Oh that they had such a heart as this always, to fear me and to keep all my commandments, that it might go well with them and with their descendants forever! ³⁰ Go and say to them, "Return to your tents." ³¹ But you, stand here by me, and I will tell you the whole commandment and the statutes and the rules that you shall teach them, that they may do them in the land that I am giving them to possess.' ³² You shall be careful therefore to do as the LORD your God has commanded you. You shall not turn aside to the right hand or to the left. ³³ You shall walk in all the way that the LORD your God has commanded you, that you may live, and that it may go well with you, and that you may live long in the land that you shall possess."

Thesis: Here is what I see in the preamble (verses 1 through 6) to the Ten Commandments:

God has declared His redemptive ownership of His people, giving us principles to live out His redemption in ways that are consistent with the norms He created into us.

Throughout the Old Testament we have several summaries of God's covenant with His people. These say, more or less, "I am your God, and you are My people." The preamble to the Ten Commandments is a long version of the covenant. It emphasizes that God owns us and that we belong to Him.

Of course, everything belongs to God. And by the great plagues which God sent upon Egypt before He brought His people out of Egypt, God was pointedly revealing that the earth belongs to God. It was specifically about the plague of hail that Moses said, in Exodus 9, that this happened "so you may know that the earth is the LORD's" (verse 29). And many of the plagues seem designed to communicate the same message, that the earth is the Lord's. But in the Ten Commandments, God is declaring His ownership of His people in a very different kind of way. God is declaring that He is not only their Creator, but that He is also their Redeemer, their Savior, and that they belong to Him as His specially redeemed people, as His community.

This is the response to people who suspect that God's commands are or ever were a way to earn God's favor or salvation. The Commandments never had that function. They were written in stone to provide an explicit foundation for the way of life of God's own community. We are at a much later point in the history of God's salvation. We live after the incarnation, death, resurrection, and ascension of Jesus, events that were far off the horizon in Moses' day. We have a much fuller revelation of God's undeserved grace, so we should never imagine the Commandments have anything to do with earning salvation or a place in heaven. But already in Moses' day, it was crystal clear that the commands of God were not to be used to earn God's favor. His people had just been saved from the house of bondage in Egypt.

The text we have read in Deuteronomy 5 is the second giving of the Ten Commandments. God first gave Israel the Ten Commandments some forty years before at Mount Sinai. The people here, in the second giving of the Law, were either children or had not yet been born during the first giving of the Law. Yet Moses spoke to them as if they had been adults at Mount Sinai; this was because they were, as a community, facing the existential choice of a lifetime as they were about to enter the promised land. Their choice would articulate their faith, way of life, identity, and destiny. They could say "yes," God specially loved and chose our ancestors and brought us out of Egypt, and therefore we will embrace the way of life He has given us. Or they could say "no" and thereby suffer the loss of everything that made them who they were as the people of God.

When we read the Ten Commandments, we face, I believe, the same existential choice faced by Israel some 3400 years ago. We can say "yes" not only to the Exodus but also to the gospel of Christ, and we acknowledge that the God who has saved us has made us His own possession, so that we know that we belong to God in Jesus Christ. And this God who has rescued us has also given us a way of life, a moral law that prescribes the meaning of our day-to-day lives. Or we can say "no" to the gospel and to the law of God, but if we say that, we are lost to wander in the meaningless desert of the post-modern world. So please, with me, say "yes!" to both the gospel and to the law of God.

Assuming that we all have said or will say "Yes!" both to the gospel of Christ and also to God's law, we need to think together. This is the hard work of faith seeking understanding. Let's get started!

When we read the Ten Commandments, we should keep in mind that the Bible itself distinguishes them from the rest of the Bible. We say that all the Bible is the Word of God, and it is; but only the Ten Commandments were delivered by God himself, in an audible voice, from Mount Sinai. Only the Ten Commandments were written in stone. It has been argued that being written in stone did not have exactly the same meaning that this image has today. Some say it was merely normal. In their day, very probably, all extremely important treaties were recorded on stone. But that really is the point: in their day, documents of extreme importance were written on stone; documents of lesser importance were written in some other way.

The Ten Commandments have an enduring character that some other commands in the Bible do not have. For example, in Deuteronomy 12:21 we read the command not to boil a calf in its mother's milk. This was probably a response to a pagan religious practice. If modern pagans revive that practice, we should not participate, but it is quite possible that command will never directly apply to any of us. So, too, in Deuteronomy 22:8 there is a command to build a railing around the roof of your house. This was related to the practice of using the roof as a patio. If any of us uses the roof as a patio, we should obey the command of God to build a safe railing, but that may never apply to some of us. The Ten Commandments are set apart within the Bible; they apply to all people everywhere. They are central to God; most of the other commands of God in the Bible seem to assume these major Ten.

In the main portion of this study, we shall look at each of the Ten Commandments. But before we do so, I want to ask what roles or functions God's standards should play in our lives. God has given us His law – what do we do with it? I believe the Ten Commandments should have at least three major functions in our lives. I did not figure this out on my own. Much of what I know on this topic came from reading Martin Luther and John Calvin some forty years ago.[2]

This is the way the question came up for Martin Luther. He spent his early years trying to earn salvation or to earn assurance of salvation. He was dreadfully afraid of God's wrath. After years of wrestling with the Bible, he became convinced that we are justified by faith alone. What a breakthrough! By trusting in the promise of God, that Jesus died and rose for us, Luther learned that we are united with Christ and stand before God clothed in Christ's righteousness. His righteousness is credited to me, while my guilt and shame are credited to Christ on the cross. Hallelujah! That is the gospel!

---

[2] For more of what I learned from Martin Luther and John Calvin see "Culturally Relevant Hermeneutics: A Return to the Reformation," Chapter 2 of Thomas K. Johnson, *Christian Ethics in Secular Cultures: Vol. 2: Culture, Hermeneutics, Natural Law, Islam, and Missions,* World of Theology Series Published by the Theological Commission of the World Evangelical Alliance (Bonn: VKW, 2022); https://www.academia.edu/74013380/Christian_Ethics_in_Secular_Cultures_vol_2_Culture_Hermeneutics_Natural_Law_Islam_Missions.

But then Luther faced more big questions. How does God want us to live? Should Luther continue to put a lot of emphasis on fasting, monasteries, chastity, pilgrimages, and indulgences? Or were God's priorities something different? What Luther learned was that:

I. The Ten Commandments, with the other commands of God in the Bible, provide the moral structure for a life pleasing to God, a life of worship to God.

By trusting in the gospel, we are justified before God; God's law teaches a way of life pleasing to God. We need to be reminded of the importance of distinguishing God's moral law from the gospel of salvation. I think Luther was right that this distinction tends to be forgotten, so we need always to talk about it.

If we want a key word to describe the way of life pleasing to God, I would choose the word *gratitude,* or *thankfulness.* It should be with gratitude for salvation that we embrace a way of life which is pleasing to God. In Romans 1:21, ingratitude for God's self-revelation and sustaining grace is seen as the root of a Godless way of life. It would be wise to say gratitude sets the direction and spirit of a life pleasing to God, a life of worship. I sometimes call this the "doxological use of God's law."

Some of us have surely traveled Luther's road, trying to earn God's favor or assurance of salvation by something we do. And we may have done some crazy things to try to gain that assurance. That is why it is so important to see and know that God's law was never given to be a way to earn salvation or assurance of salvation. It should be with gratitude for salvation that we embrace God's law as the moral structure for a life of worship to God.

There are a couple of things I should say at this point. The first is that the moral law and love for people go together like hand and glove. Sometimes people want to separate the moral law from love for others, but that is a mistake. When we look at the preamble, we see that loving God's law is to be a response to having been loved by God. And it is surely not loving to other people to bear false witness against them or to commit murder, robbery, or adultery.

The second is that God's moral law helps life to flourish. When I was a teenager, I spent what seemed like long hours wondering if God's moral law is destructive for us, a question very similar to what I heard from my students a generation later. Then I found 1 John 5:3, which says, "... his commandments are not burdensome." This echoes an Old Testament theme that we are to obey God, "that it may go well with you" (for example,

Deuteronomy 4:40 and 5:29). As a teenager, I accepted this principle by faith alone. But now, after half a century of study and travel, it is a matter of both faith and reason for me. When people embrace God's law with gratitude for salvation, His law tends to make life flourish. A main exception is when people are severely persecuted for their biblical faith.

There is a second use of God's moral law, which Luther also knew about.

II. God's moral law shows us our sin.

In Romans 3:20 we read, "... through the law comes knowledge of sin." If I drove down a city street at 200 kph, all sensible people would know I was doing something horribly wrong; I might kill someone. The official speed limits make the sin clearer, but the sin would be real even if there were no written speed limits. So, too, without the Ten Commandments, people are somewhat aware of sin, but the commandments make sin much clearer.

In fact, that may be one of the reasons so many of the commandments are phrased in the negative, "You shall not ..." With this phrasing, they stand as a protest against sin, a confrontation with our sin. It is assumed the reader will be doing some of these things, and he must be told to stop. The law points out and protests against our sinfulness.

In Christian history it is common to compare this use of God's law with a mirror. Some people may look into a mirror to see how "beautiful" they are. But generally, in history, Christians have thought we look into a mirror to see what is wrong with our appearance. So, too, we look into God's law to learn what is wrong with ourselves. You might say we get to know ourselves through God's law.

This may occur in different ways at different times in life. When we first come to faith, when we are converted, one of the things that has to happen is that we need to recognize that we are sinful. And we recognize our own sin by God's law.

A step in this process of being convinced of sin is that God's law may prompt us to become even more sinful. When encountering God's law, some people react: "I don't care what God says. I will do what I want!!" This seems to be what Paul has in mind in Romans 7:5 when he mentions, "... our sinful passions, aroused by the law." When that happens, we hope it is a step toward being personally convicted of sin and repenting and coming to faith.

I have heard a story that has the ring of truth, even if it might be a parable. There was a nice hotel on an island in a lake, built so that the windows of the hotel rooms were directly above the edge of the lake. The manager put "No Fishing!" signs by the hotel windows, yet he had repeated problems with the windows being broken, with the breaks apparently happening when people were fishing from their windows. His expensive consultant recommended he try removing the "No Fishing!" signs to see what happened. When the signs were removed, there were no more broken windows. Without the signs, no one thought of fishing from the window of a nice hotel. The law was prompting the sin. And that can happen to us in ways more important than fish and broken windows.

One of the things Martin Luther discovered as he was studying God's Word is that repentance is usually described as an ongoing or frequently repeated process of changing one's mind or renewing one's mind. In the first of his famous 95 Theses of 1517 he wrote, "When our Lord and Master Jesus Christ said, 'Repent' (Matthew 4:17), he willed the entire life of believers to be one of repentance." That includes getting a new perspective on things. Repentance is not only an event at the beginning of the life of faith, and it is not only an occasional special event. That is why Luther made repentance a constant theme in worship.

Being shown our sin has to continue in order for us to grow in the Christian life. We need to be convicted regularly regarding sin, so we can live lives of continual repentance. This is not the whole of the Christian life, but it is a part, and it is partly why we should read God's law.

There is another use of God's moral law.

III. God's moral law can help to restrain sinful actions.

In Christian history this was alternately called the "civil use" of the moral law or the "political use" of God's law. In Exodus 20:20 we read, "... that the fear of [God] may be before you, that you may not sin." And this fear is related to God's law.

It would be nice to think that Christians would follow God's law simply out of love and gratitude. But quite honestly, it does not work that way all the time. Sometimes gratitude runs low. At those times we may obey God out of fear or habit or motivated by what other people will think. Certainly, this is not as good as obeying God out of gratitude, but it would be terrible if you murdered someone because your gratitude was low today. And the Bible is realistic about our motivations.

It may be good to distinguish this use of God's law among believers in the church from its use in society, which is religiously mixed. Even among people who do not believe in God and who may never have read the Bible, God's law helps restrain sin, at least a little. And this comes in several ways.

In Romans 2:14-15 Paul writes, "For when Gentiles, who do not have the law, by nature do what the law requires, they are a law to themselves, even though they do not have the law. They show that the work of the law is written on their hearts, ..." Through conscience people are somewhat aware of God's law, and sometimes this really restrains sin. One of the most morally sensitive people I have known was a man who claimed to be an agnostic.

Another way this happens is through law enforcement. Even some terrible governments have laws about killing and stealing that partly correspond with God's law. When government breaks down, there will always be a few people who have no other restraint to keep them from killing, stealing, and destroying. The "war of all against all," sometimes described by political philosophers, is a constant danger.[3]

This restraining influence of God's law in society also comes through believers. In Exodus 19, just before the first proclamation of the Ten Commandments, we are told that God's people are to be a priestly people. A priest is a go-between. The giving of the law constituted God's people as a priestly people who bring God's law into the world. Through the words and example of believers, God's law can have a substantial good effect on a whole society, even if unbelievers do not know what that influence is or where it comes from. Among unbelievers, God sometimes remains anonymous while His law guides parts of life. Across two thousand years of Christian history there have been many times when God's people became serious about God's law, and this flowed over into the surrounding community, reducing theft, murder, and sexual assault. Some themes from God's moral law have found a place in civil laws and legal systems in many countries. In this way, God's people have been serving in a priestly role, bringing some parts of God's law into societies and cultures, and this has visible effects. This is why I write books about human rights. We have a lot to do here, but a first part includes getting to know God's law quite well.

Sometimes believers have terrible feelings about God's law, perhaps because they have tried to earn God's favor or because they only know its condemning use. But once we really know God's grace, we can see what a treasure God's law is. Unlike some of our neighbors, we are not at sea without a compass or a rudder. We can say with the psalmist, "Oh, how I love your law" (Psalm 119:97).

I want to close with a liturgical question that requires an answer from you. The right answer is for you to stand up and say "Yes!" with a loud voice. The question is similar to the existential question faced by the Israelites at this second giving of God's law. Here is the question:

---

[3] This slogan was made famous by Thomas Hobbes in his book *Leviathan* (1651).

People of God: The Lord your God has brought you out of Egypt, out of the house of bondage. He sent His Son to be born as a baby, to live, to die, to rise again, and to ascend into heaven for your complete salvation. He has sent His Holy Spirit to empower you to live for Him in this world. Will you now accept His gospel and His moral law as providing the meaning of your lives, as the destiny to which He has called you? What is your answer?

Note: At this point the congregation, which included Christians from around the globe, arose to their feet and shouted "Yes!" to the glory of God, affirming their comprehensive discipleship.

The Ten Commandments: Given by God?

Pierre Berthoud, France

How do we know that the Ten Commandments as we have them in the Pentateuch were actually given to us by God? This is an important question not only for the Ten Commandments but also for the Bible as a whole considered as the Word of God. To express it differently, how do we know that we do not live in a silent universe, that we are not alone, and that we are not left to fend for ourselves as many of our contemporaries, at least in the West, are convinced?[1] Within such a mindset, at best God is considered to be a psychological crutch or a figment of one's imagination, which may help some to cope with the tribulations of life, but in fact, He is irrelevant to the tragic condition of human existence. As to the expression "Thus says the Lord," used to communicate purported divine revelation, many understand it as a mere stylistic device to enhance a literary piece and to give authority to a human discourse.

As for those who acknowledge the existence of God, can one know His character, and does divine communication as expressed in the categories of human language exist? Or must the believer be content with a mystical union that is beyond the scope of reason since it belongs to the realm of faith? Such a viewpoint, implying a divided field of knowledge, leaves the believer with a subjective and immanent experience of God which at best sheds light on his private life and conduct.

If we take the Ten Commandments seriously, they are meant to speak to the individual disciple as he seeks to walk with the Lord and to honor Him in this life, but they are also guidelines for the church, for the body of Christ, and even for civil society! A study of church history would show the extent of the influence of the Ten Commandments on the ethical private and public conduct of Christians over the centuries.

For example, in a Protestant Reformed Church in Lourmarin just 30 km from Aix-en-Provence, where we live in the south of France, on the inner front wall of the church on both sides of the pulpit, the two tables of the

---

[1] Actually, this is true to a lesser and greater degree in other parts of the world. While in South Korea some years ago, I had the opportunity of entering a major bookstore in Seoul. I headed for the English section, and to my amazement, all the major works of Western authors were on display. I noted the same thing in Brazil. Secular humanism and ultramodern thought are very much alive on all the continents!

law are represented, inviting the Christian congregation to consider carefully the Ten Words of God as they relate to both the believer's and the church's lives.

Another example is a monument in Aix-en-Provence. Joseph Sec, a local inhabitant, had a most intriguing monument built that *he dedicated to the municipality of the city, observer of the law.* This happened in 1792, just a few years after the French Revolution; but in the midst of the growing impact of humanism, the Christian mindset still had a major influence on society. The transcendent Word of God had not yet been relegated to the private sphere of human experience! As one considers the façade of the monument, the reference is clearly to the Ten Commandments. The statue of Moses holding the tablets of the law in his hands is in the center of the frontage, and in the midst of different figures and symbols reflecting the cultural influence of both the biblical and Greco-Roman worlds, one can read the following inscriptions:

> Come inhabitants of the earth/nations, listen to the law.
> You will love the Lord your God and your neighbor.
> - Having escaped from cruel slavery
>   I have no other master but myself,
>   But of my freedom I want to make use,
>   To only obey the law.
> - Faithful observer of these admirable laws,
>   that a God himself deigned to dictate to us,
>   every day in my eyes they are more amiable,
>   and I would rather die than deviate from them.

These are amazing statements, for they imply a biblical worldview: the existence of a personal God who communicates His word of truth; an autonomous creature who is nevertheless accountable to the Lord, entailing both form and freedom; the love of God and His word of life calling for commitment and self-sacrifice. It is as if Sec were saying to the governing body of Aix-en-Provence, "If you want loyalty, justice, well-being, and peace to flourish in the city, you must draw from the wisdom of these Ten Words!"

More than 200 years later in our ultramodern, secular, and pagan cultural environment, the Christian influence on civil society has largely disappeared. Nevertheless, our generation still holds to some of the core values inherited from its Christian heritage, ideals such as truth, justice, freedom, beauty, and love. But being severed from their supernatural worldview and unrelated to one another, these values are reinterpreted within a purely horizontal perspective and thus significantly distorted.

What the Catholic philosopher G. K. Chesterton said at the beginning of the twentieth century is even truer within our present cultural climate: "The modern world is full of old Christian virtues gone mad."[2] The new generations do not even have the memory of the past Christian consensus! We thus need to win back lost ground and to reverse the course of history in order to allow the *The Magna Carta of Humanity*[3] to contribute to the restoration of civil society, conducive to more peaceful living together. To allow this to happen, we need to know that the Ten Commandments are indeed a divine communication that continues to shed light on the tragic condition and plight of our contemporaries and to offer them a way to happiness and genuine freedom within the covenant relationship.

In the following sections of this paper, we will address the questions of being, revelation, and knowledge as we seek to argue that the Bible and specifically the Ten Words were indeed given by the Lord.

A. The question of being

In contemporary thought one usually postulates the existence of being rather than of non-being. Thus, for example, the display of stained-glass windows, devoted to the theme of Genesis, which took place some years ago in Aix-en-Provence. On the poster for the exhibition, inspired by one of the works of Dominique Masset entitled "Preamble to Genesis," one could read this most significant question: "Why does something exist rather than nothing?" Such a query invites us to consider the "why" of this something or the origins of this reality and its significance. This question brings to mind Paul Gauguin's famous (last) painting entitled *"What are we? Where do we come from? Where are we going?"*[4] The artist's questions relate to the origin, the meaning, and the finality of human destiny and existence.

If something exists, what is its nature?

We will begin by exploring some aspects of the present discussion, both theological and scientific. Historically, the different stages of this debate

---

[2] G. K Chesterton, *Orthodoxy* (New York, NY: Doubleday, 1959/1908), 30. Chesterton remains until this day a thought-provoking and stimulating author. His insights are still helpful to understand the modern mind, though he was very critical of the Reformation, considering it one of the major roots of modernity!

[3] Title of Os Guinness's recently published book: *The Magna Carta of Humanity: Sinai's Revolutionary Faith and the Future of Freedom* (Downers Grove: InterVarsity Press, 2021).

[4] Gauguin's painting is in the Boston Art Museum (USA).

are connected to the advent of the philosophy of the Enlightenment and to its impact on natural sciences, thus leading science to become, in due course, an end in itself. Such an influence gradually gave birth to a science cloaked in a modernist dress. Having become captive to different rationalistic philosophies, the sciences were then used to undermine the biblical and classical Christian view of creation. As a matter of fact, from Copernicus until the advent of Marxist materialist ideology, through Darwin and Freud, those two worldviews, "scientific" and "religious" (Christian), developed side by side without much contact with one another. In the Christian community, without denying the existence of a Creator and the doctrine of creation, the tendency has been, to various degrees, to recognize and to accept the "scientific" explanation of the origin of the universe and of man. As a consequence, the church and Christians have placed the emphasis progressively on redemption to the detriment of creation.

As time went by, it became evident that it was inappropriate to speak about redemption without bringing creation into the picture. But renewed interest in this doctrine carefully avoided the questions related to origins. It was thus argued that the biblical narratives of creation purposed to shed light on the fragile human existence. Human life unfolds in a dangerous and hostile environment. In light of this dramatic threat, the stories of creation appease, comfort, and reassure, but they only have existential value. They fulfill a threefold purpose, doxological, polemical, and soteriological; creation texts invite the believer to praise the unique God, to reject idols, and to welcome salvation offered by the Lord, but without specific truth claims about God or the universe.[5]

However, to confess the Creator God is only significant if the biblical perspective is intellectually true, tenable, and trustworthy. The answer that we bring to the question of being necessarily bears upon that of meaning and purpose. Is belief in the Creator and in creation only the product of my imagination, of my philosophical-religious perspective, or is such a belief based on the fact that God has really taken the initiative to create the universe and that this work is of an objective nature? To be sure, the first chapters of Genesis are not to be compared to a scientific treatise as defined today, but when the biblical narrative bears witness to the intervention of God in the realm of reality and history, we can expect it to speak in truth. God is also the Lord of science. If questions with regard to origins

---

[5] We clearly see in these two paragraphs a dichotomy between the realms of the sciences and of existential experience. Cf. Claus Westermann, *Genesis 1-11: A Commentary* (London: SPCK Press, 1984), 11; Samuel Amsler, *Le secret de nos origines* (Poliez-le-Grand: Editions du Moulin, 1997), 8-9.

still fascinate our contemporaries, it is no doubt because they make up the DNA of our identity as men and women who live in the midst of this world. The question of origins is indeed linked to that of the finality of the human being!

The astrophysicists' pertinence

While much of contemporary theology of creation eludes the question of the origin of being, curiously, astrophysicists have made a significant contribution to the debate. Their discoveries have led them to reconsider the question of being and of the origin of the universe. They have had to face the challenge of the zero moment of the universe with all its implications. Thus, to postulate that the universe has a beginning introduces the Creator God at the center of the debate from which scientists thought He had been definitely excluded!

Anglo-Saxons call the zero moment of our universe the Big Bang in the hypothesis that this universe would be in constant expansion.[6] Trinh Xuan Thuan argues:

> Recent discoveries of cosmology have shed a new light on the most fundamental and oldest of questions. And it matters that any serious reflection on the existence of God take this new evidence into account. After all, the questions asked by the cosmologist are strikingly close to those that concern the theologian: how was the universe created? Is there a beginning to time and space? Will the universe have an end? Where does it come from and where is it going? The sphere of God is that of mystery and of the invisible, that of the infinitely small and of the infinitely large. This sphere no longer belongs exclusively to the theologian; it also belongs to the scientists; science is there; it adds up discoveries and disrupts preconceptions. The theologian has no right to remain indifferent.[7]

---

[6] This explanation of the origins of the universe represents an interesting, stimulating, and helpful point of contact in the present discussion and does not imply my agreement with this theory.

[7] Trinh Xuan Thuan, *La mélodie secrète* (Paris: Gallimard, 1991), 296-297. The author advocates the Big Bang theory and does not believe in chance and necessity, but he is careful to confine God to the realm of mystery and of the invisible. He is somewhat reluctant to draw the consequences of what he has discovered: the existence of a personal Creator. In fact, Thuan opts for the impersonal "principle of creation" and says his view corresponds largely to the pantheism of Spinoza: "Table ronde avec Trinh Xuan Thuan, Anne Dambricourt et Alexandre Jollien," Paris, Collège des Bernardins. *Et Dieu dans tout ça?* June 29, 2015. Podcast. https://www.youtube.com/watch?v=1oyd_lfXlF0. Cf. John J. Davis, *The Frontiers of*

But neither should astrophysicists sidestep the question of God, as many do. Indeed, the ultimate issue is not the encounter between God and modern cosmology but the Davidic acknowledgment that "The heavens declare the glory of God, and the sky above proclaims his handiwork" (Psalm 19:1). In fact, this is what Robert Jastrow does in his own way when he states, not without humor:

> The scientist's pursuit of the past ends in the moment of creation. ... It is not a matter of another year, another decade of work, another measurement or another theory; at the moment it seems as though science will never be able to raise the curtain on the mystery of creation. For the scientist who has lived by his faith in the power of reason, the story ends like a bad dream. He has scaled the mountains of ignorance; he is about to conquer the highest peak; as he pulls himself over the final rock, he is greeted by a band of theologians who have been sitting there for centuries.[8]

While many modern theologians have sought to avoid the obstacle embodied by the question of origins, astrophysicists, confronted by scientific evidence witnessing to the beginning of the universe, have been led to reconsider the question of the existence of God and have gone as far as to challenge theologians to take part in the examination and study of the fundamentals of reality and its bearings on creation. It is important to recognize, though, that these scientists remain somewhat vague as to the nature of this being.[9] But to meet such a challenge is to consider as possible the correspondence between this ultimate being and reality as it stands before us and to seek to understand it. It also suggests a potential link between the issue of the finality and meaning of life and the existence of this infinite Being. Could it be that divine revelation is one link and that its various complementary components shed light on the world that we behold?

Science and Faith (Downers Grove, IL: InterVarsity Press, 2002), 11-36. For interesting input on the contribution of physics and mathematics to the debate, cf. I. and G. Bogdanov, *La pensée de Dieu* (Paris: Grasset, 2012), 9-39, 337-351. But what does the *"pensée de Dieu" (the divine thought)* apparent in reality refer to: The ultimate principles or absolutes, a distant divinity (deism), the infinite personal Creator? The question remains open!

8   Robert Jastrow, *God and the Astronomers* (New York, London: W. W. Norton, 1992 [1978]), 115-116.
9   Cf. Footnote 7.

Two options

There are two main options open to a number of variations in answer to the question of being. On the one hand, the materialistic and humanistic worldview of many of our contemporaries leads them to postulate that ultimate reality is infinite and impersonal and is primarily defined in terms of matter and energy. This conception is also inherent to Hinduism, which is in many ways akin to pantheism. But how can such a perspective account for the complexity of the universe overflowing with intelligence and for the unique character of man qualitatively distinct from other living creatures, the unique character of the human creature within the realm of creation? The despair expressed by Gauguin's masterful painting hints at the gap between such a philosophical outlook and reality. On such a humanist basis, he could not find the universal that would have given him the key to the finality of human existence and opened the door of genuine meaning and serenity.

On the other hand, the biblical perspective postulates that the ultimate reality is the infinite and personal Being. This is the starting point of all philosophy and of the system of moral values based on the divine character and thought as revealed in Scripture. Such a global outlook offers an answer to the question of origins which takes into account the unity and diversity of reality and highlights the dignity of human beings since they are created in the image of God. No doubt there is an infinite distance between the Creator and the creature; however, like God, man is a personal being. Gifted with intelligence and creativity, he is a free and responsible being with a moral conscience. He thinks and communicates, loves faithfully and is loyal, and possesses an entrepreneurial drive and a creative spirit. This daring comparison allows biblical writers to use anthropomorphisms as metaphors to speak of God and to conceive of Him in terms of the image of man. It is precisely the mystery of the Trinity that makes it possible to emphasize the personal character of God and to conceive of an intimate relationship with Him in which communication, communion, and love are the essential components. It takes into account the unity and the diversity within the Godhead, of reality as well as of cultures, and highlights a unique anthropological concept in its psychological, social, and cultural aspects. By rejecting this doctrine, Islam, Judaism, and deism accentuate the oneness of God and thus His transcendence and majesty to the detriment of His personal character, with, as a consequence, the weakening of the personal character of human beings.

Blaise Pascal provides a good summary of the point we are making when he says in his *Pensées*:

God of Abraham, God of Isaac, God of Jacob, not of the philosophers and of the learned. Certitude, certitude. Feeling. Joy, Peace. God of Jesus Christ. My God and your God. Your God will be my God. Forgetfulness of the world and of everything, except God.[10]

Since the universe is not an extension of divinity and divinity is not to be confused with the energy of the universe, God, the infinite, living, and personal Being, took the initiative to create all things *ex nihilo* by the sole power of His word![11] This key notion is expressed in the first chapter of Genesis. The verb "to create" (bārā), used only with God as subject, describes a unique creative activity.[12] The Hebrew root is used three times: in relation to the creation of the universe, of aquatic and flying beings, and of the human being: man and woman (Genesis 1:1-2; 20-21; 27-28). God's specific intervention is apparent in the realms of physics, biology, and anthropology. Consequently, the answer given to the question of being bears on the way the universe and the destiny of man on earth are understood.

B. A silent God?

Thus far we have argued that the infinite and personal God is the most appropriate and relevant answer to the question of being insofar as it accounts for the complexity of the universe overflowing with intelligence, as well as for the uniqueness of the human being and his mandate in the midst of the created environment. Thus, our basic presupposition is that God has not remained silent! He has chosen to communicate. Such a communication is of crucial importance, for it indicates that the infinite and personal God is truly capable of conveying His thoughts and design according to the categories and words of human language so that His image bearers can truly understand Him. This is what we call divine revelation; it is personal and varied and reflects the character of God while shedding light on all of reality. Indeed, this notion is but a shallow formula, and even meaningless, if it does not convey a message which finds its origin in an existing Being, the infinite and personal God. We will now consider the

---

[10] Blaise Pascal, *Pensées*, Œuvres complètes, Bibliothèque de la Pléiade, (Paris: Galimard, 1954), 554.

[11] For a detailed argument of this theme, cf. P. Berthoud, *En quête des origines: les premières étapes de l'histoire de la révélation: Genèse 1-11* (Cléon d'Andran: Excelsis; Aix-en-Provence: Kerygma, 2008), ch 7, p. 177 ff.

[12] It is important to indicate that *bārā* does not usually express the idea of a creation *ex nihilo*. The emphasis is on the unique divine creation, whether God creates starting from nothing or from pre-existing matter.

nature of such a revelation as given to mankind in both creation and the Scriptures, which are complementary.

The living God reveals Himself in creation.

This living God took the initiative to create all things, including human beings, by the power of His word alone. Creation therefore has its own existence, while depending on God, and is subject to His providence. Such an outlook makes it possible to distinguish between the first cause and secondary causes. Though nothing escapes the sovereign will of God, everything "proceeds according to the rules which govern causalities within the created domain."[13] From its very beginning, the Bible affirms the non-autonomy of the whole of creation. Human beings live in the world of God, and the whole of reality invites the creature to turn his gaze toward his ultimate Vis-à-vis (Psalm 19:1-6; Romans 1:19-20). The analogy between a work of art and creation is age-old. We find it, for example, in a beautiful passage from the book *The Wisdom of Solomon*, in which the author engages in a controversy with idolatry and the deification of the elements of nature: "Foolish by nature were all who were in ignorance of God, and who from the good things seen did not succeed in knowing the one who is, and from studying the works did not discern the artisan;" (Wisdom 13:1).[14] The same thought is expressed by the apostle Paul when he writes: "For what can be known about God is plain to them, because God has shown it to them. For his invisible attributes, namely, his eternal power and divine nature, have been clearly perceived, ever since the creation of the world, in the things that have been made" (Romans 1:19-20). Thus God, who is totally other and yet so close, in disclosing Himself in creation, invites His creatures to seek Him (Acts 17:25-28). This implies that without an infinite reference point, man cannot give lasting meaning to his existence. When the human creature stops believing in God, he does not believe in nothing, but he believes in something else. Saint Augustine makes a similar point in a prayer he addresses to God: "You stir man to take pleasure in praising you, because you have made us for yourself, and our heart is restless until

---

[13] L. Jaeger, *Pour une philosophie chrétienne des sciences* (Cléon d'Andran: Excelsis, 2000), 59.

[14] The quotation is drawn from the New American Translation (revised edition). This verse is set within a section (verses 1 to 9) in which the author argues that the beauty and power of the created world should have directed, by analogy, the gaze and mind of the creature toward the Creator. Instead, the natural elements became the object of his attention and worship. This is the essence of folly from a biblical perspective and is the antithesis of wisdom.

it rests in you".[15] By revealing Himself in this way, the Lord of the universe and of history reminds man that he is a responsible party vis-à-vis God. He is therefore inexcusable, since he cannot appeal to his being ignorant (Romans 1:20b-21).

The saving God reveals Himself in the Word.

However, due to the creature's state of sin, this revelation is insufficient to overcome the rupture in his relationship with the Creator. The human creature is in need of a special divine revelation in order to clearly position himself in the universe, to understand his dilemma, and to give meaning to his existence. The passages just mentioned above, with their emphasis on the folly, anxiety, and wickedness of man, testify to the plight inherent in the human condition ever since the first couple's rebellion against God in the Garden of Eden. In this regard, the diagnosis of Ecclesiastes is relevant: "... God made man upright, but they have sought out many schemes" (Ecclesiastes 7:29). Another translation reads, "... but man invents endless inventions of his own" (New English Bible). In other words, human created beings have pursued their own thoughts and plans and have thus emancipated themselves from the wisdom of God. Sin consists in choosing to be one's own finality, the measure of all things, whereas the chief end of mankind is to take on his destiny before the Creator. The dilemma of man is therefore not metaphysical, and evil is not intrinsic to his being. If that were the case, he would be excusable, since there is no way to overcome such a fate! According to the Genesis narrative of the Fall, the dilemma of man is moral and thus "proceeds from the subsequent historical use of human freedom" (Genesis 3; Romans 5:12-21).[16] As a consequence, the responsibility of human creatures is involved, implying that true guilt is at the very heart of his existence. But it also means that the human being is not the prisoner of his fate, and there is thus hope for a solution. Since sin is incompatible with the holiness of God (Isaiah 6:5) and its destructive influence touches all aspects of human life, both private and public, man can in no way offer an answer to this dilemma. As a consequence, without a specific divine intervention in the realms of knowledge and existence, there is no true, decisive, and lasting outcome:

---

[15] Saint Augustine, *Confessions,* trans. Henry Chadwick (Oxford: Oxford University Press, 1991), Book I.i (1), 4.

[16] For a more detailed presentation of the problem of evil, cf. Berthoud, *En quête,* Ch. 8, *Le mal, la mort et la vie,* 229-276; Henri Blocher, *Révélation des origines* (Lausanne: PBU, 1988 [1977]), Ch. VII, *La Rupture,* 130-167.

- In the sphere of knowledge, in order to reverse the harmful impact of sin, God uses the word of truth. The darkened intelligence of man is in need of divine communication in order to establish a diagnosis, induce a change of mentality, and identify a cure.
- In the sphere of existence, in order to remedy the disastrous consequences of a lifestyle that is in opposition to His Wisdom-Law, the Lord favors the transforming word of redemption. His grace and compassion procure a cure to a wounded and bleeding heart.

More than a collection of testimonies, the Scriptures are the disclosure, in word and in deed, of divine wisdom and salvation destined to ailing men and women. This revelation, which God chose to unveil progressively, was fully manifested in Jesus Christ, "the Lamb of God, who takes away sin of the world" (John 1:29). Indeed, Jesus Himself said during His ministry on earth: "I am the way, and the truth, and the life. No one comes to the Father except through me" (John 14:6). It is thus by the grace of the Lord and the illumination of the Holy Spirit that we can know and be reconciled to our heavenly Father. The church, the community of the covenant, continues to receive the joyful mandate to proclaim both the written and incarnate word at the crossroads and in the heart of cities. This is vitally important for our contemporaries who live under the shadow of death.

A united field of knowledge

The object of knowledge[17] which leads to redemption is thus the revelation God has given us in creation and history as well as in Scripture. Both spheres give us information that our minds can grasp and understand. It

---

[17] In the light of a careful study of the biblical evidence, it is possible to draw, in summary form, the following characteristics of the biblical concept of knowledge: *1. The doctrine of creation, specifically the Covenant of creation, forms the setting for a biblical understanding of knowledge; 2. The human process of knowledge within the realm of reality (the realm of creation) implies both integration and differentiation for the human creature; 3. This notion of knowledge is personal and implies the unity of the human nature; 4. The knowledge of the human creature is limited by both his finiteness and his rebellion. These characteristics imply a united field of knowledge including both the visible and invisible worlds and reality. This means that reason and faith, having different functions, are not opposed but complementary and work hand in hand.* This is true for the Hebrew Bible and the New Testament Greek as well as the common usage as found in Classical Greek. The differences between the Greek and Hebrew concepts of knowledge have too often been overstated. The divergences are attested essentially in the philosophical writings. I have further developed these different aspects of epistemology in an article, "L'autorité et l'interprétation de l'Ancien Testament," *La Revue Réformée* N° 135 (1983): 1-10.

follows that in order to come to a true understanding of such a divine communication, we must hold to a united field of knowledge.[18] But because the effects and marks of sin are so deep, the human person is also in vital need of the illumination of the Holy Spirit. It follows that God is the foundation of man's cognitive process, not only because of His work of creation, but also because of His solicitude manifested in His work of redemption in favor of the broken and lost human creature.

When God knows man, this means that He seeks him, remembers him, chooses him, calls him, and blesses him. This divine initiative establishes the unique value and the raison d'être of the human person. The Lord graciously offers to his human *vis-à-vis* the knowledge that leads him to the fountain of wisdom and life. The Spirit of wisdom and power quickens the cognitive faculties of man and restores the full scope of the covenant relationship.

As we conclude this section, we can say with Gerhardus Vos that the context of divine revelation and human understanding "is not a school but a 'covenant'." All that God reveals of Himself is in response to the concrete and religious needs of His creatures and people such as they appear in the course of their lives and history. This view of epistemology, which emphasizes both its personal and rational aspects, in denying philosophical autonomy, dissociates itself from the purely horizontal view of the theory of knowledge that arose with the rationalism of the Enlightenment.[19]

C. The guarantee offered by the Lord

The Bible as a unit

We will begin by quoting a few passages of the New Testament, because for the early church, the Old Testament bore the status of Holy Scripture and was therefore the reference and norm in matters of doctrine and faith. In

---

[18] With regard to Greek epistemology, one of the most able French Hellenists, Jacqueline de Romilly, who died in 2010, argued convincingly that the Greek understanding of reason was very different from "the systematic rationalism of the Enlightenment." Less arrogant, the Greek mindset was aware of its limits and its need of other resources. She also recognized that Greeks functioned within the context of a united field of knowledge since both the "rational and the irrational were closely united and intertwined." Jacqueline de Romilly, *Ce que je crois* (Paris: De Fallois, 2012), 29-33. Though not a Christian, she realized the need of a form of transcendence in order to truly understand the humanity of the human being.

[19] G. Vos, *Biblical Theology, Old and New Testaments* (Grand Rapids, MI: Eerdmans, 1975), 17. Cf also P. Berthoud, *En quêtes*, 60, 61.

his second epistle to Timothy, Paul argues that "All Scripture is breathed out by God and profitable for teaching, for reproof, for correction, and for training in righteousness, that the man of God may be competent, equipped for every good work" (2 Timothy 3:16-17). The word *theopneustos* literally means that the Scriptures[20] are the work of the breath of God, who has acted through the biblical authors. In the second epistle of Peter, we read: "For no prophecy was ever produced [carried] by the will of man, but men spoke from God as they were carried along by the Holy Spirit" (2 Peter 1:21). It is for that reason that "no prophecy of Scripture comes from someone's own interpretation"[21] (v. 20). In His debate with His opponents, Jesus called upon the authority of Scripture, which cannot be abolished or annulled, to support His argumentation (John 10:34-35).

However, this notion of revelation, divine communication, is also found in the Old Testament. The following examples will illustrate my point. In Exodus 4, we are told that "Aaron is the mouthpiece of the god-Moses." The text is very clear: "... you shall be as God to him" (v. 16b), and "You shall ... put the words in his mouth" (v. 15a). Aaron is literally the mouthpiece for Moses, who acts toward him as "God." The objective character of the communication and the infallibility of the result are safeguarded since God added, "I will be with your mouth and with his mouth and will teach you both what to do" (v. 15b); God watches over His word so that it reaches its beneficiary and is understood and is effective (Exodus 4:15-16). In a neighboring passage of Exodus, Aaron is called "prophet." He is a "prophet" because a "god" has spoken to him, that is to say, Moses. The latter is, through Aaron, "like God to Pharaoh" (Exodus 7:1-2). The impact of their speech on Pharaoh is related to the fact that God has communicated with both Moses and Aaron (v. 2). Such is the Lord's answer to Moses, who is "of uncircumcised lips" (6:30) and "not eloquent" (4:10).[22] A third example is related to Jeremiah's call to practice a tragic ministry in the

---

[20] The Scriptures designate primarily the Old Testament. Some have thought that this term could also refer to collections of texts pertaining to Jesus, including His words which spread in the early Christian communities. Some of Paul's letters have also been included/mentioned [1 Timothy 5:18 (Deuteronomy 25:4) and 1 Corinthians 9:9; 2 Peter 3:15-16]. These passages indicate that Paul's letters have the same authority as the writings of the Old Testament, but also, that the canon of the New Testament was still in the process of being recognized and thus, far from closed.

[21] It has also been translated "is not the fruit of a personal initiative" (Bible du Semeur: BS), but the Greek word *èpilusis* is better translated by *explanation, interpretation*.

[22] In Exodus 4:10b Moses adds, "I am slow (heavy) of speech and of tongue."

midst of the people of Judah. Having heard the reluctance voiced by the young man who did not consider himself fit for such a task, the Lord "touched [the prophet's] mouth"[23] and said: "Behold, I have put my words in your mouth" (Jeremiah 1:5-9). The power and authority of the prophet and his message are related to the divine intervention. Without minimizing the literary dimension of these texts, they convey the idea of a divine communication that man can grasp and understand. The infinite and personal Being, whose action far surpasses our understanding, has truly, but not exhaustively, chosen to unveil and communicate His thought to us. As we stand before Him and are confronted by such a divine revelation, no one can remain indifferent. As creatures of the Creator, we are indeed all personally concerned and involved (Romans 1:18-23).[24] This fundamental starting point being clarified, we will now consider the three principles that will further help us to understand that the Bible's message, and specifically the Ten Commandments, were actually given to us by the Lord: the objectivity, inspiration, and infallibility-reliability of the divine word.[25]

1. The objectivity of revelation

What we have already suggested and just stated enables us to recognize the objective character of revelation. The Bible shows us an authentic communication of God to man (*ab extra*). The word which the human creature receives has an external origin. God chooses to share His thoughts and designs with His *vis-à-vis*, who, being in His image, can really understand what He seeks to convey to him. This act of divine communication can go as far as including the idea of dictation.[26] Thus it is feasible to imagine that a man of God was able to put in writing, under divine dictation, the message which he was expected to impart to the people or to an individual. Jeremiah dictated "... all the words of the LORD ..." Baruch wrote them "... in a book ..." (Jeremiah 36:4; 45:1).

This approach, needless to say, in no way excludes a subjective and personal means of revelation. What we are referring to here is the inward activity of the Holy Spirit acting upon the depths of human

---

[23] Jeremiah probably also experiences his own impurity before the Lord, because the act of God touching his lips is also a gesture of purification (Isaiah 6:5-8).

[24] In this passage Paul is speaking of general revelation, which leaves all human beings "without excuse" (v. 20b).

[25] For this section, cf. P. Berthoud, *En quête*, 61-66; G. Vos, *Biblical Theology*, 20-23.

[26] When a manager writes a letter in which each sentence and word must be weighed, he doesn't hesitate to dictate it to his secretary. We find that normal, and the secretary's dignity and significance are in no way questioned or negated.

consciousness and creating thoughts that, in fact, proceed from God Himself (*ab intra*). It is, in fact, the usual pattern of divine revelation. The Psalms offer a good example of such communication. This conception of revelation, far from weakening its objective character and divine authority, emphasizes the incarnate character of the Word and the significance of human agents in such a process. The prophet Jeremiah, as God's spokesman, illustrates both the passive and active aspects of his prophetic ministry. A careful reading of his writings enables us to discover the profound humanity of revelation, including the literary dimension of the oracles the prophet has imparted to his contemporaries. We are also touched by all that we learn about the man, Jeremiah: his sensitivity and suffering, his faithfulness and audacity, his vulnerability and anguish, his inward battles and doubts, his amazing talent and creativity! On the basis of what we read in his writings, it is, in fact, possible to have a personal and moving appreciation of the man Jeremiah. One can think of the marvelous portrait drawn by the Dutch painter Rembrandt van Rijn or of the beautiful book written by the Jewish French author André Neher.[27] If the objective nature and the authority of revelation were mitigated, we would then have less than a divine communication. In fact, such an approach is confirmed in some trends of modern theology that limit revelation to the acts of God or consider the headings introducing the divine oracles as literary fictions and therefore devised by their authors. For instance, Old Testament scholar D. J. A. Clines suggests that we see in the expression "The LORD ... proclaimed" (Exodus 34:6) only the words of the narrator! But R. W. L. Moberly has rightly remarked that beyond the literary aspect of the formula, the question of the reality and of the truth of the divine proclamation remains.[28] In fact, the two aspects (literary form and divine communication) need to be kept together. If the two are separated, we are then left with a narrative or a discourse that derives from human reflection upon acts of God or from an account of one's own spiritual experience and encounter with Him. In other words, the biblical texts offer us at best a creative formulation of the theology and spirituality of their authors. This approach favors the relativizing and the questioning of the idea of divine

---

[27] The painting *Jeremiah lamenting over the destruction of Jerusalem* is in the Rijksmuseum, Amsterdam, Holland. Rembrandt captures with great sensitivity the plight of the prophet as he witnesses the fulfilment of the divine oracles. A. Neher, *Jérémie*, (Paris: Plon, 1960). The author presents a very vivid, warm, and dramatic portrait of the prophet.

[28] R.W.L. Moberly, "Theology of the Old Testament" in D. W. Baker and B. T. Arnold eds., *The Face of Old Testament Studies* (Grand Rapids, MI: Eerdmans, 1999), 465.

conceptual communication. What actually remains is a discourse that finds its origin in the human being and is therefore entirely submitted to him. How are we then going to verify the divine origin of an act that purports to be revelation, or the authenticity of a mystical encounter of a believer or a prophet with the Lord? Why favor one theological tradition rather than another? It is precisely for this reason that this objective-subjective concept of divine personal communication gives the most adequate interpretation of the biblical data and enables us to receive the full value of its words, contents, and meaning, without neglecting its human and spiritual flavor as well as its formal and literary aspects.

2. The inspiration of revelation

In an article written in 1914, H. Gunkel, questioning the validity of Old Testament studies, attacked the doctrine of inspiration. Here is what he said: "When the Christian Church came into existence, it accepted not only the Old Testament writings, but also the doctrine that that book was a work of God, given and inspired by the Holy Spirit. ... But biblical research which came into existence about the middle of the eighteenth century and gradually gathered strength and confidence, first challenged that view, then attacked it, and finally shook it to its foundations ... if it has not completely destroyed it."[29] The author's concern is to emphasize the literary and human riches and beauty of the biblical texts, but he begins by a radical attack on the doctrine of the inspiration of Scripture. At best he criticizes a doctrine that undervalues the humanity of Scripture. He even speaks of "revelation in history," but the presuppositions that underscore his approach to the texts are hardly compatible with a high view of Scripture. In light of Gunkel's comments, we better understand the importance of the doctrine of inspiration and the issues that are at stake,[30] in particular the question of the authority and authenticity of the Word of God.

---

[29] H. Gunkel, "Why Engage the Old Testament?" in H. Gunkel, *Water for a Thirsty Land*, translated from German by A.K. Dallas and J. Schaaf, (Minneapolis, MN: Fortress Press, 2001 [1914]), 1ff.

[30] R. de Vaux understood this very well when he argues that the Bible is the Holy Scripture "because it is written under the inspiration of God to express, to preserve and to transmit God's revelation to men." But by allowing major concessions to the historical-critical method, he weakens the foundation upon which this doctrine rests. Once again, it is essential to tackle the historical and literary issues while respecting the biblical perspective and remain focused on the witness of the

This approach, emphasizing the doctrine of inspiration, implies that the subject to be studied is the revelation of God Himself. We are not primarily concerned in recounting the history of beliefs and customs practiced by individuals or communities who lived in the past. Neither is it our concern to account for the theological reflections of individuals or communities on the revelatory acts of God. If that were the case, we would be pursuing a study either in the history of religions, in anthropology and in sociology, or in "historical theology" and in the religious thought of a people, Israel. Since we are dealing with the communication of the Lord's thought and design that has been transmitted according to the categories of human language, the idea of inspiration becomes essential. Thus God, by His authority, guarantees and confirms the truth of the object of what we read and study. This does not exclude, however, the key idea of a rational verification and of an intelligent appropriation of truth, but it enables us to stress that God's own authority, by the means of inspiration, establishes the truth of the object of our study, the Scriptures. Let us remember that revelation encompasses both the contents expressed in the categories of human language and historical facts. Without the confirmation of inspiration, without the mark of the Lord's authority and competency, a full conviction with regard to the truth of the divine word cannot emerge and blossom. Rather, doubt and uncertainty linger on relentlessly.

3. The infallibility of revelation

The recognition of the infallible and sure character of divine communication springs from the two principles we have just considered. If God is an infinite and personal Being, a conscious Being, it follows logically that, as the guarantor of the authenticity of His objective revelation, He is able to disclose to human beings a perfect expression of His character and purposes. The communication of His thought bears the marks of His divinity. If it were not so, we would have to find the reason in the fact that God is bound by the finitude of the world. This is, in fact, what H. Gunkel argued when he wrote: "The Old Testament is not the perfect revelation of the Christian view: it is only revelation taking place in history."[31] We agree with him when he emphasizes the progressive character of revelation, but what he really implies is the imperfect and therefore fallible character of revelation linked to its historical contingencies. R. E. Murphy heads

---

texts as they have been transmitted to us. R. de Vaux, « Peut-on écrire une 'théologie de l'Ancien Testament'? » in *Bible et Orient* (Paris: Le Cerf, 1967), 68.

[31] H. Gunkel, loc. cit., p. 26.

in the same direction when he upholds that "the Bible contains divine words in a garment of human words and that there are, consequently, limitations concerning the way the divine mystery can be perceived in the humanity of biblical expression."[32] Once again, the emphasis is placed upon the fallible character of God's revelation, since it is conditioned by its human limitations. It therefore follows that the means of expression impedes the divine communication with the world. God's sovereignty over creation and history being limited, it follows that His revelation can only be fallible. But according to the biblical perspective, in both the Old and the New Testaments, God is in no way bound by worldly contingencies. He is supremely free in regard to His own creation and in His interaction with it, and especially with the human creature (Amos 3:7-8; Habakkuk 3:1-19). This implies, though, that we keep in mind both the idea of adaptability when we mention God's communication with man and the analogical character of our knowledge of divine mysteries. The Lord condescends to speak to His creatures so that they can truly understand Him. His word is embodied, according to the periods of history, in different linguistic expressions, in a variety of literary forms, and in a multiplicity of cultural settings, but in so doing, God does not alter the truth and the infallibility of His own statements. God watches over and accompanies the transmission of His thought in such a way that His recipients can enjoy a just and true understanding of what He intends to communicate to them.

The Ten Commandments

What we have just said with regard to the Bible as a whole applies also to the Ten Words: the divine communication, inspiration, and perfect disclosure are the guarantee that they are indeed given by the Lord of the Covenant. But there is a major difference in the fact that it is God Himself who addresses the people (Exodus 20:22), without the mediation of Moses,[33] though the latter is completely involved in an intensive dialogue with his divine partner and in communicating His instructions.[34] Not only does the

---

[32] R.E. Murphy, "Reflections on a Critical Biblical Theology" in *Problems in Biblical Theology*, eds. H. T. C. Sun; K. L. Eades (Grand Rapids, MI/Cambridge, UK: Eerdmans, 1997), 273.

[33] While "the Lord spoke face-to-face with the people at the mountain," Moses remained the mediator between God and His people (Exodus 19; 24:1-8; Deuteronomy 5:4-5).

[34] Independently of the Ten Words, Moses is told to write that which the Lord has communicated to him (Exodus 17:14; 24:4; 34:27; 39:30).

Lord address His people, but we are told repeatedly that He has "written [the law] for their instruction" on tablets (Exodus 24:12); "he wrote on the tablets the words of the covenant, the Ten commandments" (Exodus 34:28);[35] "And he gave to Moses ... the two tablets of the testimony [charter], tablets of stone, written with the finger of God" (Exodus 31:18).[36] We are also told that "The tablets were the work of God, and the writing was the writing of God, engraved on the tablets" (Exodus 32:16), thus underscoring "the sublime worth of the gift that Moses was to bring to the people."[37] While recognizing the use of metaphors, the emphasis is on the Lord's specific and direct action as He "talks from heaven" and "writes His instructions." Umberto Cassuto summarizes this unique divine intervention very well: "Just as they [the Ten Words] were proclaimed by God, so their writing must necessarily be the writing of God, graven upon the tables (Exodus 32:16)."[38]

This is indeed a major moment in the history of Israel and in the history of the covenant community, for it is within the setting of a theophany, the glorious and spectacular manifestation and presence of the Lord on Mount Sinai, that the Lord reveals Himself (Exodus 19-24). The fact that "the people heard his words and his voice"[39] and that His declaration was engraved on the tablets of stone prepared by Moses represented the fullest divine guarantee of the authenticity and truth of the Sinai Magna Carta (Exodus 20:1-17)!

It is important to add that these Ten Words are designated as a "testimony" or "witness" and thus testify to the covenant that was made between the Lord and the community of Israel. The Hebrew word ʿedouth has also been translated as "charter,"[40] suggesting that the Lord graciously initiated a constitution guaranteeing both duties and rights. But in fact, it is the word *covenant* that designates the personal and formal relationship the Lord chose to establish with Israel. Such a bond implies a mutual commitment between the two partners.

---

[35] Deuteronomy 4:13; 5:22. In Exodus 34:28, the subject is clearly the Lord (34:1), while the subject in 34:27 is Moses.
[36] The expression refers to a specific intervention of God (Exodus 8:19; Deuteronomy 9:10).
[37] Umberto Cassuto, *A Commentary on the Book of Exodus*, trans. I. Abrahams (Jerusalem: The Magnes Press, 1974), 418.
[38] Ibid., 315.
[39] J.A. Motyer, *The Message of Exodus: The Days of Our Pilgrimage*, (Downers Grove, IL: InterVarsity Press, 2005), 212.
[40] La Bible Bayard, (Montrouge, FR: Bayard Editions, 2015).

Thus, the Ten Commandments, placed in the ark with the jar of manna and Aaron's rod, testify and bear witness[41] to the ratification of this covenant (Exodus 24:1-8; 34:27), a major landmark in the history of revelation. In fact, the Ten Words are often considered to be a condensed version or the basic stipulations of the Mosaic covenant[42] that were to be of utmost significance for the history of Israel, for the Christian church, for Western civilization, and beyond. Already on the occasion of the renewal of the covenant, the Lord declared the amazing impact and extent they would have in Israel and among the nations:

> "Behold, I am making a covenant. Before all your people I will do marvels, such as have not been created in all the earth or in any nation. And all the people among whom you are shall see the work of the LORD, for it is an awesome thing that I will do with you" (Exodus 34:10).

Conclusion

As we come to the end of this study on the Ten Words, so masterfully encapsulated by the Lord Jesus Christ in the greatest of commandments, the love of God and of one's neighbor (Matthew 22:34-40), I would like to mention the beautiful work of art entitled *Invitation/Decalogue* created by Liviu Mocan, a Romanian artist, on the 500th anniversary of John Calvin's birth. It was first exhibited in Geneva in 2009.

According to Jonathan Tame, the monumental sculpture "consists of ten pillars, resembling human fingers. Set in a circle, the pillars have two sides: a smooth, well-rounded side facing inwards, creating a sense of peace and well-being within the circle. On the other side, facing outwards, each pillar narrows to a sharp, vertical blade, expressing a somber warning." Tame then indicates that the sculpture's aim is to generate "encounter with God and others." In order to do so, the statue presents "four metaphors in the form of invitations" to the visitors: "the ten fingers represent *an invitation*" to relationship with God and one's neighbor; the "contrasted sides of each pillar are *an invitation to ethical reflection;*" as to "the space

---

[41] Witness, in reference to stone tablets (Exodus 25:16; 21; 34:28); to the ark as containing the tablets (16:34; 27:21); to the tabernacle as containing the ark (30:6, 26, 36; 40:21; Numbers 17:4, 7, 8-10); to the veil as screening the ark (Leviticus 24:3), *The Dictionary of Classical Hebrew*, Volume 6, (Sheffield: Sheffield Phoenix Press, 2007), 279

[42] M. Kline, "The Two Tables of the Covenant" in *The Structure of Biblical Authority* (S. Hamilton, MA: Meredith Kline, 1989), 113-130; K.A. Kitchen, *On the Reliability of the Old Testament*, (Grand Rapids, MI: Eerdmans, 2003), 242, 283 ff.

created by the circle of pillars, it is *an invitation to freedom" within form; lastly,* the height of the "columns is an *invitation to hope."*[43] What an amazing and challenging invitation to reconsider and practice, within a dismantled and broken world that has lost its bearings, the "law of Christ" as fully manifested and accomplished in Jesus of Nazareth!

---

[43] Liviu Mocan, *The Ten Commandments*; Jonathan Tame, "Laws of Life and Love," ArtWay Visual Meditation, July 25, 2010, https://www.artway.eu/content.php?id=757&action=show&lang=en, (emphasis added).

Are the Ten Commandments Still Valid?

Risimati S. Hobyane, Republic of South Africa

The importance of the Decalogue in the modern world may seem obvious, at least to normal Christians; after all, much of what we hear in the news demonstrates how ignoring those ancient commandments is wreaking havoc in the lives of individuals, families, and societies. However, the application of the Ten Commandments is being questioned among contemporary believers exactly when these words from above seem most needed. The questions among Christians about following the Decalogue are largely based on misunderstanding certain texts in the New Testament. These texts include:

1. Matthew 5:17: "Do not think that I have come to abolish the Law or the Prophets; I have not come to abolish them but to fulfill them."
2. Romans 6:14: "For sin will have no dominion over you, since you are not under law but under grace."
3. Romans 7:6: "But now we are released from the law ..., so that we serve in the new way of the Spirit and not in the old way of the written code."
4. Romans 8:3: "For God has done what the law, weakened by the flesh, could not do. By sending his own Son in the likeness of sinful flesh and for sin, he condemned sin in the flesh."

The general observation here is that a superficial reading of these texts has the potential to undermine the importance of the Decalogue. After reading the texts cited above, the central question may be: Is God's law still important? We have heard it said, "If, according to Matthew 5:17, the Lord Jesus Christ has fulfilled the law, is it still necessary to read it and call Christians to observe it? How is it even relevant to read it during our weekly worship services?" In reaction to the writings of Cornelius Vonk, Karel Deddens (1993:88) remarked, "In recent years we have been hearing suggestions to the effect that we should trade in the reading of the Ten Commandments for other passages of Scripture in which the Christian rule of life is laid out, preferably passages drawn from New Testament admonitions." Vonk claims that the Sinai covenant is no longer valid. Therefore, it follows to suggest that the Ten Commandments should not be read during a worship service of the New Testament church.

To be clear, this is not the view of this author. The current article aims at discussing the essentiality and importance of the Decalogue by considering three points: the treatment of the Decalogue in the New Testament; some exegetical vantage points from the Scriptures; and the stance/teaching of the traditional Protestant confessions, which provide an historical point of reference for interpreting Christian ethics. The quest here is to ensure that believers understand the importance of the Decalogue in our time.

The Treatment of the Decalogue in the New Testament

Is there teaching about the Decalogue in the New Testament? If so, how should New Testament believers view or understand it? To these questions, P. J. De Bruyn (1998:18) helpfully states that "the way the Decalogue is treated in the New Testament (Matthew 19:18-19; Romans 12:20; 13:8-9) makes it clear that it has a universal intent and meaning, in other words, that it applies to all Christians, in every part of the world, both in their relations with each other, as well as with non-Christians." This assertion is critical for our discussion. It underscores the fact that the Decalogue, in its nature, is not time-bound but is time-directed. It is the law of God that is valid and applies to all Christians regardless of time and age.

Over and against negative views (e.g., that of Vonk highlighted above), Deddens (1993:69) points out "that we must not surrender the validity of the Ten Commandments for our time. In the whole of God's covenantal revelation, they occupy a special place. Unlike other laws given by God in the Old Testament, they were written on two stone tablets and were kept and preserved in the Ark of the Covenant." He further mentions that "Calvin speaks of the Ten commandments as an 'eternal rule of justice' which God has prescribed for human beings of all times and places as a way for them to live their lives in accordance with His will."

Apart from one commandment (see footnote 1 regarding the Sabbath), nine of the laws found in the Decalogue are explicitly reiterated as part of the New Covenant (New Testament). This repetition underscores their importance/relevance and their binding nature for all believers, and they must be obeyed today. These laws are binding today, not because they were a part of the Old Covenant but because they are a part of the New Testament and God's holy Word (canon). Their reiteration in the New Testament can be summarized as follows:

- Commandment 1: Exodus 20:3; reiterated in Acts 14:15
- Commandment 2: Exodus 20:4; reiterated in Acts 17:29

- Commandment 3: Exodus 20:7; reiterated in Matthew 6:9
- Commandment 4: Exodus 20:8-11; **not reiterated in the NT**[1]
- Commandment 5: Exodus 20:12; reiterated in Ephesians 6:2
- Commandment 6: Exodus 20:13; reiterated in Romans 13:9; Revelation 21:8
- Commandment 7: Exodus 20:14; reiterated in Romans 13:9; Revelation 21:8; and Hebrews 13:4
- Commandment 8: Exodus 20:15; reiterated in Romans 13:9; Ephesians 4:28
- Commandment 9: Exodus 20:16; reiterated in Romans 13:9; Ephesians 4:25
- Commandment 10: Exodus 20:17; reiterated in Romans 13:9; Colossians 3:5

As the reader may notice, one New Testament verse, Romans 13:9, is referenced multiple times as reiterating commandments from the Decalogue. It merits quotation, with additional context, because of the way in which the Apostle Paul integrates love for other people with several commandments. Romans 13:8-10:

> Owe no one anything, except to love each other, for the one who loves another has fulfilled the law. For the commandments, "You shall not commit adultery, You shall not murder, You shall not steal, You shall not covet," and any other commandment, are summed up in this word: "You shall love your neighbor as yourself." Love does no wrong to a neighbor; therefore love is the fulfilling of the law.

---

[1] With regard to the lack of reiteration of the Sabbath Law in the New Testament, M. G. Easton (1893: 591-592) helpfully says, "If any change of the day has been made, it must have been by Christ or by his authority. Christ has a right to make such a change (Mark 2:23-28). As Creator, Christ was the original Lord of the Sabbath (John 1:3; Hebrews 1:10). It was originally a memorial of creation. A work vastly greater than that of creation **has now been accomplished by him**, the work of redemption. We would naturally expect just such a change as would make the Sabbath a memorial of that greater work.

"True, we can give no text authorizing the change in so many words. We have no express law declaring the change. But there are evidences of another kind. We know for a fact that the first day of the week has been observed from apostolic times, and the necessary conclusion is, that it was observed by the apostles and their immediate disciples. This, we may be sure, they never would have done without the permission or the authority of their Lord.

"After his resurrection, which took place on the first day of the week (Matthew 28:1; Mark 16:2; Luke 24:1; John 20:1), we never find Christ meeting with his disciples on the seventh day. But he specially honored the first day by manifesting himself to them on four separate occasions (Matthew 28:9; Luke 24:36, 13-35; John 20:19-23). Again, on the next first day of the week, Jesus appeared to his disciples (John 20:26)."

When underscoring the importance of the Decalogue and its reading in our weekly worship meetings, Deddens (1993:70) points out that the law is also God's Word. It is not just one of the responses of the congregation but forms part of what the Lord says to His people. He correctly concludes, "Hence the reading of the Ten Commandments makes a great deal of sense as part of the service. It gives the law the opportunity to function as the source from which we know our misery (Romans 7:7) and also as the rule of our gratitude."

In a world infested with greed and corruption, one cannot underscore enough the importance of the teaching of the Decalogue. For example, P. J. Buys[2] addresses the question of bribery from the law perspective. He says, "Bribery is a phenomenon both acknowledged (Proverbs 17:8) and warned against (Proverbs 15:27) in the wisdom tradition and condemned in the Law (Exodus 23:8; Deuteronomy 16:19)." Modern men are warned against the act of bribery (and many other wrongdoings/sins) by the law of God.

The Decalogue and Jesus Christ in the New Testament

In His teaching, Jesus indicates that He did not come to abolish the law or the Prophets (the authority and principles of the Old Testament) but to fulfill them. This utterance cannot and should not be understood to suggest any invalidation of the law[3]. By fulfilling, Jesus did not mean to subvert, abrogate, or annul, but to unfold them, to embody them in living form, and to enshrine them in the reverence, affection, and character of men (R. Jamieson, et al., 1997). The text in which Jesus addressed this question merits our attention, Matthew 5:17-19:

---

[2] Phillipus J. (Flip) Buys, "Corruption, Bribery, African Concepts of God, and the Gospel," *Unio cum Christo* (2019): 10.

[3] The concept of "law" in this context should be understood to refer to the three categories of law, i.e., **the ceremonial law** (related specifically to Israel's worship – Leviticus 1:2-3, and its purpose was to point forward to Jesus Christ and is no longer necessary after Jesus' death and resurrection), **the civil law** (applied to daily living in Israel – Deuteronomy 24:10-11; these laws do not apply to our modern society and culture, but the principles behind the commands are timeless and should guide our conduct), and **the moral law** (this refers to the Decalogue. It is the direct command of God, and it requires strict obedience. It reveals the nature and will of God, and it still applies today. Jesus obeyed the moral law completely.) (*Life Application Study Bible*. Carol Stream, IL: Tyndale House.)

> "Do not think that I have come to abolish the Law or the Prophets; I have not come to abolish them but to fulfill them. For truly, I say to you, until heaven and earth pass away, not an iota, not a dot, will pass from the Law until all is accomplished. Therefore whoever relaxes one of the least of these commandments and teaches others to do the same will be called least in the kingdom of heaven, but whoever does them and teaches them will be called great in the kingdom of heaven."

In the following portions of the Sermon on the Mount, Jesus makes specific reference to several of the Ten Commandments in a way that affirms their foundational role in life. For example, in Matthew 5:21-22 Jesus says:

> "You have heard that it was said to those of old, 'You shall not murder; and whoever murders will be liable to judgment.' But I say to you that everyone who is angry with his brother will be liable to judgment; whoever insults his brother will be liable to the council; and whoever says, 'You fool!' will be liable to the hell of fire."

We could discuss whether Jesus is stripping away a misunderstanding of the commandment to get to its original meaning or if He is making a demand of His disciples that is deeper than the original commandment. Regardless of our conclusion to that question, Jesus is clearly teaching that we must not murder.

As a second example, we can take Matthew 5:27-28, where Jesus says:

> "You have heard that it was said, 'You shall not commit adultery.' But I say to you that everyone who looks at a woman with lustful intent has already committed adultery with her in his heart."

Again, we could debate exactly how Jesus is using the commandment that forbids adultery. Is Jesus adding a deeper dimension to the original commandment, or is He clarifying the original intent of the commandment? Regardless of the answer to this question, Jesus clearly teaches that the commandment regarding adultery is still foundational for New Testament Christians. Therefore, the Decalogue is still valid and applicable to the lives of Christians in the modern world.

Historic Protestant Confessions on the Decalogue

I belong to a family of churches that uses two historic confessions written during the Protestant Reformation to provide a professional standard for our pastors as they apply God's Word and especially the Ten Commandments, which we are now considering. Those confessions are the Belgic Confession of 1561 (hereafter referenced as BC) and the Heidelberg Catechism of 1563 (hereafter referenced as HC). The BC is divided into 37 short articles; the HC is divided into 129 questions and answers which are grouped into 52 "Lord's Days" for convenient study each Sunday of the year. The teaching of the BC and of the HC regarding the Decalogue is very similar to the teaching found in other classical documents of the Protestant Reformation. (Our churches also use the historic Canons of Dort of 1619, but that text addresses other issues and says less about interpreting the Ten Commandments.)

Our church confessions are unequivocal on the necessity and the value of the Decalogue in the lives of believers. First, when elucidating our confession regarding the "written word of God," BC Article 3 points out that "God, with his own finger, wrote the two tables of the law. Therefore, we call such writings holy and divine Scriptures." Unlike the ceremonial laws, which contained specific directions for the special service of the Lord among the Israelites, such as sacrifices, special clothing for the priests, and festivals, the Decalogue was meant for all times (De Bruyn: 2013:14; see also BC Article 25). The reference and acknowledgement of the holiness and divine nature of the Decalogue by the BC is special (cf. 2 Peter 1:21) and without doubt highlights the value it places on it and its relevance and applicability to the modern world.

Secondly, in HC Lord's Day 2, many things are said regarding the importance of the Decalogue, including its value and binding, pedagogical nature. We confess that the law is significant in our lives as believers. Lord's Day 2, Question 3 asks: "How do you come to know your misery?" Answer: "The law of God tells me." The reference to the term "law of God" points back to the Decalogue, as outlined in Exodus 20:1-17 and Deuteronomy 5. The Scripture further elucidates in Romans 3:20, "For by works of the law no human being will be justified in his sight, since through the law comes knowledge of sin." Without going into the exegetical details of the texts indicated, we can point out that the Apostle Paul broadly and deeply lays the foundations of his teaching of the great doctrine of justification by free grace and not justification before God by obedience to the law (R. Jamieson, et al., 1997). Nonetheless, the text puts forward the importance of the law in the lives of believers, that is, "for through the law comes knowledge of sin." First, the law shows us where we go wrong. Because of the law, we know that we are helpless sinners and that we must come to our Lord Jesus Christ for mercy. Second, the moral code revealed in the law can serve to guide our actions by holding up God's moral standards. The message should be clear in this regard: Yes, we do not earn salvation by keeping the law, but we do please God when our lives conform to His revealed will for us (see also the *Life Application Study Bible* on these texts).

It suffices to point out that Lord's Day 2 provides us with the answer regarding the significance of the Law of God (the Decalogue) in the lives of believers in the modern world. Furthermore, the third major part of the HC, Lord's Day 33, Question 91, reminds us of the relevance of the Law in our lives as believers. Part of our gratitude toward the Lord for our salvation is our obligation to do that which is good, namely: "Only that which arises out of true faith, conforms to God's law (Leviticus 18:4) and is done for his glory and not that which is based on what we think is right or on established human tradition (1 Corinthians 10:31)." Notice again how the reference to God's Law has a central role in the confessional teaching of the church in which I am a member.

From the above highlighted points on the teaching of our confessions regarding the Decalogue, one can conclude without hesitation that the law of God is not obsolete but is still relevant and applicable in the lives of believers today. The Decalogue (with the exception of the Sabbath law[4]) is the Word of God and must be obeyed and observed.

Conclusion

This article has aimed at discussing the importance of the Decalogue in the modern world by looking first at the way in which the New Testament treats and reiterates the Decalogue, with the exception of one of the commandments. Second, a brief discussion has been provided regarding the question of the fulfilment of the law by Jesus Christ in the New Testament and how it impacts Christians in the modern world. Third, we have looked at selected historic Protestant confessions and how they approach the teaching of the Decalogue. In all these discussions, one must conclude that the Decalogue is the revealed Word of God, which is useful for teaching, rebuking, correcting, and training in righteousness (2 Timothy 3:16).

Bibliography

Buys, Phillipus J. (Flip). (2019). "Corruption, Bribery, African Concepts of God, and the Gospel." Unio cum Christo, 5(2), 1-12. https://doi.org/10.35285/ucc5.2.2019.art10.

---

[4] See footnote 1 for M. G. Easton on change to the first day of the week from the seventh day.

Carson, D. A. (1994). *New Bible Commentary: 21st century edition.* (Rev. ed. of: *The New Bible Commentary.* 3rd ed. D. Guthrie and J.A. Motyer, eds. 1970). Leicester, England; Downers Grove, IL., USA: InterVarsity Press.

De Bruyn, Paulus Jacobus. (2003). *The Ten Commandments.* Potchefstroom: Potchefstroom Theological Publications.

Deddens, Kavel. (1993). *Where Everything Points to Him.* Michigan: Inheritance Publications.

Easton, M. G. (1893). In *Illustrated Bible Dictionary and Treasury of Biblical History, Biography, Geography, Doctrine, and Literature* (pp. 591–592). New York: Harper & Brothers.

The Holy Bible: New Revised Standard Version. 1996, c. 1989. Nashville: Thomas Nelson.

Jamieson, R., Fausset, A. R., and Brown, D. 1997. *A Commentary, Critical and Explanatory, on the Old and New Testaments.* Oak Harbor, WA: Logos Research Systems, Inc.

Life Application Study Bible. 2013. Carol Stream, IL: Tyndale House.

The New King James Version. 1996, c. 1982. Nashville: Thomas Nelson.

Wiersbe, W. W. (1996). *The Bible Exposition Commentary* (Vol. 1, p. 535). Wheaton, IL: Victor Books.

The Relation between Biblical Law and Christian Faith

Glenn N. Davies, Australia

The covenant dynamic of the Old and New Testaments is the interaction between grace and response. God is the giver of grace, which He lavishly pours forth upon His people, and He delights in their response of obedience. This characteristic dynamic is present in each of the covenants of the Old Testament as well as in the promised new covenant, which unfolds in the New Testament.

The two parts of the Bible would have been better called the Old Covenant and New Covenant, rather than using 'testament' to translate *berît* or *diathēkē*. However, the most important thing to understand is the continuity between the covenants with respect to God's dealings with humankind, notwithstanding the discontinuity or, more properly, the fulfilment of the old in the new. In particular, we should recognize the similarity in the response to God's grace under either the old or the new covenant: it should always be characterized by a faith which issues in obedience or, as Paul describes it, the obedience of faith (Romans 1:5; 16:26).[1] This article will explore the content of that obedience for the Christian – the place of the Decalogue in the Christian life.

Old covenant law

The Ten Commandments evidence the nature of the grace-response dynamic. The obedience required of Israel in the Decalogue is an obedience which flows from God's grace. Hence, "'I am the Lord your God who brought you out of the land of Egypt, out of the house of slavery'" (Exodus 20:2; Deuteronomy 5:6) is the necessary preamble to the giving of God's law. Israel had seen the goodness of the Lord in their departure from Egypt and redemption from slavery, and the response God required of them was to trust and obey Him.

As they stood on the banks of the Red Sea, with Pharaoh's army behind them, Israel had to trust God's word, delivered through Moses, so that the salvation of the Lord would be manifested (Exodus 14:13). Yet to display

---

[1] In this phrase, "of faith" is rightly translated as a genitive of origin, as per the translation by the NIV: "the obedience that comes from faith."

trust in God, as the waters divided, they had to walk through it themselves. God did not transport them across the sea or provide a travellator, with no effort or activity on their behalf. Rather, they had to respond by getting up and walking across. This was their obedience of faith. Yet such obedience could never be seen as the ground of their salvation, but merely as the means of the salvation which God alone had provided.

In God's infinite wisdom, He ordained not only the act of salvation, but also the means. Israel's journey across the Red Sea is exemplary of the life of faith, a faith that issues in obedience. The Ten Commandments thereby became the blueprint for Israel's obedience both in the wilderness and in the Promised Land.

However, it is not as if the knowledge of these commandments was new to Israel. Moses' narrative throughout the Pentateuch bears witness to infractions of each of these commandments prior to Mount Sinai, with the attendant disapproval of God. The first commandment was broken by Adam and Eve, the tenth and sixth by Cain, and the fourth was violated by the Israelites in the wilderness en route to Sinai (Exodus 16:26ff). Shem and Japheth knew to honor their father, Reuben knew the sin of false witness, and Joseph knew adultery was wrong. Indeed, God describes Abraham as one who "obeyed my voice and kept my charge, my commandments, my statutes, and my laws" (Genesis 26:5).

Therefore, one might ask: what is the significance of God's promulgation of the Ten Commandments at Mount Sinai if these laws were already known? The answer the Bible supplies is that the law of God is here given to Israel with the attendant penalties attached for breaking God's law. For this reason, the apodictic laws of Exodus 20 are followed by the casuistic or case law of the following chapters, where Moses outlines which penalties apply to specific breaches of God's law. Prior to Mount Sinai, the penalty for law-breaking had not generally been revealed. The declaration of the death penalty for murder, as recorded in Genesis 9:6, is an exception, but the death penalty was not applied to Cain's murder of Abel.

This is no doubt the reasoning of the apostle Paul in Romans 5:12-15.[2]

> Therefore, just as sin came into the world through one man, and death through sin, and so death spread to all men because all sinned – for sin indeed was in the world before the law was given, but sin is not counted where there is no law. Yet death reigned from Adam to Moses, even over those whose sinning was not like the transgression of Adam, who was a type of the one who was to come.

---

[2] All quotations are from the ESV unless otherwise specified.

Paul identifies the similarity between the law given to Adam and the law given to Moses, along with the dissimilarity of sins committed between the time of Adam and Moses. In the latter case, sins were "not counted," not being like the sin of Adam. The law given to Adam came with its own sanction, namely, the penalty of death should he eat from the tree of the knowledge of good and evil (Genesis 2:17). Similarly, there was an array of penalties for the breaking of the Mosaic law, with capital punishment being the overriding sanction. Yet, says Paul, death reigned from Adam to Moses because of the culpability of humanity's participation in Adam's sin. This teaching is amplified later in Romans 5, as Paul exclaims that "... as one trespass led to condemnation for all men, so one act of righteousness leads to justification and life for all men" (5:18).

An illustration of the lack of knowledge as to the penalty for breaking God's laws may be found in Numbers 15:32ff. The event recorded there is most likely prior to Mount Sinai, as the penalty for Sabbath-breaking was not revealed until after Moses had descended from the mountain (Exodus 31:12-14). Thus, before Moses could deal with the offender, God needed to tell him the specific sanction for Sabbath-breaking, as the penalty had not previously been disclosed (Numbers 15:34).

The association of the Mosaic law with the penalty of death enables Paul to describe it as "... the ministry of death, carved in letters on stone" (2 Corinthians 3:7). However, in the same verse, Paul can also claim that it "came with such glory that the Israelites could not gaze at Moses' face because of its glory." In other words, we should not lose sight of the glory of God's law as given to Moses, even though it brought a sentence of death upon those who broke it. Yet the law promised life (Leviticus 18:5; Nehemiah 9:29) and so could be described as "living oracles" (Acts 7:38), "spiritual,"[3] "holy and righteous and good" (Romans 7:12, 14). In fact, the law of God is full of grace - "More to be desired than gold, even much fine gold; sweeter also than honey and drippings of the honeycomb" (Psalm 19:10).

Old covenant grace

Central to the nature of the Mosaic law was the sacrificial system. This was where God's grace was manifested in the life of Israel. For God in His wisdom knew that sin was a present reality in the life of His righteous people (Ecclesiastes 7:20), indeed, a reality for every human being (Psalm 143:2).

---

[3] Paul characteristically uses *pneumatikos* as a reference to the Holy Spirit, except in Ephesians 6:12, where the context demands otherwise. See R. B. Gaffin, *The Centrality of the Resurrection* (Grand Rapids: Baker, 1978).

Hence, the provision of forgiveness by way of animal sacrifice was a necessary part of the Mosaic law. The law never envisaged sinless, perfect observance by Israel. On the contrary, *the law presupposed sin*. For the offering of sacrifices was part and parcel of keeping the law. If people thought they had not committed sin and so declined to offer a sacrifice, then they would be breaking the law (since offering sacrifices was mandatory) and would therefore be bound to seek forgiveness by offering a sacrifice!

When the priest offered a sacrifice on behalf of an Israelite, the forgiveness was real and immediate, as the oft-repeated refrain in Leviticus 4-5 testifies: "The priest shall make atonement for him for the sin that he has committed, and he shall be forgiven." Likewise, on the Day of Atonement, the High Priest would offer sacrifices for his own sins and then for the sins of the people: "For on this day shall atonement be made for you to cleanse you. You shall be clean before the Lord from all your sins" (Leviticus 16:30).

Of course, the offering of sacrifices was in response to the offender's repentance. The only sin that could not be forgiven was sinning "with a high hand" (Numbers 15:30), or "sinning defiantly" (NIV), i.e., a sin without repentance. The writer to the Hebrews warns his readers that even under the new covenant, defiant sin without repentance cannot receive forgiveness but merely a fearful prospect of judgment (Hebrews 10:27). God does not forgive sin where there is no repentance (Hebrews 12:17).

Yet forgiveness, like salvation, is all of grace. The faith exercised by repentant Israelites in offering a sacrifice was their response to God's grace, His promise of forgiveness. As this dynamic was reflected in the lives of individual Israelites, it was also the underlying contour of Israel's entry into the Promised Land. Their inheritance of the land of Canaan was not the result of their achievement but was due to God's grace. Hence, in Deuteronomy 9:4-5 Moses warned the Israelites against the folly of presumption.

> Do not say in your heart, after the Lord your God has thrust them out before you, 'It is because of my righteousness that the Lord has brought me in to possess this land,' whereas it is because of the wickedness of these nations that the Lord is driving them out before you. Not because of your righteousness or the uprightness of your heart are you going in to possess their land, but because of the wickedness of these nations the Lord your God is driving them out from before you, and that he may confirm the word that the Lord swore to your fathers, to Abraham, to Isaac, and to Jacob.

Nonetheless, Israel still had to enter into battle. In fact, their victory over Amalek (Exodus 17:8-16) dramatically portrayed their dependence upon God for the victory, as Israel prevailed only when Moses' hands were lifted in prayerful dependence upon God. When Moses' hands weakened, Amalek prevailed. Yet when Aaron and Hur held up Moses' hands, we see the symbolism of all Israel trusting in God, which gave them the victory. Accordingly, Moses built an altar and named it "The LORD Is My Banner," saying, "A hand upon the throne of the LORD." "Doing" is not antithetical to grace, as James emphatically teaches: "... faith by itself, if it does not have works, is dead" (James 2:17).[4]

Old covenant obedience

Israel's obedience to the Mosaic law, generated by faith and the regeneration of the Holy Spirit,[5] was a genuine possibility, which the elect accomplished, though the majority of Israelites failed to achieve it (Romans 11:7). Stephen, citing Exodus 33:3 and Jeremiah 6:10 and 9:26, described disobedient Israel (including his hearers) as "You stiff-necked people, uncircumcised in heart and ears, you always resist the Holy Spirit. ... you who received the law as delivered by angels and did not keep it" (Acts 7:51, 53).

Christian commentators often overlook the fact that whereas most Israelites were breakers of God's law (Romans 2:23), it *was* possible to keep God's law (Romans 2:26). Yet one can understand this only in the light of the law's provision for forgiveness through sacrifice, as the gift of grace. Hence, in Deuteronomy 30:11-14, Moses encourages Israel to keep God's law, by which they shall live (see also Leviticus 18:5):

> Now what I am commanding you today is not too difficult for you or beyond your reach. It is not up in heaven, so that you have to ask, "Who will ascend into heaven to get it and proclaim it to us so we may obey it?" Nor is it

---

[4] J. C. Ryle's comment on Luke 12:41-48 is worth noting. "The lesson is one which many, unhappily, shrink from giving, and many more shrink from receiving. We are gravely told that to talk of 'working' and 'doing' is legal, and brings Christians into bondage! Remarks of this kind should never move us. They savour of ignorance or perverseness. The lesson before us is not about justification, but about sanctification – not about faith, but about holiness; the point is not *what a man should do to be saved*, but *what ought a saved man to do*. The teaching of Scripture is clear and express on this subject. A saved man ought to be 'careful to maintain good works' (Tit. 3:8). The desire of a true Christian ought to be, to be found 'doing.'" J. C. Ryle, *Expository Thoughts on the Gospel of Luke*, vol. 2 (Cambridge & London: James Clarke & Co., 1969), 90.

[5] The circumcision of the heart is the usual description of a regenerate heart in the Old Testament. See G. N. Davies, "The Spirit of Regeneration in the Old Testament," in *Spirit of the Living God*, part 1, ed. B. G. Webb (Homebush West, NSW, Australia: Lancer, 1991), 23-43.

beyond the sea, so that you have to ask, "Who will cross the sea to get it and proclaim it to us so we may obey it?" No, the word is very near you; it is in your mouth and in your heart so you may obey it. (NIV)

The apostle Paul recognizes that such intended obedience to the law of Moses was possible only by faith (Romans 10:6).[6] Just as Abraham obeyed all the ordinances of the (pre-Sinai) law by faith (Genesis 15:6; 26:5), so did David, as he testifies in Psalm 18:20-24 (NIV).

> The LORD has dealt with me according to my righteousness;
>   according to the cleanness of my hands he has rewarded me.
> For I have kept the ways of the LORD;
>   I have not done evil by turning from my God.
> All his laws are before me;
>   I have not turned away from his decrees.
> I have been blameless before him
>   and have kept myself from sin.
> The LORD has rewarded me according to my righteousness,
>   according to the cleanness of my hands in his sight.

Many readers find such claims by David to be questionable, if not outrageous, given his adultery with Bathsheba and other sins recorded in 1 and 2 Samuel. Yet despite David's clear violation of God's law, God in His mercy had forgiven David, notwithstanding the fact that his sin deserved death (Leviticus 20:10). For David repented of his sin (Psalm 51) and sought the Lord for mercy. In Psalm 18, David did not claim that he deserved God's mercy, for he was aware of his own frailty and of his need of a Savior (vv. 2-3, 35, 46) as much as he was aware of the promises of God to all who take refuge in him (v. 30). However, he was also aware of the need to manifest the obedience that comes from faith.

When he introduces the story of Zechariah and Elizabeth, Luke is equally aware of the importance of obedience in relation to God's covenant promises. As a priest, Zechariah knew the significance and value of Levitical sacrifices, just as he also knew the importance of acting in obedience to God's law.

> In the time of Herod king of Judea there was a priest named Zechariah, who belonged to the priestly division of Abijah; his wife Elizabeth was also a descendant of Aaron. Both of them were righteous in the sight of God, observing all the Lord's commandments and regulations blamelessly (Luke 1:5-6 NIV).

---

[6] For an explanation of Romans 9:30 -10:13, see G. N. Davies, *The Obedience of Faith: A Study in Romans 1-4* (Sheffield: Sheffield Academic Press, 1990), 177-204.

The importance of this description of two Old Testament saints should not be underestimated. They were righteous in the sight of God (echoing Genesis 15:6) but also obedient to the Mosaic law – observing *all* the Lord's commands. Neither of them was sinless, but each of them was blameless, because the guilt of their sin had been removed through the appointed sacrifices. They were blessed in their obedience, like David, with the declaration of Psalm 32:1-2, that the Lord had forgiven their transgressions and covered their sins.[7]

Faithful Israelites kept God's law as their response to His grace. They understood that the essence of grace was God's love toward them (Deuteronomy 7:8), just as the essence of their response was love of God (Deuteronomy 6:4-6) and love of their neighbor (Leviticus 19:18). It is therefore not surprising that Jesus should declare that all the law and the prophets hang on these two commandments of love (Matthew 22:37-40).

New covenant law

The parting words of Jesus to His disciples constitute what has become known as the Great Commission, calling for the making of disciples through the waters of baptism in the Triune name and teaching those followers to obey all that Jesus had commanded. This demand of discipleship in terms of obedience to the Lord Jesus is echoed in our Savior's words to His apostles in the upper room: "If you love me, you will keep my commandments" (John 14:15). Just as the commandment to love God was central to the old covenant, so it is with the new covenant. Love and obedience hang together; Jesus abides in the Father's love by keeping the Father's commandments. Accordingly, Jesus declares, "If you keep my commandments, you will abide in my love" (John 15:10). Moreover, the converse is true; if anyone does not love Jesus, he or she will not obey His teaching:

> Jesus replied, "If anyone loves me, he will obey my teaching. My Father will love him, and we will come to him and make our home with him. He who does not love me will not obey my teaching. These words you hear are not my own; they belong to the Father who sent me" (John 14:23-24, NIV).

---

[7] "The necessity of obedience to God's commands, as the expression of faith in God's promises, is therefore not works righteousness, since both the promises of God and the power to trust them are gifts of God's unmerited, saving grace. God gives what he demands, and what he demands is the obedience of faith (Romans 1:5; 16:26)." Scott Hafemann, *2 Corinthians* (NIV Application Commentary; Grand Rapids: Zondervan, 2000), 139.

However, although Jesus could summarize the law by the two great commandments of loving God and loving one's neighbor, we must not assume that this love is devoid of objective content or that it amounts simply to what one feels to be right. On the contrary, Jesus did not come to abolish the law and the prophets but to fulfil them (Matthew 5:17-19).

Similarly, in Jesus' revelation to John, He encourages His readers with these telling words: "Here is a call for the endurance of the saints, those who keep the commandments of God and their faith in Jesus" (Revelation 14:12).

New covenant grace

Yet, just as grace was plentiful under the old covenant, grace overflowed under the new covenant. In Jesus, we see the first and only sinless observer of God's law. His maturation as an adult in His humanity required leading a life of reverent submission to His Father. By so doing, He was perfected by His obedience to God's law: "Although he was a son, he learned obedience through what he suffered. And being made perfect, he became the source of eternal salvation to all who obey him" (Hebrews 5:8-9).

Note that those who are saved are those who obey. By Jesus' obedience unto death on a cross (Philippians 2:8), He thereby "destroyed death and has brought life and immortality to light through the gospel" (2 Timothy 1:10, NIV).

As we have seen in the promulgation of the Ten Commandments at Mount Sinai, whereas the law was graciously given to Israel as their means of responding to God's grace, at the same time the law brought condemnation to those who disobeyed. Strictly speaking, this condemnation rested upon all Israel, including Moses, but in God's mercy, provision was made for forgiveness within the very structure of the law, enabling sinful Israelites to be forgiven. As the writer to the Hebrews acknowledges, "... without the shedding of blood there is no forgiveness of sins" (Hebrews 9:22). However, he is also aware that "... it is impossible for the blood of bulls and goats to take away sins" (Hebrews 10:4). For "... the law has but a shadow of the good things to come" (Hebrews 10:1). The shadow, of course, is removed by Christ through His sinless obedience to the law, as well as taking upon Himself the law's punishment, which belonged to God's people. As Paul puts it, "For our sake, [God] made him to be sin who knew no sin, so that in him we might become the righteousness of God" (2 Corinthians 5:21).

In other words, the condemnation of the law is removed for those who are in Christ, because Christ has set us free from the law of sin and death

(Romans 8:1-2). Paul does not say that Christ has set us free from the ethical demands of the law, but that He has set us free from its condemnation. As Luke records Paul's words to the Jews in Pisidian Antioch:

> Let it be known to you therefore, brothers, that through this man forgiveness of sins is proclaimed to you, and by him everyone who believes is freed from everything from which you could not be freed by the law of Moses (Acts 13:38-39).

The law of Moses could not ultimately free Israel from judgment, as the sacrifices were not effective in themselves but only inasmuch as they prefigured the salvation that was to be procured by Christ's sacrifice:

> Therefore he is the mediator of a new covenant, so that those who are called may receive the promised eternal inheritance, since a death has occurred that redeems them from the transgressions committed under the first covenant (Hebrews 9:15).

Paul expresses a similar thought in Romans 3:25-26, where he defends God's righteousness in passing over former sins, committed under the Mosaic covenant, because God has definitively dealt with sin, once and for all, through the sacrifice of Christ. In other words, Christ's sacrifice is retrospective as well prospective for God's people throughout redemptive history.

New covenant obedience

In Romans 6, Paul is at pains to counter misunderstandings about God's grace that could encourage believers to sin more, so "... that grace may abound" (6:1). Similarly, his dictum that "... we are not under law but under grace ..." in Romans 6:15 is often misunderstood today by those who conclude that keeping God's law is no longer required of the Christian. Yet the next verse speaks of our slavery to Christ, which comprises an obedience that leads to righteousness (6:16). Paul thereby encourages his Roman readers to realize that God has made them "... obedient from the heart to the standard of teaching to which [they] were committed ..." (6:17). Moreover, in the following chapter, whatever position one takes on the identity of the man of Romans 7, Paul clearly indicates that obedience to the law of God is still the goal, for the law is spiritual; indeed, he says "... I delight in the law of God ..." (7:22), despite his natural inability to keep it.

Paul's statement that we are not under law but under grace is a shorthand way of saying that we no longer live under the judgment of the law (a ministry of death) but under the reign of grace, whereby Christ has taken the penalty of law-breaking upon Himself for us. This is the burden of Romans 8:1: "There is now no condemnation for those who are in Christ Jesus." For "the just requirement of the law has been fulfilled in us" (8:4).[8]

Paul eloquently reminds Timothy of the removal of judgment for the believer, while highlighting the stark reality that the condemnation of the law continues to fall upon the unbeliever:

> Now we know that the law is good, if one uses it lawfully, understanding this, that the law is not laid down for the just but for the lawless and disobedient, for the ungodly and sinners, for the unholy and profane, for those who strike their fathers and mothers, for murderers, the sexually immoral, men who practice homosexuality, enslavers, liars, perjurers, and whatever else is contrary to sound doctrine, in accordance with the gospel of the glory of the blessed God with which I have been entrusted (1 Timothy 1:8-11).

At first sight, Paul's words appear problematic. He seems to be suggesting that the law has no application to the just (i.e., the righteous), but only to the ungodly and sinners. Yet the words "not laid down" are significant for understanding Paul's meaning.[9] The use of *keitai* in this context suggests that the laying down of the penalty of the law is in view. The full force of the law's judgment is laid upon the ungodly, the law-breakers. For Paul prefaces his remarks by saying that "... the law is good if one uses it lawfully (*nomimōs*)" – that is, in the way it was intended, to provide the right response to God's grace. For Timothy and the saints at Ephesus, the law continues to provide guidelines for their behavior. Yet the law's condemnation does not fall upon the righteous, those who by faith are declared righteous in God's sight, because the judgment that would have belonged to them has been satisfied by the death of Christ. Christians no longer live under the law but under grace. However, the judgment of the law does fall on those who persist in unbelief and disobedience – for them there is no sacrifice for sins.[10]

---

[8] The Greek word *dikaiōma* is in the singular, as it is in 1:32, where the death penalty is in view. Its appearance in the plural, however, can refer to the precepts of the law as in 2:26, which has caused some commentators to assume that 8:4 is a reference to the fulfilment of the precepts of the law, whereas the context and the grammar indicate the fulfilment of the judgment of death that Christ has undertaken on our behalf. While both the NIV and ESV rightly translate *dikaiōma* as "righteous decree" in 1:32, they unhelpfully translate it as "righteous requirement" in 8:4.

[9] The NIV's translation of *keitai* as "made" is inadequate, if not misleading.

[10] If the warning of Hebrews 10:26 applies to those who sin deliberately after receiving knowledge of the truth, how much more does it apply to those who wilfully ignore the truth?

Moreover, in his exhortation to Timothy, Paul refers to specific commandments from the Decalogue that apply to the believer, as he does in Romans 13:8-10. Although in the latter passage Paul declares that the demands of love sum up these commandments, he does not thereby mean to say that the commandments no longer have any applicability. Rather, these commands are "sound doctrine" and "in accordance with the glorious gospel" which was entrusted to Paul (1 Timothy 1:10-11).

Application of God's law under the new covenant

When the prophets foretold the new covenant, they included obedience to the law as part of God's new economy. In Jeremiah 31:33ff, the prophet speaks of God writing His law on the hearts of His people. Isaiah 42:4, referring to the ministry of the Servant of the Lord, states, "He will not grow faint or be discouraged till he has established justice in the earth; and the coastlands wait for his law."

Similarly, in Ezekiel 11:19-20, the prophet reinforces the importance of following God's laws:

> 'I will give them an undivided heart and put a new spirit in them; I will remove from them their heart of stone and give them a heart of flesh. Then they will follow my decrees and be careful to keep my laws. They will be my people, and I will be their God' (NIV).

Yet, since the new covenant envisages an international community, not the theocracy of a nation-state, clearly law under the new covenant must be seen through the prism of Christ. This is the perspective of Paul's description of the "... law of Christ" (Galatians 6:2), or in James's words, "... the perfect law, the law of liberty" (James 1:25) or fulfilling "the royal law" (James 2:8, where he cites Leviticus 19:18). For example, the food laws of the Old Testament no longer apply under the new covenant (Mark 7:19), nor does the requirement of circumcision. Yet the fact that we are still required to keep God's laws, without being subject to the whole Mosaic economy, is expressed clearly by Paul: "For neither circumcision counts for anything nor uncircumcision, but keeping the commandments of God" (1 Corinthians 7:19).

The irony of this statement is that circumcision was a command of God, yet Paul exhorts his readers (some of them uncircumcised) to keep the commandments of God. How then should we understand which commands to keep? The Reformers faced this question in the sixteenth century. The Church of England therefore adopted Article VII of the Thirty-nine Articles as a solution to the problem:

The Old Testament is not contrary to the New: for both in the Old and New Testament everlasting life is offered to Mankind by Christ, who is the only Mediator between God and Man, being both God and Man. Wherefore they are not to be heard, which feign that the old Fathers did look only for transitory promises. Although the Law given from God by Moses, as touching Ceremonies and Rites, do not bind Christian men, nor the Civil precepts thereof ought of necessity to be received in any commonwealth; yet notwithstanding, no Christian man whatsoever is free from the obedience of the Commandments which are called Moral.[11]

The recitation of the Ten Commandments in the Administration of the Lord's Supper in the *Book of Common Prayer* demonstrates the continuing application of the Decalogue in the life of the believer. After each commandment is read, the congregation responds, "Incline our hearts to keep this law."

Such a response is worthy of all God's people, not just Anglicans, as the words of the psalmist indicate:

> If your law had not been my delight,
>   I would have perished in my affliction.
> I will never forget your precepts,
>   for by them you have given me life. (Psalm 119:92-93)

---

[11] The Church of Scotland, on the other hand, adopted Chapter 19 of the Westminster Confession of Faith, which declares a similar distinction between the moral law, as expressed in the Ten Commandments, and the ceremonial and judicial laws of Israel.

God's Commandments Require Us to Read and Think Carefully[1]

Thomas Schirrmacher, Germany

The Bible is not a collection of rules and regulations one can memorize and quickly apply in every situation. The Bible, the written source of God's commandments, is a small library with literary diversity and different forms of reasoning.[2] There are universally valid, positive commandments such as "You should love …," as well as universally valid, negative commandments such as "You shall not steal …" Such prohibitions should protect God's order for humanity at places where it is vulnerable, regarding, e.g., property, marriage, and truth-telling, whereas the positive commandments set the meaning and direction of life before God and in society.

In addition to universal positive and negative commandments, the Bible contains nuanced directives. These include case studies which apply to similar situations, along with commands that declare the priority of obligations (such Hosea 6:6, "I desire mercy, not sacrifice," which is quoted in Matthew 9:13 and 12:7; and 1 Samuel 15:22, "to obey is better than sacrifice," which is referenced in Psalm 51 and Jeremiah 7). Some commands, such as regulations regarding divorce, give instructions for a situation where other commandments have already been violated. A few commands define exceptions to general rules, such as killing in self-defense (see Exodus 22:1-2, quoted below). Some do not mention exceptions though exceptions are known from other texts or are seen as self-evident.

There are even practices which Holy Scripture endorses but never raises to the level of a commandment. Fasting is a good example. While great blessing rests upon fasting, and we find many biblical models for it,

---

[1] This chapter is adapted from Thomas Schirrmacher, *Leadership and Ethical Responsibility: The Three Aspects of Every Decision*, translated by Richard McClary, edited by Thomas K. Johnson, Vol. 13 of the WEA Global Issues Series (Bonn: VKW, 2013), 54-68; https://www.academia.edu/83724725/Thomas_Schirrmacher_Leadership_and_Ethical_Responsibility_The_Three_Aspects_of_Every_Decision_edited_by_Thomas_K_Johnson.

[2] See the overview by Walter C. Kaiser, *Towards Old Testament Ethics* (Grand Rapids, MI: Zondervan, 1983), 64-66. Quotations from the Bible in this chapter are from the New International Version.

fasting is never presented as a general duty.³ This manner of presentation of God's commandments requires us to seek wisdom; this means we must read and think very carefully about God's commandments.

Five levels of law in the Bible

The Bible does not give us God's commandments in a unilinear fashion; the Bible gives us God's commands through a spectrum which runs from foundational statements to case examples. One can distinguish five levels of Old Testament law: 1) ultimate principles; 2) foundational commandments, often one or more of the Ten Commandments; 3) rules for implementation; 4) case studies in relation to people; and 5) case studies regarding nonhumans. Other levels could also be delineated, and one does not find every level represented for every topic. The point is not the number; rather, the point is the nature of law and commands as they range from entirely general statements to completely concrete examples.

Sometimes two or more levels are addressed together in one verse, as we will see in 1 Timothy 5:17-18. Many times, a principle is formulated generally and exemplified through a case example. This can be seen, for example, in Proverbs 15:16-17: "Better a little with the fear of the Lord than great wealth with turmoil. Better a meal of vegetables where there is love than a fattened calf with hatred" (also cf. Proverbs 16:8; 17:1).

An example: five levels of law regarding murder

- 1st level, ultimate principle: Love of neighbor
- 2nd level, foundational commandment: Do not murder
- 3rd level, rule for implementation: Manslaughter at the time of burglary
- 4th level: Human case law of a railing around a roof
- 5th level: Nonhuman case law of cisterns

Detailed explanation:

- 1st level: Leviticus 19:18: "... but love your neighbor as yourself."
- 2nd level: Exodus 20:13: "You shall not murder."

---

[3] See R. T. Foster, "Fasting," in David J. Atkinson and David H. Field (eds.), *New Dictionary of Christian Ethics and Pastoral Theology* (Downers Grove, IL: IVP, 1995), 376-378.

- 3rd level: Exodus 22:2-3: "If a thief is caught breaking in and is struck so that he dies, the defender is not guilty of bloodshed; but if it happens after sunrise, he is guilty of bloodshed."
- 4th level: Deuteronomy 22:8: "When you build a new house, make a parapet around your roof so that you may not bring the guilt of bloodshed on your house if someone falls from the roof." This command naturally applies to parallel cases: It is also manslaughter if one does not think about others and allows them to endanger themselves.
- 5th level: Exodus 21:33-34: "If a man uncovers a pit [or a well] or digs one [or lets it be opened] and fails to cover it and an ox or a donkey falls into it, the owner of the pit must pay for the loss." This is an example of case law where the example has to do with animals, yet it applies all the more to people. Jesus also argued about the Sabbath with laws relating to animals. He did this to justify people's actions (e.g., Luke 13:15-17; 14:4-6; Matthew 12:10-12).

Case law and an ethic of principles

Regarding a railing around a roof, Luther wrote, "This can be a proverbial and general law, that in public community things are so built, and one behaves in such a manner, that one does not cause others to be exposed to any dangers, disadvantages or damages."[4]

Since case law applies to similar situations and illustrates the central principle – even in the case of manslaughter – this command also applies in cultures that have other types of roofs. It applies to life situations in which it is necessary to take preventative measures to protect people. That a railing should be a protection on a flat roof, and that a pit should have a

---

[4] Martin Luther. "Anmerkungen zum fünften Buch Moses," column 1565 in Martin Luther, *Sämtliche Schriften*, vol. 3, edited by Johann Georg Walch (Groß Oesingen: Verlag der Lutherischen Buchhandlung, 1986, 1910² reprint). In Old and New Testament times houses had flat roofs that were also used. Grass, that animals were sometimes allowed to eat, grew on the roof (Isaiah 37:27; Psalm 129:6). Women spread things out on the roof so that they would dry (Joshua 2:6), and in the summer, tents were put up on the roof and people slept there (2 Samuel 16:22; cf. Nehemiah 8:16; 1 Samuel 9:25). A person was safe on the roof (Matthew 24:17). Important news was called out from roofs (Isaiah 15:3; Jeremiah 48:38; Matthew 10:27), which led to people subsequently meeting on roofs (Isaiah 22:1). When people gathered in a house, the roof could be uncovered and people could get to the center of the house as the friends of the paralytic were able to do in Mark 2:4; Luke 5:19, in order to bring him to Jesus.

barrier around it, means that every person is responsible for injuries and death in the case where one does not protect or warn others. In all legislation that is influenced by Christianity, there are corresponding provisions, for instance, that areas around road construction sites and pits and manholes be clearly sealed off.

A case law (casuistry, from the Latin *casus*, the case) is a law that illustrates a general principle by using a particular example.[5] Martin Honecker rightly writes: "Casuistry is the 'explanation of individual cases' in morals and jurisprudence. The word is largely used as a negative label when it is understood as a synonym for 'hairsplitting' and 'sophistry,' but casuistry primarily means – and this matter of fact is quite well justified – to apply rules to an individual case."[6]

Biblical case laws are not case laws only in the sense of precedent decisions. They are basic commands, enacted once and for all; the canon of these case laws does not expand. Biblical case laws illustrate foundational principles in relation to a particular case, and we must transfer the principles to similar cases.

Examples of similar case laws

The command that a millstone should not be given as security (Deuteronomy 24:6) naturally does not mean that only millstones may not be given as security. Rather it refers to everything that is required for survival.

The commands regarding blind and deaf people, "Cursed is the man who leads the blind astray on the road" (Deuteronomy 27:18) and "Do not curse the deaf or put a stumbling block in front of the blind, but fear your God," refer not only to these examples but convey the idea that people are not to take advantage of others' disabilities. One must be considerate of their limitations. Job was for this reason "eyes to the blind and feet to the lame" and "a father to the needy" (Job 29:15-16). These provisions have strongly shaped our culture.

In the Old Testament petty larceny of food is not theft: "If you enter your neighbor's vineyard, you may eat all the grapes you want, but do not put any in your basket. If you enter your neighbor's grain field, you may pick kernels with your hands, but you must not put a sickle to his standing grain" (Deuteronomy 23:24-25). This is a typical case law that does not

---

[5] Cf. P. D. Toon. "Casuistry," in R. K. Harrison (ed.). *Encyclopedia of Biblical and Christian Ethics* (Nashville, TN: Thomas Nelson, 1987), 52-53.

[6] Martin Honecker, *Einführung in die Theologische Ethik* (Berlin: Walter de Gruyter, 1990), 170; also 170-175.

apply only to grapes and grains. Rather it establishes that the amount needed to meet one's needs is exempt from punishment.

Case law points to the fact that biblical ethics are an ethic of principles. It is decisive that for each commandment out of which external visible application arises, an ultimate divine principle is first recognized. The highest principle is love toward God and neighbor. This lies at the bottom of all commandments, and they are only properly understood from that standpoint. From this basis principles are derived which form the basis for more specific moral rules and civil laws.

Understanding the principles at the highest level of Old Testament commandments is crucial to properly understanding how the New Testament builds on Old Testament ethics. The New Testament emphasizes the principles in the Old Testament commandments.

An ethic of principles is also of importance for the application of biblical commands in the present, in the ever-new cultural situations we face. What is decisive is how the basic principle is put into practice. Old Testament law, for example, requires "righteousness in the gates." This is because the Israelites' courts met "in the gates." What is decisive is the principle of righteousness, along with the public character of holding court, not the city gate as such, which many cultures do not have.

Regarding casuistry, one must differentiate the Old Testament from later Jewish casuistry. Old Testament casuistry illustrates a basic command with specific cases and examples, showing how the principle should be applied to similar cases. For this reason, the cases discussed represent only a portion of the imaginable cases. *Casuistry alone is too concrete to derive truly basic principles from it, but to do without casuistry leaves ethics and law too abstract and distanced from reality.*

Furthermore, inner-biblical casuistry, which can call upon the authority of God's Word, must be distinguished from interpreters' casuistry, which tries to apply biblical ordinances to present-day cases. The latter is acceptable, but the conclusions drawn from it cannot be placed in the same category as a command of God, such as was claimed in the Jewish Talmud or in Catholic canon law.

Principles and commandments provide a framework for life, not life itself

"All human thought and action hang together with a worldview. Everyone arrays themselves and their actions within the framework of a comprehensive interpretation of man and the world, within which behavior first achieves meaning."[7] The word "framework" is crucial. As important as absolute moral principles are, an individual cannot live with them alone, making decisions solely based on them. We must think to make decisions about how we live. God's Word sets a framework for our life, thought, and planning, but it does not fill out this framework. This is responsible freedom. God does not live our lives nor treat us like robots; He produces the conditions so we can live. Essential principles are often illustrated for us in the Holy Scriptures via case examples. But the Bible summons us to weigh our plans, think through them, consider, seek counsel, and then take responsibility for our decisions.

That is why large portions of the Old Testament law are formulated negatively ("You shall not ..."). The precise thing that disturbs many people has to do with freedom. The "not" sets boundaries without prescribing details. Gustav Friedrich Oehler observes, regarding Old Testament law: "The stipulations of the law are mainly found in detail in negative terms. The requirements go into detail regarding what an Israelite is not allowed to do ... However, it is easy to recognize that in respect to positive duties, the law in many cases only expresses things generally. The intention is not to expressly mandate, but rather to put forth facts, examples, and institutions which allow the positive aspects to freely flourish."[8]

Job acknowledges (23:12): "I have not departed from the commands of his lips; I have treasured the words of his mouth more than my daily bread." Job's love for the poor, who are described in this connection, goes well beyond what was required. Still, based on this fact, one may not come to the opposite conclusion that love can get along without moral order and rules.

Weights and measures

When the Old Testament calls for uniformity and reliability regarding weights and measures for business, the values involved are not simply private values. These principles form the basis for every functioning economy and are the precondition for equitable prosperity. Two principles are at work that are referenced in the Ten Commandments, but these are also generally recognized in secular societies. These principles are,

---

[7] Hansjörg Hemminger, *Psychotherapie: Weg zum Glück? Zur Orientierung auf dem Psychomarkt*, Münchener Reihe (Munich: Evangelischer Presseverband für Bayern, 1987), 5.

[8] Gustav Friedrich Oehler, *Theologie des Alten Testaments* (Stuttgart: J. F. Steinkopf, 1891³), 289.

namely, honesty over against lying ("You shall not give false testimony") and the right to property ownership over against theft ("You shall not steal") as well as the internal attitude ("You shall not covet"). Whoever deceitfully infringes upon these principles destroys not only personal relationships but potentially an entire society. In Amos 8:4-6 God warns about oppressing the poor and the weak by using dishonest weights and measures.

Question 110 of the 1563 Heidelberg Catechism deliberately refers to the Old Testament standards of honest weights and measures in its explanation of the commandment against stealing. It also binds the state to monitor this and indeed shows just how comprehensively the Reformation viewed the Old Testament commandment against theft: "What does God forbid in the eighth commandment? He forbids not only outright theft and robbery, punishable by law. But in God's sight theft also includes cheating and swindling our neighbor by schemes made to appear legitimate, such as: inaccurate measurements of weight, size, or volume; fraudulent merchandising; counterfeit money; excessive interest; or any other means forbidden by God. In addition he forbids all greed and pointless squandering of his gifts."[9]

Although the principles in the Bible are unambiguous, the Bible does not speak about measurements, weights, and currency units that are valid for all times and cultures. The Bible does not tell us to use ancient Middle Eastern units of measurement instead of modern measures such as kilograms or pounds, kilometers or miles. Yet the principle of reliability of the data a seller reveals is at all times of foundational importance for the economy and for all of life in society.

Biblical texts regarding measures and weights

Commands

- Proverbs 16:11: "Honest scales and balances are from the Lord; all the weights in the bag are of his making."
- Proverbs 20:10, 23: "Differing weights and differing measures – the Lord detests them both. ... The Lord detests differing weights, and dishonest scales do not please him."

---

[9]   Quoted from http://www.crcna.org/pages/heidelberg_commandments.cfm#Q andA%20110.

- Leviticus 19:35-36: "Do not use dishonest standards when measuring length, weight or quantity. Use honest scales and honest weights, an honest ephah and an honest hin."[10]
- Deuteronomy 25:13-16: "Do not have two differing weights in your bag – one heavy, one light. Do not have two differing measures in your house – one large, one small. You must have accurate and honest weights and measures, so that you may live long in the land the Lord your God is giving you. For the Lord your God detests anyone who does these things, anyone who deals dishonestly."
- Ezekiel 45:9-12: "... do what is just and right ... You are to use accurate scales, an accurate ephah and an accurate bath. The ephah and the bath are to be the same size, the bath containing a tenth of a homer and the ephah a tenth of a homer; the homer is to be the standard measure for both. The shekel is to consist of twenty gerahs. Twenty shekels plus twenty-five shekels plus fifteen shekels equal one mina."[11]

Criticism based on these commands

- Hosea 12:7: "The merchant uses dishonest scales; he loves to defraud."
- Amos 8:4-5: "Hear this, you who trample the needy and do away with the poor of the land ... that we may sell grain ... skimping the measure, boosting the price and cheating with dishonest scales."
- Micah 6:10-11: "Am I still to forget, O wicked house, your ill-gotten treasures and the short ephah, which is accursed? Shall I acquit a man with dishonest scales, with a bag of false weights?"

Further principles for business

The famous saying, "the worker deserves his wages" (1 Corinthians 9:9; Luke 10:7; cf. Deuteronomy 25:4) makes every type of work valuable and creates an obligation for equitable pay that may not be withheld (Mark 10:19; Deuteronomy 24:14; Leviticus 19:13; James 5:4). The command is understood in the New Testament equally as an obligation toward church elders and toward working animals, illustrating the organic unity of the several levels of ethical principles. "The elders who direct the affairs of the church well are

---

[10] These are Hebrew measures.
[11] The terms are more Hebrew designations of measure.

worthy of double honor, especially those whose work is preaching and teaching. For Scripture says, 'Do not muzzle an ox while it is treading out the grain,' and 'The worker deserves his wages' " (1 Timothy 5:17-18). This principle touches a foundational temptation of business-people and of materialism: "Look! The wages you failed to pay the workmen who mowed your fields are crying out against you. The cries of the harvesters have reached the ears of the Lord Almighty" (James 5:4). Not to pay wages or not to pay them completely or too late is grievous theft: "Do not steal ... Do not deceive one another ... Do not defraud your neighbor or rob him. Do not hold back the wages of a hired man overnight" (Leviticus 9:11-13).

The Old Testament very generally and rather often warns about oppressing others by paying low wages and uses clear formulations that even Karl Marx could not outdo: "Do not defraud your neighbor or rob him" (Leviticus 19:13). "Do not take advantage of a hired man who is poor and needy, whether he is a brother Israelite or an alien living in one of your towns [within your jurisdiction]. Pay him his wages each day before sunset, because he is poor and is counting on it. Otherwise, he may cry to the Lord against you, and you will be guilty of sin" (Deuteronomy 24:14-15). "Woe to him who builds his palace by unrighteousness, his upper rooms by injustice, making his countrymen work for nothing, not paying them for their labor" (Jeremiah 22:13).

The biblical statements about the binding nature of agreements relating to labor, as well as the necessity of and entitlement to payment, are of wide-ranging importance. Still, they are not so formulated that we concretely know exactly how a labor agreement is supposed to look and what wage is appropriate. God alludes to the necessity of the legal certainty of a labor agreement and to adequate compensation. However, the concrete configuration reached between the contractual parties as well as the institutions in charge of overseeing the legal aspects are items that are entrusted to others and may change in times and cultures.

Comments:

When we read God's commandments carefully and think deeply about them, life should begin to change. We may need to repent, and this repentance may go far beyond the hidden realm of our souls to change our actions. And once we begin to think deeply about God's commands, we will see that such obscure references to ephahs, homers, gerahs, and railings around roofs were applications of eternal principles to local situations, and we can articulate those principles in our secular and multi-religious societies. Then we can be much more confident to proclaim God's Word in our time.

The First Commandment:

YOU SHALL HAVE NO OTHER GODS BEFORE ME

David Zadok, Israel

The invitation by Dr. Sam Logan to write this paper arrived in my inbox minutes after I watched the inauguration of the 46th President of the United States, Joe Biden. The ceremony, which in Israel was titled the "Celebration of Democracy," was broadcasted live, and many watched the event, as it was of interest also in our part of the world. According to the long tradition, both the President and the Vice President were sworn into their respective offices by putting their hand on a Bible and repeating the oath that ends with the words "So help me God." But which God did each of them mean, and which God do people mean when they so easily use the name of God? Is it indeed the same God who revealed Himself to Moses and the people of Israel, as found in Exodus 20 and then repeated in Deuteronomy 5? And is He the Father of Jesus Christ, the Son of God?

While we may rightly consider the Decalogue as a Judeo-Christian code of ethics and conduct, we find that part of it is embedded in the criminal laws of many nations and countries. The sixth commandment, "You shall not murder," and the eighth commandment, "You shall not steal," are obvious examples of this; and violation of the seventh commandment, "You shall not commit adultery," in its various interpretations, is regarded a criminal offense in some countries and even as a capital crime in a few Muslim countries that abide by the Sharia. Of course, in its narrowest interpretation, the first commandment is not enforced in the same way that the commandments mentioned above are considered a judicial offense. There is a difference between the first commandment and some of the others, and as we will see later, that is not the only difference.

A Brief Background of the Ten Commandments

The Decalogue was given to a specific people at a particular time, though it has a universal reach. When God brought the people of Israel out of slavery in that first Passover and eventually brought them to the land promised to Abraham and his descendants, He gave them His law. In Exodus 19, we read that it was in the third month after the children of Israel had come out of Egypt, while they were in the wilderness of Sinai, that God called Moses to the mountain. The memories of the ten plagues, the sight of the parting sea for their passage, and the destruction of the Egyptian army in the same sea were still vivid and unforgettable. On the mountaintop God reminded Moses and the people of Israel of the miraculous way He had brought them out and of how He had borne them "on eagles' wings" to Himself (Exodus 19:4). They belonged to Him now. And they were to keep His covenant and obey His voice, to be unto Him "a royal priesthood, a holy nation" (1 Peter 2:9). Before giving the law, God required the people of Israel to sanctify themselves, to set themselves apart and to cleanse themselves for two days, and on the third day He would "come down" (Exodus19:11).

The drama continued as God warned Moses that the people should not come close to the mountain or touch it, for they would surely be stoned and not live (Exodus 19:13). On the third day, "there were thunders and lightnings and a thick cloud on the mountain and a very loud trumpet blast, so that all the people in the camp trembled" (19:16). God came down and called Moses to the mountaintop. God was present with Moses, and the people heard His voice as He gave the Ten Words. The Hebrew word for the Ten Commandments is עֲשֶׂרֶת הַדִּבְּרוֹת (aseret ha-dibberot), which means the "ten words."

Immediately after God delivered His Ten Words, the people who heard His voice were fearful and asked Moses, not God, to talk to them (Exodus 20:19); they wanted a mediator, because they were fearful of God. While they stood afar from the mountain and from the presence of God, Moses related the words God spoke immediately after the tenth and last commandment. In Exodus 20:22-23, we read, "You have seen for yourselves that I have talked with you from heaven. You shall not make gods of silver to be with me, nor shall you make for yourselves gods of gold." God's first words after He delivered His law echo the first commandment, "You shall have no other gods before me." And later, in chapter 21, God set before them the implication of His laws as He provided in-depth laws for their observance. In these two chapters, we have the immediate context of the before and after of the giving of the Decalogue. Now we can turn our attention to the foundation of God's commandments.

The Foundation of the Ten Words

The foundation of the Ten Commandments is the act of God. By way of introducing the commandments to His people, God tells them, "I am the

LORD your God, who brought you out of the land of Egypt, out of the house of slavery" (Exodus 20:2). In these brief and profound introductory words, we learn two essential characteristics of God and two demands of the people of God. The first characteristic that we observe is that the Lord is God, and He is "your" God. While He is the God of the universe and the Creator of heaven and earth, He is in a specific way the God of His people, Israel. He is a personal God near His people, an immanent God, and not only a transcendent God.

The second characteristic of God seen here is that the Lord God is the One who acts, who brought His people out of Egypt and out of slavery. He is not a passive God but an active God. And He acts before He speaks or demands – just as it was in the very first verse of Genesis – "In the beginning, God created ..." And the act of God in the context of giving His law was that of deliverance. He brought the children of Israel out of the land and the house where they had been enslaved for 400 years, namely the land of Egypt and the house of slavery. His deliverance came before the demands. It is only after saving and delivering His people from slavery that God gives them commandments to obey. There is new ownership of the people of Israel – they are no longer slaves to the Egyptians; they belong now to God. They are His. The preamble of the Ten Words communicates the very nature of the One who gives them His words; He is their Lord and their God and their deliverer and their Savior. Out of His graciousness alone, God delivers and sets them free. These are the two essential characteristics of God that are foundational in giving His law.

God's two demands of His people are that they are to hear His commandments and to love Him, which means to obey Him (Deuteronomy 6). God gave the law to the people of Israel not because He needed it for His benefit or to fill something lacking in Him, but rather for the benefit of His people. In the famous *Shema* in Deuteronomy 6:4-5, God says: "Hear, O Israel: The LORD our God, the LORD is one. You shall love the LORD your God with all your heart and with all your soul and with all your might." The commandments of God do not add or take away anything from Him, and they do not increase or decrease any part of His being. They are purely for the benefit and the good of man and not of God. God is perfect in all His being and in all that He is, and therefore the commandments do not change Him or make Him happier or better. He is not dependent on us; rather, we are dependent on Him, and He gave us His law for our good. When, in the *Shema*, He commands us to love Him with all our being, it is for our good and advantage. Our love and obedience do not make Him more or less perfect; He is forever the same perfect God. The Ten Words are for our good and for that of the society in which we live; they were given to protect us from ourselves and from each other. King David, the psalmist of Israel, puts it poetically and beautifully in Psalm 19:7-11:

> The law of the LORD is perfect, reviving the soul;
>   the testimony of the LORD is sure, making wise the simple;
> the precepts of the LORD are right, rejoicing the heart;
>   the commandment of the LORD is pure, enlightening the eyes;
> the fear of the LORD is clean, enduring forever;
>   the rules of the LORD are true, and righteous altogether.
> More to be desired are they than gold, even much fine gold;
>   sweeter also than honey and drippings of the honeycomb.
> Moreover, by them is your servant warned;
>   in keeping them there is great reward.

Imagine a society where murder was not punishable. The fear in which members of that society would have to live every moment of their lives would be horrible. Or imagine a community in which adultery was a norm. When spouses were not committed to fidelity in marriage and could not be certain their children were their own, what kind of family life could be enjoyed? Though some see God's law as a burden, the Scripture shows us the benefit of the law. Psalm 119, the longest chapter of the Bible, conveniently placed in the center of our Bibles, celebrates the benefits and the beauty of the law. This unique psalm, in which each stanza of eight verses is an acrostic based on the order of the Hebrew alphabet, shows the place and the prominence of the law in our lives. To the psalmist, the commandments of God are a delight (119:47), not a burden, and he loves the ordinances and the statutes of God.

However, the more significant benefit of the law of God is that it points us to the gospel and to the only One who can make the law a delight. The law and, in particular, the Ten Commandments, shows us how incapable we are of keeping it and how often we fail to uphold it. In fact, because the law condemns us and shows our inability to do the right thing in the eyes of God, it pushes us into the arms of the gospel, where we can find refuge and comfort. The story of Martin Luther helps us to see this point dazzlingly. As a devout monk who wanted to be right with God and righteous in His sight, Luther reached the point where he began hating God because of His total demands of righteousness, something Luther could never achieve no matter how hard he worked at it. Also, the apostle Paul became an enemy for the monk, because in his epistles, Paul emphasized the righteousness of God, something that was unreachable for Luther, and it agonized him. He would spend hours each day confessing his sins to the priest and then later would run back to him again to confess yet another sin. But one day he read Romans 1:17: "For in it the righteousness of God is revealed from faith for faith, as it is written, 'The righteous shall live by faith.'" These words "leaped out from the chapter, stood alone, the key to the whole problem."[1] What Luther could not do for himself, the gospel did for him. The failure to maintain the law by his own efforts pushed him toward the message of the gospel and the finished work of Christ. The righteous live not by works but by faith. This truth, justification by faith alone, became the foundation of Luther's theology and, in fact, of the whole Reformation. That is why Luther loved to emphasize the "Law and Gospel" distinction. "Lutheran theology is well-known for the sharp antithesis it draws between Law and Gospel. This finds its root to some degree in the teaching of Luther, who emphasized what is often called the 'pedagogical' use of the Mosaic law, its use as a schoolmaster to accuse us of sin that we might look to Jesus to save us."[2]

This is why the Old Testament cannot have the last word. The story cannot end there. It must continue, and thank God, it does continue. The Ten Words and the law are not the end. That is why John, in his prologue to his Gospel, tells us that "the law was given through Moses; grace and truth came through Jesus Christ" (John 1:17). The last word is Jesus, through whom the Father spoke to us, as the writer of Hebrews clearly proclaims. The apostle Paul conveys the same idea in Romans 10:4 when he tells us that "Christ is the end [τέλος (télos)] of the law ... to everyone who believes." It is by grace that we are saved and not through the works of the law, and yet we see how the law is a tutor (guardian, Galatians 3:24) leading us to Christ and His grace.[3]

The structure of the Ten Commandments guides our attention and our relationship vertically, with God, and horizontally, with people. The first four commandments concern our relationship with God, and the final six speak to our relationship with one another. Only when we are in right relationship with God and maintain the Creator-creature distinction can all other human relationships fall into their right place. Jesus summarized all of the Law in these two commandments: Love God, and love your neighbor

---

[1] Brian Lunn, *Martin Luther: The Man and His God*, (London: Butler & Tanner Ltd., 1934), 41.
[2] https://www.ligonier.org/learn/devotionals/law-and-gospel/.
[3] We are assuming the distinction among the moral, ceremonial, and judicial laws in the Old Testament. The moral laws, such as the Ten Commandments, apply throughout human history, whereas the ceremonial and judicial laws applied directly to a limited time in history. This should not lead us to neglect the ceremonial and judicial laws, since they teach us what proper worship and proper justice looked like in that time.

as yourself (Mark 12:29-31). In this, Jesus confirms the structure of the Ten Commandments – God first and then others.

The Text and the Meaning of the First Commandment

The Hebrew text of the first commandment starts with the negative word לֹא (lo), "no," just as do the second, third, and last five commandments. The only two commandments that do not start with the negative word are the fourth and the fifth, keeping the Sabbath day holy, and honoring your father and your mother, respectively. Why do the majority of the commandments begin with "no"? The word *no* limits our having any other gods besides the God who introduced Himself in the introduction to the commandments. Starting with the negative word sets the boundary for us as to who is God and who is a false god. Since the Lord God is the One and only One, it is easier to use the negative word rather than provide a comprehensive list of what is prohibited. In general, the nature of the Ten Commandments is such that it is easier to describe what is prohibited than to list what is not prohibited. They are absolute, e.g., "You shall not commit adultery" is clear regarding what the commandment prohibits.

The first commandment tells us there are no other gods and we should not have any other gods. This commandment speaks about the one true God versus false gods; the second commandment follows it and prohibits us from worshiping the one true God falsely. In other words, the first two commandments ban us from false gods and false worship of the one true God.

In Sinai, God made the covenant with the people of Israel, and part of that covenant was the relationship He established with His people. We can see in that relationship that God is the One who not only initiates but, as has been mentioned, also acted on behalf of His covenant people by bringing them out of slavery. In his classic work *The Ten Commandments*, Thomas Watson, a seventeenth-century English Puritan, writes these words in his introduction to the first commandment: "The message of this commandment is that we should sanctify God in our hearts and give Him precedence above all created things. There are two parts to this commandment: 1. We must have God for our God. 2. We must have no other God."[4] Watson brings out the two-part implication of the first commandment, i.e., who our God is and who are false gods. The one true God is a jealous God. In the second

---

[4] Thomas Watson, *The Ten Commandments*, Rev. ed., (Abbotsford, WI: Aneko Press, 2019 – first edition published in 1692), 19.

part of the second commandment, when God commands us not to bow to any graven images, the reason given is that He is a jealous God, and He will not share His glory with anyone else. Because He is the only God, it is His prerogative not to share the devotion due to Him *alone* with anyone or anything else. Earlier, in the introduction, we saw that the Decalogue was given in the third month after the Israelites had come out of the land of Egypt, which was a polytheistic culture. Philip Ryken explains, "... and in this, the Egyptians were unsurpassed. They worshipped the gods of fields and rivers, light and darkness, sun and storm. Swearing their alliances to the gods and goddesses of love and war, they bowed down to worship idols in the form of men and beasts."[5] Now that the Israelites had come out of Egypt and slavery, they needed to come out of their relationship with the foreign gods of Egypt as well.

I earlier mentioned how the President and Vice President, at their inauguration, put their hand on a Bible, and when they took the oath, they ended it by saying "So help me God." Today in our post-modern and post-almost-anything world, the name of God is misused and thrown around so very easily. Many would say they believe in God or gods, and some may even use the name Jesus; however, to whom do they really refer? And do they sincerely and honestly mean the LORD God, the One who brought Israel out of the land of Egypt, out of the house of slavery? He, and only He, is the one true God, though many in societies from all corners of the world may use the name, the same name but mean someone or something else. In our conversations with people, we need to make sure we understand to which God they refer and that it is the God of the Scriptures, because there is much confusion; Satan is working hard to convince people who believe in a false god and worship a false god that they are worshiping the one true God. And this brings us to the next question: Is Allah, or the god in which other monotheistic religions believe, the same god?[6]

Do We All Worship the Same One True God?

Now that we have discussed the Ten Commandments in their larger context, and also the first commandment specifically, we ought to ask this

---

[5] Philip Graham Ryken, *Written in Stone: The Ten Commandments and Today's Moral Crisis*, (Phillipsburg, New Jersey: P&R Publishing, 2010), 58.
[6] We know that some Christians have long used the Arabic word "Allah" (and similar words in other languages) to refer to the Trinitarian God of the Bible. We are not criticizing them for doing this. Here we are only discussing the Muslim understanding of God.

important question. Is the God of the Old and New Testaments, and more specifically, the God who gave the Ten Words, the same God whom Jews and Muslims worship? This is a sensitive question for both a Jew and a Muslim to answer, but we ought to look to the only reliable source we have to answer the question, and that is the Scriptures. In answering the question, we need to put our prejudice aside (which is difficult for me as a Jew) and look at the core of the issue, and that is the true and full identity of the one true God. Since both Islam and rabbinic Judaism teach that there is one and only one God and that their God is not Trinitarian, can it be the same God?

At the core, the answer is no, but it needs to be qualified and explained.[7] While there is some commonality between the God of the Bible and Allah, there is also a huge chasm between the two. Both Islam and the Bible describe God and Allah as one, and they are both the Creator of the universe, and Creator *ex nihilo*, who created all things out of nothing. However, the Allah that the Qur'an describes is a being who is unknowable in his essence; he is a transcendent God who is so immense that we cannot know him. He is a God who is way up there and out there and who really does not concern himself with the affairs of man in the world. In his being, he cannot be known, unlike the God of the Bible, who is close to His people.

The God of the Bible is so close that He came down to save His people (Exodus 3:6-8); of course, the Son also took on human flesh to come and "tabernacle" among us (John 1:14). He became one of us. He revealed Himself to us in such a way that we can know Him personally. And while Allah has 99 names in the Qur'an, all of these names tell us what he *does*, not who he *is*. According to the Qur'an, Allah's revelation of himself is limited to his actions; it does not concern his being. Again, this is related to the fact that Muslims see Allah as so transcendent that he is unknowable and does not tell who he is; he only tells what he does. In contrast, the God of the Scriptures not only reveals Himself to us, but He tells us He *is* love and He *is*

---

[7] Editor's note: In this essay we are not suggesting that the understanding of God in rabbinic Judaism and Allah in Islam are the same, and, we believe, our Christian knowledge of God as the Trinity (including the Incarnation, Crucifixion, and Resurrection of the Son of God) is different from non-messianic Judaism. Christians normally make distinctions among people who have a general sense that there is a Creator, those who have bits and pieces of true information about God from the Bible, people who have more complete information about God from Biblical teaching, and people who have a saving knowledge of God by faith in Jesus Christ. Some also distinguish between a rejected knowledge of God (whether of God's general revelation or of both general revelation and special revelation) and a saving knowledge of God by faith in the gospel. TJ

light, among many other characteristics.[8] The Scriptures describe who God is, not only what He does. And that is an important distinction and difference between God and Allah.

In addition, the Qur'an tells us that Allah is the one who created evil (Qur'an 113:2, which attributes to Allah the creation of darkness).[9] This, of course, completely contradicts the God of the Bible, who created all things good, and the whole creation was very good. Furthermore, Allah is not under any rules that he set for himself, and neither is he obligated to his covenants – in other words, he is a capricious being who does what he likes and, if he desires, can even go against his own character. Not so with the God of the Bible, who is unchangeable and who always acts according to His character. While He is the God who can do all things, of His own choice, He has determined not to act contrary to His character, and in His faithfulness, He will keep His promises and covenants.

The most important distinction between Allah and the one true God is that the God of the Scriptures is a Trinitarian God. From the very first chapter, the Scriptures show that God is a Trinity, and from eternity He is Father, Son, and Spirit; He is One indivisible Being in three irreducible Persons. In the very first verse of the Hebrew Bible, we come across the word אֱלֹהִים, (Elohim), which is plural, and only a few verses down in that first chapter, verse 26, God said: "Let *us* make man in *our* image, after *our* likeness." (emphasis added) The Hebrew words are plural, and though that is not the only reference to the Trinitarian God in the Old Testament, it is important that God reveals Himself in such a way in the very first chapter of His revealed and written words. In other passages in the Pentateuch, there are indications and hints of the plurality of God, as we read that the angel of the Lord is identified with God Himself. This happens in the conversation of the angel of God with Hagar (Genesis 16:7-13; 21:17-18), with Abraham (Genesis 22:11-18), with Jacob (Genesis 31:11-13), and later with Moses and the burning bush. Furthermore, when the commander of the army of the Lord appears to Joshua, though He appears as a man, or maybe as an angel, yet Joshua is not rebuked when he worships Him, though such worship is due only to God (Joshua 5:13-15). In Psalm 110:1, "The LORD says to my Lord: 'Sit at my right hand, until I make your enemies your footstool.'" What is seen in the Old Testament in shadows and types is seen clearly in the New Testament; the substance is seen clearly in the

---

[8] Among many others, He is holy, just, righteous, good, shepherd, provider (Jehovah-Jireh), peace, and faithful.
[9] Alexander Pierce, *Facing Islam, Engaging Muslims: Constructive Dialogue in an Age of Conflict*, (Enumclaw, WA: Redemption Press, 2012), 66.

incarnation of the Son, who took on a human body. It is only in the incarnation that we can interpret and explain the above passages and others in the Old Testament in the most obvious, clear, and true way. The Christian church is called to go and make disciples of all nations and to baptize them in the name of the Father, the Son, and the Holy Spirit (Matthew 28:19), a very clear presentation of the Triune God in Scripture.

One of the 99 names of Allah is "The Loving." However, the question arises as to how Allah could be such, in eternity past, before he created the world and humankind. Michael Reeves, in his small but fascinating book, raises this question.[10] Reeves's answer is that since there was nothing else that Allah could love, the only option is that he eternally loves his creation, which means that Allah needs the creation to be who he is in himself – loving.[11] However, the Triune God from eternity past had perfect fellowship among the Father, the Son, and the Holy Spirit; God loved truly and fully apart from His creation. This is the one true God, the God of the first commandment. And since the one true God is a Triune God, Christians and Muslims do not worship the same God. In John 14:6, Jesus clearly said, "I am the way, and the truth, and the life. No one comes to the Father except through me." This bold statement of Jesus about being the *only* way to get to the Father flies in the face of our post-modern culture that has totally rebelled against absolute truth. In post-modern culture, the truth is now relative and flexible and can be made into anything anyone wants it to be. However, the claims of Jesus are the very truth of the Word of God. If Jesus is the only way, the truth, and the life, then one must conclude that other gods, who are not the Triune God, cannot lead us to the Father, and they are not the same.

While there might be some similarity in the description of the God of the Ten Commandments and Allah, in essence, they are not the same. The God of Abraham, Isaac, and Jacob is Father, Son, and Holy Spirit. If Allah, or for that matter, the God of Rabbinical Judaism, is not Triune, neither of these Gods is the same as the God who gave the First Commandment.

Conclusion

The best way to conclude is by citing the Heidelberg Catechism, written in 1563 in Germany and still used as the confession of many Reformed

---

[10] Michael Reeves, *Delighting in the Trinity*, (Downers Grove, IL: InterVarsity Press, 2012), 40. This is a short and very delightful and thought-provoking book that is worth reading.
[11] Ibid.

churches. Question number 94 of the catechism asks: "What does the Lord require in the first commandment?" And it concisely and precisely answers: "That for the sake of my very salvation I avoid and flee all idolatry, witchcraft, superstition, and prayer to saints or to other creatures. Further, that I rightly come to know the only true God, trust in Him alone, submit to Him with all humility and patience, expect all good from Him only, and love, fear, and honor Him with all my heart. In short, that I forsake all creatures rather than do the least thing against His will." May we fulfill this first and fundamental commandment as answered to this question and give God the glory due to Him alone.

Suggested Resources:

Cole, R. Alan. *Exodus: An Introduction and Commentary.* Tyndale Old Testament Commentaries. Downers Grove, Illinois: InterVarsity Press, 1973.

Durham, John I. *Exodus.* Word Biblical Commentary. Waco, Texas: Word Books Publisher, 1987.

Estelle, Bryan D. *Echoes of Exodus: Tracing a Biblical Motif.* Downers Grove, Illinois: InterVarsity Press, 2018.

Lunn, Brian. Martin Luther: *The Man and His God.* London: Butler & Tanner, Ltd., 1934.

Pierce, Alexander. *Facing Islam-Engaging Muslims: Constructive Dialogue in an Age of Conflict.* Enumclaw, WA: Redemption Press, 2012.

Pink, Arthur W. *Gleanings in Exodus.* Chicago, Illinois: Moody Press, 1981.

Reeves, Michael. *Delighting in the Trinity.* Downers Grove, IL: InterVarsity Press, 2012.

Ryken, Philip Graham. *Written in Stone: The Ten Commandments and Today's Moral Crisis.* Phillipsburg, New Jersey: P&R Publishing, 2010.

Schaeffer, Edith. *Lifelines: The Ten Commandments for Today.* Westchester, Illinois: Crossway Books, 1982.

Wallace, Ronald S. *The Ten Commandments: A Study of Ethical Freedom.* Edinburgh and London: Oliver and Boyd, 1965.

Watson, Thomas. *The Ten Commandments: Life Application of the Ten Commandments,* first ed. Published in 1692. Rev. ed. Abbotsford, WI: Aneko Press, 2019.

The Second Commandment:

YOU SHALL NOT MAKE FOR YOURSELF A CARVED IMAGE ...

Robert Norris, United States

> *The principle crime of the human race, the highest guilt charged upon the world, the whole procuring cause of judgment, is idolatry.*
>
> Tertullian, *On Idolatry*

In a year in which the whole world has experienced the disruption and fear engendered by a pandemic that has consumed millions of lives, we have also witnessed protests in stable and democratic societies that expose the strains upon those established societies. While these strains have been different in various societies, protests have been widespread against perceived injustice. Both the pain and the protests have been presented by the media in such vivid ways that no Christian could have escaped being brought face-to-face with the woes of our world. The response, however, has often been that of anger, which causes political views and convictions to grow in intensity. The growth of that intensity has led to division between friends and to ruptures in families and communities and even in churches. There is little doubt that this anger has been inflamed by the media, but the result is that alienation and a disparaging of those who hold divergent views have taken place among believers and unbelievers alike. Believers in Jesus Christ who publicly own His Lordship have sadly engaged in this process and, in doing so, have sometimes confused their obedience to Christ with obedience to political leaders or to a political party or ideology, coming close to violating the second commandment with its stark warning against idolatry.

Idolatry is much deeper issue than simply creating "graven images" as did both Israel and its enemies in the Old Testament.[1] Any reading of the commandments given by God to His people as they are recorded in Exodus 20:1-17 and in Deuteronomy 5:6-12 immediately impresses us with the

---

[1] Editor's note: Notice that Dr Norris mentions the problem of worshipping physical idols. In the 21st century I have seen physical idolatry and have visited a pagan temple. It has long been a standard Protestant criticism of the Roman Catholic Church that the use of images in a church building infringes on the commandment against idolatry. TJ

intimate relationship that exists between the first and second commandments. It has often been posited that they belong together. The first commandment reveals God as the object of the worship and obedience of His chosen people. The second commandment reveals the way that obedience is to be rendered.

In the first commandment (Exodus 20:2), the Lord identified Himself as *Elohim*, indicating that He is the judge of the entirety of the created order. Implicit is the idea that He is the only God, who is master of the universe:

> "I am the LORD your God, who brought you out of the land of Egypt, out of the house of slavery. You shall have no other gods before me."

The second commandment (Exodus 20:4-6) contains prohibitions against a variety of aspects of idolatry:

> "You shall not make for yourself a carved image, or any likeness of anything that is in heaven above, or that is in the earth beneath, or that is in the water under the earth. You shall not bow down to them or serve them, for I the LORD your God am a jealous God, visiting the iniquity of the fathers on the children to the third and the fourth generation of those who hate me, but showing steadfast love to thousands of those who love me and keep my commandments."

Having other gods is idolatry. The first part of the second commandment is clear that those who received these commandments were to attribute all power to the one true God alone. It was not meant to affirm the reality of other gods besides the God of Israel. The translation of the phrase "al-panai" is "before my face," which means "forever and every place." It suggests that the prohibition against idolatry of any kind applies to all times and to all generations. God identifies Himself as "a jealous God," indicating His relationship with His people is like marriage. The marriage is between Himself and His chosen people. Therefore, we can liken idolatry to adultery; idolatry is spiritual adultery.

Idolatry Defined

An idol is anything we depend upon to meet the deep needs of the heart, such as personal worth, significance, and security. Sadly, as John Calvin said, "The human heart is an idol factory."[2] The human mind is contami-

---

[2] John Calvin, *Institutes of the Christian Religion*, ed. F. L. Battles (Louisville, KY: Westminster John Knox Press, 2001), I. xi. 8.

nated by sin in such a way that it is filled with pride, and as a result, whenever it thinks about God, it will always create a god after its own image. It will imagine, as Calvin observed, "an unreality and empty appearance as God."

In his letter to the Romans, the Apostle Paul exposes our hearts and minds when he makes clear that sin is much deeper than mere behavioral violations. Sin begins at the motivational level. The ultimate issue of our life is the unwillingness to glorify God and to give Him the centrality which is not only His due but His command. The sin of idolatry is ultimately a sin of the heart. When we seek to find identity and security in anything other than God, we have made it an idol. Failure to give God the prime place in our thinking results in idolatry. Paul writes, "... they exchanged the truth of God for a lie ..." (Romans 1:25). And in doing this:

> "... they became futile in their thinking, and their foolish hearts were darkened" (Romans 1:21).

Idolatry is the ultimate indicator of our rejection of the God who is. It replaces the worship that is due to the Creator with worship of something less than God. When we adopt any idol, we do not abandon worship, because we are created to worship. We remain true to our design, making all manner of other gods take the place of the Creator of heaven and earth. The idol we adopt, however, distorts our thinking with the lie that it can give us that for which we are looking. In adopting an idol, we not only adopt the false belief system that is centered on the idol; we give it control of our lives and imagine that it can give us what only God truly can give.

God gave the Ten Commandments in the immediate context of addressing a people who had demanded a visible representation of their God – they had made a golden calf. As it was constructed, the people announced: "'These are your gods, O Israel, who brought you up out of the land of Egypt!'" (Exodus 32:8b)

Fashioning a golden calf constituted an attempt to equate the idol they had created with their own hands with Yahweh, the living God, who alone had been the Savior of His people and whose power had brought them from their life of bondage. Israel wanted to claim that they remained loyal to Yahweh, while at the same time they were creating and submitting to an idol. The ultimate issue was that the people looked to something besides the God-given promise that He was the Savior.

The issue was clearly that the people were afraid. Their leader, Moses, had disappeared, leaving the people surrounded by nations who were their enemies. In their fear, they demanded, "Up, make us gods who shall go before us" (Exodus 32:1). In their fear and search for security, they created and submitted to an idol. It is a phenomenon as modern as it is ancient – an idol is created when something of finite value is elevated to a place of centrality and becomes the basis against which every other value is judged. Fear and the need for security were running high, and they displaced the invisible, but nonetheless real and powerful, true God. Instead of finding freedom from their fears in the secure protection of the living God, they found themselves captive.

People are compelled to serve whatever they worship. Even after conversion, Christians find false saviors and lords, together with their attendant false belief systems. These continue to distort their lives as much as they distorted the lives of the children of Israel. Among the many idols we create, political idolatry is common and can be used to illustrate the results of idolatry in all the spheres of life. Its effects upon our relationships with God and society are profound. It is summed up in the 95th question of the Heidelberg Catechism which asks:

"What is idolatry?" The answer:

"Instead of the one true God who has revealed Himself in His Word, or alongside of Him, to invent or have some other thing in which man puts his trust."[3]

Idolatry Denounced

The second commandment communicates the significance which idolatry has to the Lord Himself. The commandment reinforces the issue that idolatry is as much about seeking to serve God in the wrong way as it is about creating false gods. Clearly there is here an overlap between serving God in our own way and creating false gods. Idols cause us to seek to serve God in a way that He has neither commanded nor of which He approves, tantamount to creating and serving a god created by our own hands and hearts. The Old and New Testaments make it clear that an idol is something elevated to function as a substitute for God Himself. Any idol shrinks the Infinite and obscures the glory of the Lord. In Deuteronomy 4, as Moses addressed the gathered people of Israel, he made clear that reliance upon imagination instead of revelation was unwholesome and courted divine anger. He reinforced the reality of judgment and its severity when he warned the people of the consequence of doing so.

---

[3] *The Heidelberg Catechism Q. and A. 95*, ed. and trans. for the Christian Reformed Church (2004).

> "... beware lest you act corruptly by making a carved image for yourselves ... beware lest you raise your eyes to heaven, and when you see the sun and the moon and the stars ... you be drawn away and bow down to them and serve them ... For the LORD your God is a consuming fire, a jealous God" (Deuteronomy 4:16, 19, 24).

Helmut Thielicke expounds on this when he writes:

> Ideology has the character of idolatry in two respects. First, in ideology it is man who sets himself up as lord and master. He sets his own goals, enunciating them in the axioms of his ideology. He is the one who has the power both to fix and to realize these goals. At one and the same time he is both the inaugurator and the functionary of the forces of life. He has a will to power and what he wills he wills not in the name of something above him but only in his own name. This is idolatry.[4]

This stands in contrast to the scriptural affirmation that God is sovereign over all the earth and directs the destinies of nations. The psalmist made this clear:

> "The LORD brings the counsel of the nations to nothing;
> he frustrates the plans of the peoples.
> The counsel of the Lord stands forever,
> the plans of his heart to all generations" (Psalm 33:10-11).

Christopher Wright argues that there are principles built into creation so that when God casts down a nation that He has raised up for His own purposes, He does so "because their arrogance, violence and depravity reach an intolerable level; God acts in judgment and they collapse, or sink into global insignificance, or even depart from the stage of history altogether."[5]

Idolatry and Its Effects

Idolatry inevitably begins as a means of power, attempting to enable us to control our circumstances, fears, or challenges, but quickly the idol overpowers us and ends up controlling us. In the case of political idolatry, it may begin with a defense of immoral or improper behavior but end up causing us to overlook the acts and impacts of what we have justified.

---

[4] Helmut Thielicke, *Theological Ethics,* vol. 2, *Politics,* ed. and trans. William H. Lazareth (Philadelphia: Fortress Press, 1969), p. 48.

[5] Christopher J. H. Wright., *Here Are Your Gods: Faithful Discipleship in Idolatrous Times* (InterVarsity Press, 2020), p. 108.

Having visited the Soviet Union while it was governed by Stalin, John Macmurray, a committed Christian, described the Soviet Union in his 1938 book *The Clue to History* as "the nearest approach to the realization of the Christian intention that the world has yet seen ... It expresses the continuity of the Christian intention in an explicit and practical form."[6] This was written after the Soviet government had brutally murdered many of its opponents, slaughtered many Christian leaders while devastating the churches, and developed a personality cult surrounding Stalin that had many quasi-religious features. Macmurray was a man whose political convictions blinded him to the reality he witnessed and mastered him into becoming a defender of the indefensible.

It is all too easy to make light of political speech and divisive behavior, but the Christian's standard is always the authority of Scripture. This demands that Christians make all their assessments in light of the truth revealed there. Failure to do this inevitably leads to distorted discipleship, because as followers of Jesus Christ, we are people who have been changed by the power of the Holy Spirit and are constantly being changed into the likeness of our Lord (2 Corinthians 3:18; 5:14-21). Political idolatry shapes words and deeds in a way that begins to shape our attitudes, words, and perception of the behaviors of our political heroes. Whether these heroes come from the right or the left does not matter. Pursuing political idolatry inevitably means that we resemble our risen Lord less and less. This in turn compromises our witness.

David Powlison describes idolatry as having the effect of creating "a delusional field", by which he means that idols begin to define good and evil in ways that are contrary to God's definitions.[7] Idols must necessarily articulate a false belief system. In the field of politics, this can translate into an exalted view of the state. With Hegel, we begin to acknowledge and live as though "the state is God marching on earth."[8] We attribute to it the ultimate value that gives everything else its meaning, and its servants, the politicians, hold a unique place in our thinking. We begin to attribute to them power and capacity that should be reserved for God. The French thinker Jacques Ellul sums it up when he describes such an attitude:

---

[6] John Macmurray, *The Clue to History* (New York: Harper and Bros, 1938), p. 206.

[7] David Powlison, "The Idols of Our Heart and Vanity Fair," *Journal of Biblical Counseling* 13, no. 2, (2009).

[8] The quote from Hegel was cited in Karl R. Popper, *The Open Society and Its Enemies*, 2 vols. (Princeton Univ. Press 1963) vol. 2, p. 31.

It [the state] is a providence of which everything is expected, a supreme power which pronounces truth and justice and has the power of life and death over its members. It is an arbiter which ... declares the law the supreme objective code on which the whole game of society depends.⁹

When we make an idol out of our politics, the power of the idol is so intense that it is often felt in our body as well as in our behavior. Idols bring bondage. We become overly anxious when, having idolized a finite value, such as a political party or leader, we find that our idol is facing some threat. In that case, we can feel ourselves shaken at the very core of our being and can behave as though experiencing emotional trauma. In the 2020 election in the United States of America, one otherwise healthy and strong Christian individual I know was so emotionally anxious that he remained curled up in a fetal position for days, even after the election had taken place.

Idolatry Exposed

Such idolatry is often excused by the argument that it is a matter of principle, which in reality is a mask for prejudice. In his Gospel, Luke records an event where our Lord Jesus Christ exposed the prejudice of the disciples, a prejudice that was masked by the appearance of principle (Luke 9:51-56). Jesus and the disciples passed through a Samaritan village on their way to Jerusalem. Luke records that the villagers refused to receive them, indicating a rejection of all hospitality. Scripture records that the reason for this rejection was that as Jews, they were on their way to Jerusalem. The antipathy between the Jews and Samaritans was well-known. When James and John heard of the Samaritan rejection, they became angry immediately and said: "Lord, do you want us to tell fire to come down from heaven and consume them?" (v. 54).

Clearly, the disciples were as prejudiced as the Samaritans, disguising their prejudice with moral outrage. We are told our Lord Jesus Christ, "... turned and rebuked them. And they went on to another village" (vv. 55-56).

We see the same issue in the Old Testament in the story of Jonah. As a prophet of the Lord, Jonah tried to avoid preaching a message of repentance to the city of Nineveh as he had been commanded. He knew that if the Ninevites repented, they could and would be used by God to bring judgment upon Israel. He was more concerned about being a loyal Jew than

---

⁹ Jacques Ellul, *The New Demons*, trans. C. Edward Hopkin (New York: Seabury, 1995), p. 80.

about being a faithful prophet of the Lord. His anger never changed, and bitterness developed. When the Lord showed mercy upon the Ninevites, Jonah was angry at the repentance of the people, and he was bitter because God had shown mercy to a Gentile nation.

> "... I knew that you are a gracious God and merciful, slow to anger and abounding in steadfast love, and relenting from disaster" (Jonah 4:2).

Anything around which a believer's affections are oriented has the potential of becoming the object of his worship and can replace God as the central motivating factor in his or her life. As with anything else, this can be the case with politics, and the effect is always sad. Jesus exposed prejudice and the idol that lay behind it.

Political idolatry can have far-reaching effects. It may begin with holding strong supportive views for one political party. Left unrestrained, this can develop all too easily into the deifying of a party and its leadership. In some cases, this takes place with a messianic enthusiasm that seems to defy restraint.

For Christians, self-examination in the light of Scripture can expose such idolatry and is part of our growth in Christ. Writing to the Corinthians, the apostle Paul enjoins Christians:

> "Examine yourselves, to see whether you are in the faith. Test yourselves. Or do you not realize this about yourselves, that Jesus Christ is in you? – unless indeed you fail to meet the test!" (2 Corinthians 13:5)

In a blog on "The Exchange," Mary Lederleitner advocates self-diagnosing political idolatry by asking some probing questions.[10]

1. How involved are my emotions in the political situation?

Regardless of how we may confess Christ as Savior, when emotions are tied up with an issue or person, whether it is government, political party, or political leader, we are in danger of creating an idol. We can find ourselves being improperly angry, perhaps at what a political opponent is saying or doing, and an idol is being formed. We know this because the indwelling presence of the Holy Spirit produces love, joy, peace, patience, kindness, goodness, faithfulness, gentleness, and self-control. When these attributes are not present in the political process and emotions become marked by

---

[10] Mary Lederleitner, "Have Your Political Views Become an Idol?" *Christianity Today*, August 4, 2020.

irritability and anger, these latter emotions are not subject to the supremacy of Christ. This does not mean anger is inappropriate in every political situation; indeed, it is justified in the face of corruption or injustice. Nor does it mean that it is idolatrous to experience disappointment at political loss. But when the central place of Christ is usurped by something else, idolatry has been exposed. The fruit of the presence of the Holy Spirit is not subject to political upheaval, providing us with an impeccable test.

2. Whom or what am I trusting to provide for my future?

People enter into political idolatry because they seek safety and security in the midst of a world where things seem fragile; they feel vulnerable and powerless. Seeking security in political parties or leaders relegates Christ and His power "to save to the uttermost" (Hebrews 7:25) to a place of secondary importance. This may not have been a conscious determination, yet it may occur. The focus of Christian security will always come from the heavenly Father, who is the true provider, not from a created messianic substitute.

3. How am I treating people who disagree with me?

We can also tell if we have moved into political idolatry by our treatment of those with whom we differ. Sadly, political opponents on the left or right of the political spectrum can be demonized and their salvation questioned because of their political positions. All human beings, despite their political views or political affiliations, are made in God's image (Genesis 1:26-28) and have an inherent right to be treated with respect. While biblical convictions should impact how Christians vote and otherwise support political differences, it should not extend into judging others in the realm of salvation.

When we interact with those who see political and social issues differently, the question we must pose to ourselves is whether we treat them with the dignity and honor that is their due as people created in the image of God. It is never appropriate to think people are saved by their political ideology, nor is it appropriate to judge spirituality based on political allegiance. When we find ourselves moving in these directions, it is an indicator of idolatry. The truth is simply that God rules over the nations, and we must restrain our excessive anxiety at the rise and fall of those who cannot thwart the purposes of God. This extends to the words we choose to speak. We protect those we love, and if our love is not centered upon Christ, our biblical focus has been lost. God will judge us for how we speak about people and for the names we call them (Matthew 5:21-24). This cannot be justified by taking cues from political leaders, whose words are often unguarded.

Idolatry Overcome

No Christian enjoys being told he has an idol in his life, or that her political views or the vehemence with which she holds and shares them are idolatrous. Yet for many people, that is the simple truth. Such a situation cannot be allowed to remain unchallenged. Like all sin, the Lord Jesus Christ has come that we might know His power of both forgiveness and healing. The answer always lies in the power of the gospel applied by the Holy Spirit. To know that our fears for the future and for our security are in the hands of God is the foundation upon which we can firmly stand. It is God Himself who is our refuge and strength. Christian confidence cannot be in the schemes or plans of governments, politicians, or the political system itself. Charles Colson put it pithily when he said, "Our salvation can never come on Air Force One."

Idolatry always distorts our view of God and diverts the worship of the people of God. Idolatry in any form steals the attention and honor that belong only to God (Jeremiah 2:5) \f "B". It also prevents true service and worship and enjoyment of God. This truth is captured in the first question of the Westminster Shorter Catechism, which asks:

"What is the chief end of man?" It answers:
"The chief end of man is to glorify God and to enjoy him forever."[11]

It is impossible to enjoy God if our view of Him is distorted, and it is impossible to glorify God if our attention is diverted away from the true worship which is His due. Idolatry may satisfy men temporally, but it can never satisfy God. It may produce enthusiastic and even warm worship, but idol worship is always worship of the creature rather than of the Creator. It ultimately produces only condemnation and pain. Political idolatry is no less dangerous, for it loses sight of the eternal and focuses exclusively upon a world that is ultimately transient.

Dismantling idols first requires that we unmask them. This is no easy task since idols create the "delusional field" which Powlison described. They have been deified, and so their power has been magnified, making

---

[11] D. F. Kelly, *The Westminster Shorter Catechism in Modern English* (Phillipsburg, N.J: Presbyterian and Reformed, 1986).

them appear more wonderful and more powerful than they are. Idols appear to offer their worshipers what they desire and even seem to meet the emotional needs of the moment. Identifying, challenging, and dismantling these idols requires a deeper appropriation of the gospel.

Many Christians have confessed Christ as their Savior, but far fewer have trusted the power of the gospel to deal with their idols. Many have attempted to meet the challenge of idolatry with the use of the law. They seek to modify their behavior only to find the task overwhelming. Because human desire is involved, dependence upon the human will alone is both wearying and ultimately ineffective. In the case of political idolatry, there is also the blindness to the folly of the exaltation of politics, political parties, and persons. The only effective means is the exaltation of Christ. This means elevating the person and place of the Lord Jesus Christ within our lives and thinking. It means we must concentrate upon the work that Jesus has done on the cross. Remembering the encompassing power of His life, death, and resurrection and appropriating the freedom from bondage that He has brought are able to challenge the idol.

That remembrance then leads to exposing the idol for what it is and to a genuine Spirit-inspired repentance which addresses the idol and its false blandishments. It restores balance to our thinking. It does not mean we abandon the political process. It means instead that the political process is rebalanced in our thought. The priority of the kingdom of God and the place of the King within the kingdom confront us. The values of the kingdom outlined in Scripture then assume their rightful place.

We forget the simple fact that being a Christian does not mean we automatically think in a Christian way, which is why we have and live with idols. The more we are confronted by the Word of God and the Spirit of God, we are transformed in thought and action. It is, of course, a description of Christian growth and maturity to which every believer is called and drawn by the Holy Spirit, who indwells and prompts. As irresistible as is the Spirit's work of leading us to Christ, He never ceases to be the "Gentle Spirit," which is why the Apostle Paul can enjoin us as he did the Ephesians, "And do not grieve the Holy Spirit of God, by whom you were sealed for the day of redemption" (Ephesians 4:30). We cooperate with Him in our sanctification as He leads and enables us to challenge our idols, calling us to listen to and follow His leading.

The Curse Placed upon Idolaters

The second commandment ends with a fearful reminder of the severity with which idolatry is treated by the Lord.

You shall not bow down to them or serve them, for I the LORD your God am a jealous God, visiting the iniquity of the fathers on the children to the third and the fourth generation of those who hate me, but showing steadfast love to thousands of those who love me and keep my commandments.

The commandment contains a warning for future generations that refusal to deal with idolatry in any form, including political idolatry, will pass down the generations to our children and to their children. Historically, it has also resulted in unspeakable horrors being committed in society. The twentieth century has seen the result of this when political ideology either supported or was silent in the face of a regime that practiced genocide. It happened in the birthplace of the Reformation with the Nazi agenda. Christians continue to commit violence in the name of Christ for ideological reasons. It happened in Kosovo and Rwanda, nations with a strong Christian heritage, where professing Christians chose political idolatry over loyalty to the teachings of Christ.

At a time when a broken world needs the witness of Christ more than ever, political idolatry clouds and disfigures this witness, and the end result is that far fewer people believe that the gospel is true or is good news at all.

The second commandment also contains a promise of blessing to those who love God: When idols are cast down, God becomes the hiding place for His people. He covenants to meet the deepest needs of His people with the fruit of the presence of His indwelling Spirit.

The Third Commandment:

YOU SHALL NOT MISUSE THE NAME OF GOD

Kin Yip Louie, Hong Kong

Among the Ten Commandments, many people regard the third commandment as rather abstract. What does it mean to misuse the name of God or to take God's name in vain (as in older translations)? After all, Western people today do not usually invoke God's name literally. When one thinks about misusing God's name, sometimes people merely think of swear words. But the implication of the third commandment is much wider and deeper than misuse of God's name in swear words. This essay begins (I.) by examining the meaning of the commandment in its original context. Then (II.) we shall consider today's culture and look at ways people are misusing the name of God. We conclude (III.) with a discussion on how Christians can stay alert to the spiritual dangers addressed by the third commandment.

I.) The Hebrew text of Exodus 20:7 can be translated literally as "Do not carry the name of the Lord your God in vain." We begin by discussing the meaning of "the name of the Lord." Unlike some ancient religions, the Old Testament never considers the mere pronouncing of the Lord's name (the so-called tetragrammaton YHWH, translated as Jehovah in the King James Version) as carrying special significance. YHWH is not a secret incantation formula. Saying the name aloud will not convey special power to the speaker or bring a curse.

Rather, the name of the Lord represents the honor and reputation of God; misusing the name of God speaks of acts and words that dishonor God. In this sense, God is very jealous about His name. The psalmists write, "Yet he saved them for his name's sake, that he might make known his mighty power" (Psalm 106:8). And "He refreshes my soul. He leads me in paths of righteousness for his name's sake" (Psalm 23:3). God does love us and acts graciously toward His creatures, but Scripture reminds us that we must never treat His grace contemptuously. His acts are proclamations of His character, and God is angry with people who deliberately misrepresent His character.

What is God's character? A succinct description by the Lord Himself is found in the passage when God gave Moses the Ten Commandments for a second time: "The LORD, the LORD, a God merciful and gracious, slow to anger, abounding in steadfast love and faithfulness, keeping steadfast love for thousands, forgiving iniquity and transgression and sin, but who will by no means clear the guilty, visiting the iniquity of the fathers on the children and the children's children, to the third and fourth generation" (Exodus 34:6-7).

This essay is not an occasion for an exposition of the attributes of God, but it is important to understand God's character in order to avoid misusing His name. In the short Self-introduction above, we see that God is compassionate and gracious. Anyone who tries to use God's name to terrify or oppress people is misusing His name. On the other hand, God is also righteous and powerful. Any attempt to deny or downplay God's will or right to avenge evil is also a misuse of His name. Lastly, God is sovereign. In confronting the sins of His creatures, God can freely choose to be merciful or to be just. This is a divine prerogative that people can neither control nor can they fathom the reasons behind God's decisions.

Next, we will examine the phrase *in vain*. In modern translations, such as the NIV, the word *misuse* represents two words in Hebrew, *carry* and *in vain*. The Hebrew word for *in vain* primarily means *futility*. Job, in his agony, declared, "I have been allotted months of futility" (Job 7:3a). His sufferings made him feel like his life was a total waste. The same Hebrew word often means deception as well. Thus, "Everyone utters lies to his neighbor" (Psalm 12:2a) can be translated literally as "Man speaks vainly with a neighbor." Perhaps the connection reflects an assumption that false words have no weight before God.

Whatever the true etymological explanation is, usage suggests that the third commandment emphasizes deliberate misuse of the divine name. The main concern is not for frivolous evocation of the divine name (such as an exclamation of "Oh, Jesus, no!"), though this kind of misuse is not totally excluded. The main concern is using the divine name deceptively. When we invoke God's name, we should be praising Him, thanking Him, pleading for help, even venting our anger or grief at Him (as exemplified by some of the psalms). If we invoke the divine name as a means to accomplish our private desires, we are invoking God's name falsely or vainly.

Lastly, the Hebrew for *carry* (as in the literal Hebrew translation mentioned earlier) is a common word in the Old Testament. Its primary meaning is *lifting up*, as water lifted up the ark of Noah (Genesis 7:17). It can also mean lifting one's voice in wailing, as Hagar did when she faced the imminent death of her child in the wilderness (Genesis 21:16). Interestingly, by using the word in the phrase "lifting your head," it carries the meaning of pardoning (Genesis 40:13). It also has the more prosaic meaning of *carrying*, as a servant carried the sick child of the Shunammite woman to his mother (2 Kings 4:19-20).

Given the broad range of meaning of the word *lift up*, it is difficult to give a more precise reading of its meaning in the third commandment. We can surmise that the third commandment has a general application, instead of referring to a specific way of using God's name (such as using it for magical incantation). The danger of misusing God's name is not limited to priests and religious workers. However, as we shall point out later, those with religious authority should be particularly careful regarding the third commandment.

Now that we have given a brief exegesis of the words, it is time to ask with what kinds of situations the original readers would have associated the third commandment. In the context of the Ancient Near East (ANE), people would probably have associated this commandment with the following situations:[1]

1. The use of God's name in sorcery was prohibited. Sorcerers invoked divine names in their incantations because they believed that the pronunciation of divine names gave them the ability to manipulate spiritual powers to change the fate of people. Sorcery was prohibited among the Israelites (Deuteronomy 18:9-12). There is no evidence that any Israelites used the Lord's name in their sorcery. But since the Israelites were not to have any God but the Lord, the third commandment implies that the Israelites were not to use any god's name in sorcery. Undoubtedly, there were Israelites who practiced sorceries, since both Jeremiah (Jeremiah 27:9) and Malachi (Malachi 3:5) warned the Israelites against listening to sorcerers. In the ANE context, the third commandment was a form of "secularization" in that Israelites were prohibited from trying to manipulate spiritual powers for their own benefit. They were to simply follow the commandments of God, lead an honorable life, and trust in the Lord for all the uncertainties in life.

2. False prophecy is prohibited. The Bible has recorded many instances of false prophecy. One of the most dramatic scenes in the Old Testament is the confrontation between Micaiah and the false prophet Zedekiah (1 Kings 22). Zedekiah had made some iron horns as a dramatic indication that the Israelite king would pierce the Arameans to death. When Micaiah confronted him with the prophecy of doom, Zedekiah rebuked Micaiah: "Which way did the spirit from the Lord go when he went from me to speak to you?" Such confrontations were not rare events among the Israelites; the book of Jeremiah contains more such stories.

---

[1] J. Douma, *The Ten Commandments: Manual for the Christian Life*, trans. Nelson D. Kloosterman (Phillipsburg, NJ: Presbyterian and Reformed, 1996), 74-75.

We know in hindsight who the true prophets were, but in their historical context, the Israelites might have been quite confused about the identity of true prophets. For example, it might not have been obvious to the Israelites whether Zedekiah or Micaiah spoke the truth. Did all these false prophets speak out of selfish pride and a desire for material gain? Or did some of them speak sincerely, though they were misguided? The Bible does not dwell on the psychology of the false prophets. Whatever the motives, the third commandment cautions us to be very careful when we speak in the name of the Lord.

3. Frivolous oaths are prohibited. The Lord denounced the people in Jerusalem in Jeremiah's time: "Search her squares to see if you can find a man, one who does justice and seeks truth, that I may pardon her. Though they say, 'As the Lord lives,' yet they swear falsely" (Jeremiah 5:2). The Lord is the Truth, so swearing falsely in the Lord's name is a direct contradiction of His character and an affront to the Lord: "You shall not swear by my name falsely, and so profane the name of your God: I am the LORD" (Leviticus 19:12).

Why might a speaker swear falsely in God's name? The speaker might be involved in a court setting, in a commercial transaction, or making some surprising claims in ordinary conversation. Swearing by the name of the Lord would increase the credibility of his claim, and he is inviting God's punishment if he knowingly makes a false claim. To swear deceptively is to belittle the judgment of God and to use the divine name as a means to establish the speaker's credibility. As in the other two misuses (sorcery and prophecy), false swearing employs the Lord's name for the purpose of private gain. Moreover, it projects a false image of God in the process. We shall return to these points when we ask the contemporary relevance of the third commandment.

The New Testament gives a few important developments of the third commandment. First, Jesus generalizes the meaning of speaking in the Lord's name: "On that day many will say to me, 'Lord, Lord, did we not prophesy in your name, and cast out demons in your name, and do many mighty works in your name?' And then will I declare to them, 'I never knew you; depart from me, you workers of lawlessness'" (Matthew 7:22-23). When Jesus said the words "prophesy in your name," He almost certainly did not mean formal prophecy, such as the confrontation between Micaiah and Zedekiah. Jesus seemed to be referring to people who claimed to teach and apply God's truth in their contemporary setting. Paul had the same meaning in mind when he talked about the gift of prophecy (Ephesians 4:11). In the context of the Sermon on the Mount, Jesus is denouncing deceptive words or fraudulent miracles. The truth proclaimed by those false teachers may have been true, and they may indeed have healed people using Jesus' name. The problem is that their lives contradicted their teaching. If we claim to follow Christ but do not turn away from wickedness, we are confessing the Lord's name in vain (2 Timothy 2:19).

Second, the name of the Lord is now particularly associated with the name of Jesus: "... so that at the name of Jesus every knee should bow, in heaven and on earth and under the earth, and every tongue confess that Jesus Christ is Lord, to the glory of God the Father" (Philippians 2:10-11). The life and death of Jesus is the ultimate revelation of the character of our Triune God. As the Philippians passage indicates, having the same humble and gracious mindset of Christ in our lives is the ultimate way to honor the name of the Lord.

Third, Jesus prohibited oath-taking altogether (Matthew 5:34). It is debatable whether Jesus had a legal context in mind or whether he was referring to swearing regarding personal affairs. In church history, there have been Christians (such as the Anabaptists in the sixteenth century) who have taken this prohibition literally. Therefore, they would not enter any profession (such as some civil servant positions) and avoided situations (such as in a court) that required people to make oaths. We shall not enter into this debate,[2] as this is seldom a major issue among Christians today. We take the position that Jesus is teaching us to be sincere in our speech rather than prohibiting all oaths even when required by the laws of the land.

Now we shall move forward in time. One of the most comprehensive confessions in the history of the church is the Westminster Confession of Faith of 1646.[3] We shall now quote at length from an associated document, the Westminster Larger Catechism (WLC):

> Q. 112. What is required in the third commandment?
>
> A. The third commandment requires, that the name of God, his titles, attributes, ordinances, the word, sacraments, prayer, oaths, vows, lots, his works, and whatsoever else there is whereby he makes himself known, be holily and reverently used in thought, meditation, word, and writing; by an holy profession, and answerable conversation, to the glory of God, and the good of ourselves, and others.
>
> Q. 113. What are the sins forbidden in the third commandment?
>
> A. The sins forbidden in the third commandment are, the not using of God's name as is required; and the abuse of it in an ignorant, vain, irreverent,

---

[2] See the extensive discussion in ibid., 87-96.
[3] The Westminster Confession of Faith (WCF) is a treasured document in the Reformed tradition. It was drawn up by theologians and church leaders at Westminster Abbey in London in 1646.

profane, superstitious, or wicked mentioning or otherwise using his titles, attributes, ordinances, or works, by blasphemy, perjury; all sinful cursings, oaths, vows, and lots; violations of our oaths and vows, if lawful; and fulfilling them, if of things unlawful; murmuring and quarrelling at, curious prying into, and misapplying of God's decrees and providences; misinterpreting, misapplying, or any way perverting the word, or any part of it; to profane jests, curious or unprofitable questions, vain janglings, or the maintaining of false doctrines; abusing it, the creatures, or any thing contained under the name of God, to charms, or sinful lusts and practices; the maligning, scorning, reviling, or any wise opposing of God's truth, grace, and ways; making profession of religion in hypocrisy, or for sinister ends; being ashamed of it, or a shame to it, by unconformable, unwise, unfruitful, and offensive walking, or backsliding from it.

The exposition given above is framed in the legal genre, making it dense and even obtuse. We shall explicate it by highlighting a few key points. First, it reminds us that the profession of God's name should bring honor to God and bring blessings to people. His name should not be used frivolously. On the other hand, we are obliged to proclaim the Lord's name when we can honor Him or when people need to hear His gracious name.

Second, compared with the Old Testament, the WLC emphasizes the cognitive aspect of honoring. Thus, we should think, speak, and write about God and God's acts truthfully. In the ANE context, spiritual and material forces intertwined tightly in daily life. Sorcery and diviners were a major concern. As the Western world entered modernity, the focus of society shifted to how we construct the world with our cognitive power. The predominant ways people honor and dishonor God tend to shift with the culture.

Third, the WLC is much more explicit than is the Old Testament regarding what is prohibited by the third commandment, and the WLC expands significantly on its applications. Irreverent (e.g., swearing or cursing) or superstitious (e.g., using divine names in incantation) usage are prohibited. But an unhealthy curiosity of divine mysteries ("curious prying into ... God's decrees") also violates the third commandment. This may reflect the bitter experiences of the Reformation, when people literally went to war to settle theological controversies. The WLC emphasizes that we should practice humility when we claim to discern the will of God, as people are too ready to speak for God. But the "misapplying of God's decrees and providences" and "perverting the word" can also mean deliberate distortions of the truth revealed in God's Word. We shall later claim that modern secularism often violates the third commandment in this sense.

Lastly, the WLC emphasizes that Christians can violate the third commandment without literally calling out God's name. The third commandment prohibits "making profession of religion in hypocrisy, or for sinister ends; being ashamed of it, or a shame to it, by unconformable, unwise, unfruitful, and offensive walking." This reflects the teaching of Jesus in the Sermon on the Mount; it also shows the influence of the Puritan tradition. This perspective on the third commandment becomes very important to Christians in the West, as contemporary Christians do not usually engage directly in sorcery or prophesy in the Old Testament sense.

II.) The WLC is a faithful exposition of the Bible, but it also reflects the needs of its time. Building on our exegesis and the wisdom of the Westminster divines, we need to ask what the implications of the third commandment are for Christians today. Immediately we are confronted with the variety of situations Christians are facing.

In the developed world, the pervasive and dominating force of secularism is a daunting challenge to keeping the third commandment. This secularism does not entirely reject some kind of spiritual or super-dimensional reality. Indeed, movies toying with spiritual forces (whether fantasies such as *Game of Thrones* or science fiction such as *Interstellar*) are quite popular. However, secularism categorically rejects that there is a God who deserves our worship, speaks to us authoritatively through revelation, and judges us in eternity.

This secularism is sometimes manifested in deliberate trivialization of traditional religious symbols. I was once driving on a highway in the U.S., and I saw a truck with the word GOD on its back. I was curious. I caught up with the truck, and I found that it is an abbreviation for Guaranteed Overnight Delivery. In 1970, when someone claimed in the U.S. Court of Appeals (for the 9th Circuit) that the phrase "In God We Trust" printed on U.S. bills is a violation of the U.S. Constitution regarding "no establishment of religion," the Court rejected the case because the word *God* in this context has nothing to do with the establishment of religion. In other words, "In *God* We Trust" is merely a feel-good phrase.

The secular culture of the West continues to use religious symbols in non-religious or even sacrilegious contexts.[4] These usages do not bring honor to God or benefit anyone, so it is taking God's name in vain. But what can Christians do in such a situation? Should we follow the example of

---

[4] One can add many examples of the demeaning portrayal of Jesus from the entertainment business, from the movie *Jesus Christ Superstar* (1973) to the Netflix series *Paradise PD* (2018 to the 2021 4th season).

Muslims who vociferously attack anyone who defames the prophet Mohammed? Contrariwise, we are Christians who follow the humble Christ. We do not conquer people's hearts with violence and coercion.

The God portrayed in secular media is most often a caricature of the true God, and the Christians (or God-believers in general) portrayed are most often caricatures of real believers. For example, in science fiction movies, religion usually disappears in the future. Those time travelers in the future only find believers in the past or in more primitive cultures of other planets. The implicit message is that theistic beliefs are only credible to people not enlightened by scientific knowledge. In Hollywood movies, clergy are often self-righteous. They dress in impeccable clergy collars, but they often turn out to be hypocrites or even psychopaths. If we Christians respond with vehement attacks (either verbally on social media or with rowdy demonstrations on the street), it will confirm the negative image of Christians to society.

Christians in the West need to engage in culture war, in which the honor of God is at stake. Moreover, negative views of God and Christians are penetrating the church. Often the most bitter critics of church are young people who have grown up inside the church. In our information age, we cannot use a firewall to protect our younger generation from the corrosive images of faith in the public media. Instead, we need to develop cultural intelligence among Christians, so we can learn to enjoy our cultural possibilities today without uncritically adopting the ideologies of secularism. How to develop such cultural intelligence is a significant topic that goes beyond the scope of this chapter. Here we shall say only that Christians need to learn to read the presuppositions lying behind various forms of discourse, from newspaper commentary to Hollywood movies.

To fight this culture war and to protect the honor of God, we cannot just play defense. We need to play offense too. Particularly in the U.S. context, Christians tend to associate offense in the public square with boycott campaigns and demonstrations. While such actions have their place in a democratic society, these are not the tactics championed by Jesus or the apostles. In fact, we believe that such types of activism among Christians may, in fact, be a reflection of the secular culture of the U.S. We shall return to this kind of political activism when we discuss the hunger for power among Christians.

Perhaps a better way is to encourage Christians to participate in the mass media industry. We should not let atheists dominate our cultural landscape. We need Christian artists who honor God by portraying the image of God and His works faithfully in the media. They do not always need to literally preach the gospel. Christians in the movie industry should not limit themselves to producing so-called "gospel movies." They can also produce movies that, for example, celebrate the goodness of providence. For example, the movie *The Shawshank Redemption* (1994) is not a gospel movie.[5] Yet it encourages people to trust in divine providence that will ultimately punish evil and reward goodness. As another example, it would be good if we could have a movie that honestly and sympathetically portrays the struggles of transgender people (instead of putting all the blame on discrimination) and the possibility of overcoming gender dysphoria. Christians need to go beyond protesting the distortions and actively engage in the creation of a culture that honors God.

III.) Thus far we have been talking about the misuse or abuse of God's name in secular society. Now we turn to the misuse of God's name among Christians. We recall that in the Old Testament context, sorcery, false prophets, and frivolous oaths were the principal examples of transgressing the third commandment. They are all instances where people tried to manipulate God's name for their private purposes. In today's context, Christians also run the danger of using God's name for private purposes, though with different methods. In particular, sorcerers and false prophets can masquerade as religious leaders in churches that appear to be respectable. We shall begin with the temptations facing pastors and preachers today.

In this age of megachurches and media explosion, pastors or preachers can suddenly find themselves becoming celebrities. Success leads to further success, as fame is one of the most marketable assets today. A famous pastor can attract many worshippers, and his success may lead to the leadership delegating most of the power in the church to that visible pastor. He may gain further fame and financial gain by publishing his writings. In this age of globalism, he may even become an international celebrity.

A megachurch is not a bad thing, nor is it bad that pastors and theologians can bless many people beyond the walls of the church if they become popular writers. Modern mass media means that good Bible teaching (or good Christian songs or other forms of expressions) can reach more people more quickly than ever before. However, with this greater possibility also comes greater danger. First, the danger is to change the gospel message so that it sells well in our culture. Sometimes, the line between a pastor and a motivational speaker is very thin. And in our age of anxiety and superficial opportunities, motivational speakers can make

---

5 We do not know the personal beliefs of Frank Darabont (director and screenplay) or of Stephen King (writer of the original story). Owing to the common grace of God, sometimes even non-Christians can proclaim God's truth powerfully.

a lot of money. A pastor who preaches a prosperity gospel sometimes brings himself a lot of money and fame.[6] The pastor may be preaching in the name of Jesus, but in fact he is exhorting human potential and profiting himself in the process. He is a false prophet, and he clearly violates the third commandment.

Secondly, the celebrity status of some pastors often implies that they have immense personal authority within their organization. Naturally, people idolize the leader, particularly when he brings success to the organization. Sometimes, this leader is also the founder of the organization and the *raison d'etre* for the organization, and any query regarding the teaching or the conduct of the leader will be sidelined in order to protect the organization. Even in a church setting where there is usually more oversight, the lay leaders are often very trusting toward the senior pastor (as they should be), and they may tend to minimize the importance of any moral irregularities of the respected pastor. This can tempt a charismatic leader to conclude that he is special in the sense that boundaries for normal Christians do not apply to him. He has worked so hard and so long for the Lord: he deserves a break from the Lord.

If one thinks that such betrayal of the Lord only happens to some rotten apples, the recent examples of Bill Hybels, Jean Vanier, and Ravi Zacharias demonstrate that no one is immune from such temptation. These were respected Christian leaders who were admired by millions of Christians worldwide; their ministries and life stories inspired many Christians. When their sexual abuses came to light, their stories were reported worldwide in both Christian and secular news sources. Non-Christians may take these as evidence that the Christian faith is a fraud, and Christians may feel discouraged in their journey of faith. Even though these charismatic leaders may not have intended to defame the name of the Lord, they in fact violated the third commandment.

Are there ways to stop this kind of abuse of God's name? Put simply, there is no foolproof way to avoid such sins. Take the seeker-friendly trap, for example. Is it safe if a preacher stays with the "old-fashioned" gospel? Not necessarily, as the preacher may be selling his message to Christians who grow up listening to this type of message. The preacher knows he is safe and well-accepted whenever he repeats the same old message. He may

---

[6] There is no clear definition of what constitutes a prosperity gospel. In general, it highlights believing in God as a means to reach material prosperity. There are no unambiguous criteria to decide who is a prosperity gospel preacher. Obvious examples include televangelist Jim Bakker. Among pastors still active today, Joel Osteen is one who comes to mind.

fail to challenge his audience to face their invisible sins.[7] The audience actually grows in self-righteousness by listening to the preaching. Therefore, both old-fashioned and seeker-friendly gospels can be just a way for a preacher to put the approval of the audience above God's truth.

There is no simple solution to the moral failures of charismatic leaders. Usually, these leaders can become global players only because they have exceptional drive and originality. However, the same drive and creativity can make them a dominating presence that makes people hesitate to challenge them. When does originality become heresy? When does trust become blind trust? These are not easy questions. When charismatic leaders start going down the wrong path, it is hard for others to discover it; and it is even harder to hold these leaders accountable for their transgressions.

Obeying the third commandment (or any of the other nine commandments) is not a simple task. That was true in Old Testament times as well. As we have said, though it is clear in hindsight who the true prophets were, the Israelites at that time might have had a hard time discerning who truly spoke for the Lord. Even the false prophets themselves might have believed they were speaking for the Lord. Today's prosperity gospel preachers may truly believe they are preaching the gospel. The moral of the story is that nobody is perfect. The media culture today exacerbates the problem by making charismatic leaders into superheroes. In other words, when many ordinary Christians violate the second commandment by idolizing leaders, the leaders are walking into the trap of failing the third commandment.

The more success a pastor or preacher has, the more he needs to remind himself that he is merely a forgiven sinner. He needs to ask God and others to constantly examine his life so that, despite his good intentions, he will not violate the third commandment. The church in general should be keenly aware of the lure of celebrity culture, and a healthy checks-and-balances system among leadership should be a priority in Christian organizations and churches.

Most Christians will not become leaders in the Christian world, but there are various prosaic ways to misuse God's name. One common way is to use the name of Christ as a means of self-glorification, as when we proclaim to others our identity as a Christian with a sense of moral superiority. Again, the age of social media exacerbates this problem by encouraging Christians with a similar sense of religious superiority to fan their passion together through the Internet. Sometimes these internal Christian dia-

---

[7] To give one example, many preachers in conservative Christian circles in the U.S. seldom challenge chauvinism or racism in the church or in society.

logues catch the attention of the secular press, and the secular press often delights in portraying the "ignorant" views of Christians. Of course, Christians should not merely bow to secular society's criteria of decency, but Christians should be aware of the dangers of a tribal mentality and of self-glorification.

As the West moves into the postmodern culture, this moral superiority can turn more militant and political. Postmodern culture is characterized by the fragmentation of cultural norms and the image of the world as a ceaseless power game. For Christians, this power game is a game of values. Under this image, the political arena can become a place of *jihad* for Christians to impose Christian values on society. For the sake of protecting the rights of Christians to practice their beliefs and to fight against the devil's plan to turn society against God, some Christians believe they must use all means to win over the governing power. However, this brings the risk of sin.

As we have said, Christians are indeed engaged in a culture war. For Christians living in a democratic society, it is good and proper for Christians to use democratic means to advocate Christian values. However, when winning becomes the paramount concern, the name of God can be hijacked in the political game. While Christians may believe that political candidate A is more congenial to Christian values than is candidate B, no political candidate can represent the voice of God. We should not identify the political campaign of candidate A as a campaign for the kingdom of God. If we make prophecy in the Lord's name part of a political campaign, we may be breaking both the third commandment and the second commandment (by idolizing candidate A).

This chapter is not the place to discuss the intricate relationships between faith and political life. However, we must recognize that both politics and religion are inspiring and totalizing activities. People will die for their religion, and many will also die for their nation. Because of the power of religion and politics in our lives, there is constant danger to utilize one for the purpose of the other. In the paragraph above, we mention the danger of Christians using their religion as a tool for political gain. Many national governments would also like to use religion to generate political support for the state.

One of the most grievous examples of the abuse of God's name is the support of Adolf Hitler by *Deutsche Christen* (the "German Christian" movement of the 1930s and early 1940s) in the name of Christianity. The *Deutsche Christen* believed Germany was the embodiment of a vigorous Christianity, and Hitler was the defender of this faith. Nowadays some state governments (particularly in the Majority World) want churches to teach their members to love the state the way they love the Lord. Christians are to be told that the existing regime is ordained by God to bless their nation. These governments will support the church (or at least let it survive) if the church will become cheerleaders for the existing regime.

We must constantly remind ourselves that although God is almighty, the power of Christians has no direct relationship to the glory of God. The glory of Jesus shines through in His apparent powerlessness of going to the cross. Perhaps one of the most important lessons the church needs to learn today is to serve in weakness. If Christians do engage in political life (as they should), their main objective should be to witness to the truth of God by words and deeds. In a democratic society, Christians must remember to live out the grace of God in the public square; their primary objective is not to gain votes in the ballet box. Christians in any society should remember that the glory of the nation is not the glory of God. The church should not become a servant to patriotism or to any political ideology. If the church has become a tool in a political agenda, it is a misuse of God's name to call herself a church.

Then there are more mundane ways that Christians misuse God's name. There are Christians who think of God only in times of trouble. Every time they pray in the name of Jesus, they are looking for God's favors. Some Christians advocate praying with a mental picture of the object they want God to provide. They claim that the more specific the mental picture, the more likely it is that God will grant that desire. Other Christians claim there are specific ways to pray that can guarantee that God will answer their prayers. While Scripture tells us to lay all our hearts' desires before God, it also emphasizes that He will answer our prayers according to divine wisdom and sovereignty. When Jesus taught the disciples to pray, His example (the Lord's Prayer, Matthew 6:8-13) exhibits a simple trust in God's provision and providence. If we think we can manipulate God into answering our prayers according to our specifications, we are dangerously close to the sorcerers in the Old Testament.

Sorcery, false prophets, and frivolous oaths are not merely things of the past. In some churches in the Majority World, syncretism is a living issue. Christianity can be easily confused with folk religion, so that the name of Jesus becomes a formula to invoke supernatural intervention. Moreover, people in this chaotic world (e.g., the Covid-19 pandemic) yearn for an authority figure. Those who proclaim with complete confidence that they are spokespersons for God often attract a large following. And while we do not usually invoke God's name in legal and business contracts, we can still parade our Christian identity as a way to gain people's trust. Whether literally or in a culturally transformed way, the Old

Testament ways of abusing God's name are still something about which Christians need to be mindful.

So how can we guard against violating the third commandment? The most effective and simple way is to go back to the basics of the Reformation: *sola Scriptura* and *sola gratia* and *soli Deo gloria*. We abuse God's name whenever we practice a syncretic faith, whether this be a syncretism with folk religions or with market capitalism. *Sola Scriptura* reminds us we must constantly examine our lives and the teaching we hear in the light of Scripture; no one is immune to the trap of syncretism. Next, we must constantly remind ourselves that we are God's children by the sheer grace of God. Whatever we can do, it does not make us more important or favorable before God. Whatever success or righteousness we achieve are gifts of God. Then we shall not be puffed up in our faith and presume to speak for God or try to use God for our purposes. Lastly, we must always remember that all glory belongs to God. We are the servants of God; God is not the servant of us or of our nation or of anything on earth or in heaven. *Soli Deo gloria*.

The Fourth Commandment:

SABBATH AND SHALOM

Fergus MacDonald, Scotland

The imperative of the fourth commandment expressly linking it with God's resting on the seventh day of the creation week and sanctifying it (Genesis 2:2-3) has prompted many Christians to follow the English Puritans in viewing the Sabbath as a "creation ordinance" of universal application and perpetual validity (Westminster Confession of Faith 21.7, 8). This view came to reflect the thinking and practice, probably, of the majority of English-speaking Protestants from mid-seventeenth century to mid-twentieth century. However, during the second half of the twentieth century, many English-speaking Protestants became more sympathetic to the views of European reformers Luther and Calvin, who regarded the Sabbath as a Mosaic institution later repealed by Christ.[1] As a result, in the early decades of the twenty-first century, most Anglophone evangelicals meet together for worship on Sunday as the Lord's Day but do not regard the day as a Christian Sabbath. This change has taken place in the face of widespread enthusiasm for the successful 1981 movie *Chariots of Fire* and the eloquent pleas of Marva Dawn, Eugene Peterson, and Walter Brueggemann to recognize the benefits of Sabbath-keeping for personal spiritual health and for the renewal of Western socioeconomic thinking and practice.[2]

Perhaps the most influential theological articulation of this transition is found in the 1982 (reprinted in 1999) anthology entitled *From Sabbath to Lord's Day: A Biblical, Historical, and Theological Investigation*, edited by D. A. Carson, with contributions from Carson and six others.[3] This theological

---

[1] R. J. Bauckham, "Sabbath and Sunday in the Protestant Tradition," in *From Sabbath to Lord's Day: A Biblical, Historical, and Theological Investigation*, ed. D. A. Carson (Grand Rapids: Zondervan, 1982), 312-17.

[2] See Marva J. Dawn, *Keeping the Sabbath Wholly: Ceasing, Resting, Embracing, Feasting*, (Grand Rapids: Eerdmans, 1989); Eugene H. Peterson, "Confessions of a Former Sabbath Breaker," *Christianity Today*, September 2, 1988; "The Pastor's Sabbath," *CT Online*, May 19, 2004; Walter Brueggemann, *Sabbath as Resistance: Saying NO to the Culture of Now* (Louisville: Westminster / John Knox Press, 2014, 2017).

[3] The D. A. Carson book represents the "majority report" of a project which broke up and issued also a "minority report," published in R. T. Beckwith and W. Stott,

reform of Sunday practice was reinforced by socioeconomic trends powered on the one hand by an emerging turbo-capitalism demanding 24/7 loyalty from workers and, on the other, by the rapid expansion of commercial and amateur Sunday sport. Both trends continue to compete with churches for popular attention, attendance, and involvement.

All the contributions in the Carson volume are of high academic caliber and merit respect. Nevertheless, they have not convinced everyone that the Lord's Day Sabbath lacks both the theological gravitas of a creation institution and the endorsement of the New Testament (NT). A substantial evangelical minority is convinced of the theological validity of the Puritan position, although they might dot their i's and cross their t's somewhat differently. This paper reflects the minority view and will examine the Sabbath in the following contexts: Decalogue, Genesis 1-3, Old Testament festivals, the book of Psalms, the prophets, the teaching and praxis of Jesus, early church practice, and finally, today's church and society.

Decalogue

The unique status of the Ten Words of the Decalogue in Old Testament (OT) legislation is highlighted in several ways. These words were given by God to Moses during a dramatic theophany on Mount Sinai (Exodus 19:16-25; Deuteronomy 5:4-5); they were inscribed on tablets of stone (Exodus 31:18; 34:1; Deuteronomy 4:13; 5:22); these words alone on their tablets were deposited in the ark of the covenant (Exodus 40:20-21; Deuteronomy 10:1-5).[4]

The Carson book has a very different take on the fourth commandment. Harold Dressler and A.T. Lincoln make the case for the Sabbath being innately Mosaic and against its being a creation institution.[5] They argue that the connection between the Sabbath of Exodus 20:8-11 and God's seventh-day rest of Genesis 2:2-3 is analogous, rather than derivative. They

---

This Is the Day: The Biblical Doctrine of the Christian Sunday in Its Jewish and Early Church Setting (London: Marshall, Morgan and Scott, 1978).

[4] Cf. C. J. H. Wright, *Deuteronomy. New International Biblical Commentary* (Peabody: Hendrik Publishers, 1996), p. 75; C. J. H. Wright, *Exodus: The Story of God Bible Commentary*, (eBook) (Grand Rapids: Zondervan Academic, 2021), p. 359; P. S. Ross, *From the Finger of God: The Biblical and Theological Basis for the Threefold Division of the Law* (Fearn: Christian Focus Publications, 2010), 51-88.

[5] H. H. P. Dressler, "The Sabbath in the Old Testament"; A.T. Lincoln, [A] "Sabbath, Rest, and Eschatology in the New Testament" and [B] "From Sabbath to Lord's Day: A Biblical and Theological Perspective," in *From Sabbath to Lord's Day: A Biblical, Historical, and Theological Investigation*, D.A. Carson, ed. (Grand Rapids: Zondervan, 1982).

justify this opinion mainly on two grounds. First, they understand the Genesis reference in Exodus 20:8-11 simply to mean: because God rested then, therefore He has blessed the Sabbath now. They see a parallel dynamic in Deuteronomy 5:15: because God rescued Israel from Egypt then, therefore He commanded them at Sinai to keep the Sabbath. The second ground is grammatical: it is claimed that the Hebrew particle 'al-ken (translated "therefore" in Exodus 20:11b and in Deuteronomy 5:15 by most English versions) creates or constitutes an etiology which "can have a verb in the past tense without implying a strictly past meaning."[6]

Both arguments are open to challenge. The linguistic argument, which Lincoln regards as "crucial," while perhaps possible, given that it is sometimes difficult to distinguish past, present, and future tenses in the Hebrew verb system, lacks support from the contextual indicators which favor the common traditional plain reading of the text. This reading is reinforced by both the Hebrew preposition *ki* ("for" or "because"), which opens verse 11, and the *wayyiqtol* form of the Hebrew verb closing the commandment ("and made it holy"), which suits a simple past, rather than present, translation.

In addition, it is doubtful if Exodus 20:11b forming an etiology supports Lincoln's claim. For B. S. Childs, "The etiology grounds the sanctity of the Sabbath in the creative act of God; it is built into the very structure of the universe."[7] Although different verbs are used (*nwḥ*, "to rest," in Exodus 20:11; and *šbt*, "to cease," in Genesis 2:2), a plain reading of Exodus 20:10 is that the commandment identifies "seventh day" and "Sabbath." Further, many commentators regard the rationale offered in Deuteronomy 5:15 as supplementing the rationale of Exodus 20:11b without detracting from it.[8]

For these reasons, a plain reading of Exodus 20:11b is to be preferred. Before moving on to examine the creation narrative to which Exodus 20 refers, it is important to note that at the renewal of the Decalogue forty years later, the fourth commandment was set in the exodus narrative (Deuteronomy 5:12-15). According to the Pentateuch, the rationale of the Sabbath lies in redemption as well as in creation. It is as relevant to life post-Fall as it was pre-Fall.

---

[6] A.T. Lincoln "From Sabbath to Lord's Day: A Biblical and Theological Perspective," 349.
[7] B. S. Childs, *The Book of Exodus: A Critical Old Testament Commentary* (Louisville: Westminster / John Knox, 1974), 416. Cf. J. H. Walton, *The NIV Application Commentary: Genesis* (Grand Rapids, Zondervan, 2001), p. 153.
[8] For example, Wright, *Deuteronomy. New International Biblical Commentary*, 75.

Creation

The fourth commandment's reference to Genesis 2:2-3 is unmistakable. But a point often missed is that, according to Genesis 1:1-2:3, the seven-day week itself is a creation institution. The seven-day week, which flows from the Sabbath, and is independent of solar and lunar calendars, is widely regarded as a unique Israelite institution.[9]

John Walton interprets the Genesis creation narratives in the context of a temple building and a temple dedication. "The face value of the account (i.e., that which is mutually understood by the biblical author and his contemporary audience) contains at least a strong undercurrent of God's setting up a cosmos intended to function not only as an environment for the people He is creating, but even more as a sanctuary for Himself. He furbishes it, puts people in it, and takes up His repose (Sabbath) in 1:1-2:3; then He sets up Eden along the lines of the Most Holy Place."[10] A similar interpretation of the creation accounts as anthropomorphic narratives is taken by the Bible Project.[11]

Walton observes that in the conceptual world of the Ancient Near East (ANE), creation, temple, and rest are inseparably linked.[12] ANE texts describing new temple initiations associate divine resting with divine enthronement.[13] This prompts Walton to determine that God's resting on the seventh day signifies His taking up the role of sovereign ruler of the cosmos. Walton finds biblical support for this conclusion in the use of the verb *nwḥ* (to rest, to settle) in Exodus 20:11b, rather than *šbt* (to cease, to stop working, to rest) as in Genesis 2:2, and in the employment in Isaiah of *nwḥ*'s derivative noun *manûḥâ* (resting place) to describe where God is enthroned within His cosmic temple (Isaiah 66:1; cf. Psalm 132:8, 14). The verbs *šbt* and *nwḥ* have distinct linguistic milieus, but in Genesis 2 and in Exodus 20, each describes the same creation seventh-day action of God.

---

[9] Wright, *Exodus: The Story of God Bible Commentary*, 366; Dressler in Carson, 24; Childs, 414. As in Israel, so too in Mesopotamia, the special status of seven-day periods is well-attested. Cf. '*Šbt*,' *Theological Dictionary of the Old Testament*, vol 14, eds. G.J. Botterwerk, H. Ringrenn (Grand Rapids: Eerdmans, 1981), 344-47.

[10] John H. Walton, *Genesis: The NIV Application Commentary: From Biblical Text ... to Contemporary Life* (Grand Rapids: Zondervan, 2001), 147-48.

[11] Shara Drimalla, "Were Adam and Eve Priests in Eden?" *BibleProject* (blog), accessed May 3, 2021, https://bibleproject.com/blog/were-adam-and-eve-priests-eden/.

[12] J. D. Levenson, "The Temple and the World," *Journal of Religion* 64 (1984): 288.

[13] Victor A. Hurowitz, "The Inauguration of Palaces and Temples in the Assyrian Royal Inscriptions," *Orient* 49 (2014): 89-105.

For Walton, the second creation account, in Genesis 2:4-3:24, is, in effect, a sequel to the first account (Genesis 1:1-2:3). He regards the *tolǝdot* formula in 2:4 to be introducing the second account.[14] The noun *tolǝdot* comes from the Hebrew root *yld*, "to bring forth" or "to generate." "What the heavens and the earth bring forth are the provision of God for the people He created and the plan of God in history."[15]

In summary, viewing the Genesis creation accounts in their own cultural context strengthens Childs's claim that the seventh-day Sabbath is, indeed, built into the very fabric of the universe. In the next three sections, we move on to explore the Sabbath in the lived experience of ancient Israel by reviewing religious festivals, the book of Psalms, and the witness of Israel's prophets.

Festivals

Keeping the Sabbath involved resting from work on the seventh day of each week and worshiping Yahweh (1 Chronicles 23:30-32; Nehemiah 10:33; cf. Isaiah 66:23), but it included more, for Sabbath observance was extended into the Sabbatical Year and into the Year of Jubilee. The Sabbatical (or seventh) Year had four features. The land lay fallow (Exodus 23:10-11; Leviticus 25:1-7); slaves went free (Exodus 21:2; Deuteronomy 15:12-18); debts were remitted (Deuteronomy 15:1-11); and the book of Deuteronomy was read aloud during the Festival of Tabernacles (Deuteronomy 31:9-13). The Year of Jubilee fell every fiftieth year, calculated as that following "seven weeks of years" (Leviticus 25:8), when the four features of the Sabbatical Year would recur (Levitikus 25:8-55). Together, these institutions, when consistently observed, would give the Sabbath significant influence on the socioeconomic life of Israel.

The Sabbath's links with creation and redemption were reinforced by holding three great annual religious festivals at the central sanctuary in Jerusalem (or Zion). These were:

- Passover / Unleavened Bread (Exodus 12:14-20; Leviticus 23:4-8; Numbers 28:16-25, 33-36)
- Tabernacles / Ingathering (Leviticus 23:33-43; Numbers 29:12-39; Deuteronomy 16:13-17)

---

[14] Some scholars regard this formula to refer retrospectively to the first creation account.
[15] Walton, 163.

- Weeks / Harvest / Pentecost (Leviticus 23:15-22; Numbers 28:26-31; Deuteronomy 16:9-12)

Passover and Weeks were week-long events, which would include a Sabbath, and Tabernacles began and ended on a Sabbath ("a solemn assembly; do no regular work;" Leviticus 23:35-36). In addition, the New Moon Festival was regarded as parallel to the Sabbath (2 Kings 4:23; Amos 8:5; Ezekiel 46:1). Also, the Day of Atonement (Leviticus 16:31) and the Festival of Trumpets (Leviticus 23:24; cf. Numbers 29:1-6) were designated a *šabbātôn*, a "Sabbath of solemn rest." The festivals were times when both creation and redemption were recalled as fundamental to Israel's life.[16] In addition, Weeks/Pentecost reflected the weekly Sabbath's humanitarian concern for the disadvantaged (Leviticus 23:22; cf. Deuteronomy 5:14).

Additionally, the origin of the Sabbath at creation was symbolized in the architecture of the Temple. The twin apartment complex – Holy Place and Most Holy Place – replicated the Garden of Eden,[17] where the pre-Fall Sabbath rest of the people of God would have been first experienced. The floral and arboreal artwork on the walls of the Temple were visual reminders of Eden.[18] The earthly sanctuary in Jerusalem was a microcosm of the Heavenly Temple where Yahweh is enthroned, ruling over the cosmos. As such, the Jerusalem sanctuary was the space on earth where Yahweh met His people.

In the OT historical books, references to the weekly Sabbath, to sabbatical years, to the Year of Jubilee, and to the festivals are relatively few. This may be due to the spiritual apathy and unbelief that seemed to prevail in successive generations, with some notable exceptions, during the historical period covered.[19] On the other hand, the 150 prayer songs of the book of Psalms, which articulate the vital faith of Yahweh's covenant people, may provide a more fruitful field for exploring the spiritual life of pious Israelites. Therefore, it is to the psalms that we turn next in our review of sabbatic practice and/or sabbatic ideas.

---

[16] C.E. Armerding, "Festivals and Feasts," *Dictionary of the Old Testament: Pentateuch*, eds. T.D. Alexander and D.W. Beber (Downers Grove: InterVarsity Press, 2003), 309.

[17] Walton, 147-50; cf. Bible Project video, The Royal Priest: Royal Priests of Eden, accessed 14 April 2021, https://www.youtube.com/watch?v=K60TAYja110.

[18] See I Kings 6:29-35; cf. Ezekiel 40:16, 37; 41:26.

[19] Maybe the events recorded in the historical books had no connection with the festivals. There is, however, evidence that a formal religiosity prevailed (e.g., Isaiah 1; Hosea 4). The exceptions were: under Joshua (Joshua 5:10), Hezekiah (2 Chronicles 30:1-27), Josiah (2 Kings 23:21-23; 2 Chronicles 35:1-19), and Zerubbabel (Ezra 6:19-22).

The Book of Psalms

At first sight, the book of Psalms isn't promising. The word *Sabbath* appears in the superscription of Psalm 92 but not at all in the text of any of the 150 psalms. On the other hand, the sovereignty of God in creation, a clear implication of the Genesis creation accounts, is pronounced. The psalm lyrics articulate a creation theology affirming Yahweh's rule over the newly created cosmos and consecrating it to His glory. A dual focus on God enthroned in heaven and also on earth, reigning in cosmos and history, is common throughout the Psalter.[20] According to J. L. Mays, the fundamental confession of the Psalter which Israel was called to proclaim to the nations is "The LORD reigns."[21] Furthermore, the "resting place" terminology employed in Psalm 132:8, 13-14, describing God's enthronement in Zion, almost certainly mirrors God's resting on the seventh creation day (cf. Isaiah 66:1). This strong psalmic perspective of Yahweh enthroned in heaven and on earth, over cosmos and history, has earned the Psalter the descriptor "the poetry of the reign of God."[22]

The sovereignty of Yahweh which congregations avowed during temple worship was also powerfully proclaimed by the prophets, so it is appropriate that we turn next to them.

The Prophets

The books of the prophets contain more than twenty references to the Sabbath. While Jeremiah is *forthtelling* divine judgment on those who desecrate this special day (Jeremiah 17:19-27), Isaiah expounds the Sabbath eschatologically. In Isaiah 56-66, he is *foretelling* both the *coming* of God's kingdom, with the arrival of the Messiah, and also the kingdom's *consummation* under the returning Messiah. The Sabbath becomes a pointer to both future events (56:1-8; 61:1-11). In chapter 56, Sabbath-keeping is a key feature, when God's righteousness (v. 1) is extended to those excluded from the Mosaic covenant (vv. 3-8; cf. Leviticus 21:20; Deuteronomy 23:1). Sabbath-keeping will be a symbol of the newcomers' allegiance to Yahweh (Isaiah 56:6; cf. vv. 2, 4). The Sabbath motif appears again in a focus on the "year of Yahweh's favor" (61:1-11). Then in the final chapter (66:22-24), the

---

[20] Psalms 9:7-11; 29:10; 47:1-9; 50:1-2; 76:2, 8; 78:68-69; 80:1, 14; 89:29; 93:1-2; 95:1-7; 96:10-13; 97:8-9; 98:4-6; 132:14; 134:3; 146:10.

[21] J. L. Mays, *Psalms: Interpretation, A Bible Commentary for Teaching and Preaching* (Louisville: Westminster / John Knox, 1994), 30.

[22] Mays, 30.

Sabbath is regarded as a feature in the new heavens and the new earth (cf. Ezekiel 46:1, 4, 12). Isaiah is, in effect, contextualizing the future orientation of the primordial Sabbath in God's redemptive purpose for the world.

Running parallel to this prophetic utilization of the Sabbath is a similar deployment of the Hebrew term šālôm, "peace," which is commonly transliterated into English as "shalom." Whatever disaster might strike Zion, Yahweh's "covenant of peace" with His people, like His love (ḥesed), will not be removed (Isaiah 54:13; cf. Numbers 25:12; Isaiah 54:10; Ezekiel 34:25; 37:26; Malachi 2:5). The Hebrew noun šālôm is derived from the verb šlm, meaning "to be whole, complete." It includes the ideas of welfare, prosperity, and security and is associated with wholeness (Isaiah 60:17c).[23] As with the Sabbath, there is an eschatological focus (66:12).[24]

This close association between Sabbath and shalom in Isaiah resonates with the role of the fourth commandment in the Decalogue. That commandment is the "crucial bridge," linking our duty to God, summarized in the first three commandments, with our duty to neighbors, expressed in the last six.[25] The fourth commandment is a fulcrum, helping us to proportion our response to God and to neighbor. In other words, the Sabbath is a catalyst of shalom. This catalytic role of the Sabbath is graphically illustrated in Isaiah 58, where delighting in the Sabbath (vv. 13-14) is accompanied by loosening the chains of injustice, liberating the oppressed, feeding the hungry, sheltering the poor, and clothing the naked (vv. 6-7) – i.e., promoting and establishing shalom.

So far in our excursus, we have discovered that God's seventh-day rest in the Genesis creation accounts is highly significant theologically. The Sabbath commandment in the Decalogue, along with the Sabbath motifs in Israel's festivals and institutions, are important reminders of God's activity in creation and redemption. The Psalms celebrate the goodness of creation and the blessings of redemption, while in Isaiah, the Sabbath stimulates social responsibility in the present and inspires hope for the future.

It is now time to pass from the Old Testament to the New. Before changing our focus, however, it is important to note that the Hebrew Bible integrates the Sabbath into the Mosaic Covenant (Exodus 31:16-17). The New Testament apostles regarded the Mosaic rituals as temporary fore-

---

[23] G.A.F. Knight, *Isaiah 40-55, Servant Theology, International Theological Commentary* (Edinburgh: Handsel / Grand Rapids: Eerdmans, 1984), 185.

[24] The oracle in Isaiah 66:1 inverts the focus in Psalm 132:13-14 on Yahweh's enthronement in Zion to Yahweh's enthronement in heaven with the earth as His footstool.

[25] P. D. Miller, *The Ten Commandments, Interpretation* (Louisville: Westminster / John Knox, 2009), 117.

shadowings of the coming of Christ (Colossians 2:16, 17; cf. Hebrews 10:1). Does that mean Jesus' life, death, and resurrection made the Sabbath obsolete? To find out, we now turn to the New Testament, first to the Gospels and Acts and then to the Epistles.

New Testament: Teaching and Praxis of Jesus

It is noteworthy that a sabbatic motif is central in Jesus' sermon in the Nazareth synagogue, which, for Luke, is the keynote address of Jesus' ministry (Luke 4:16-21). The focal point of the sermon is "the year of the LORD's favor" which would be proclaimed by the Messiah (Isaiah 61:1-2). We have already noted that this special year featured the release of slaves, the cancellation of debts, and resting the land (Leviticus 25:8-55). In making the dramatic claim, "Today this scripture has been fulfilled," Jesus is utilizing Sabbath associations.

Perhaps it is not surprising, then, that Jesus' observing and interpreting the Sabbath are highlighted in all four Gospels. Most of His teaching on the Sabbath arose in response to heavy criticism of the Jewish religious leaders, mainly the Pharisees, who considered that Jesus and His disciples were repeatedly breaking the Sabbath. The evangelists had at least three reasons for giving high visibility to these confrontations. The first is that these clashes elicited significant Christological claims; second, they appear to have contributed to the decision of the religious authorities to persecute Jesus; and, thirdly, the focus on the Sabbath controversies in the Gospels may well reflect tensions about Sabbath observance among believers in the churches for which the Gospels were originally written.

The Pharisees' criticism of Jesus and the Sabbath revolved around two types of activity. The first was the disciples' picking and eating heads of grain on a Sabbath as they passed through some grain fields (Mark 2:23-28; Matthew 12:1-8; Luke 6:1-5). The second activity was Jesus' readiness to heal non-emergency illnesses on the Sabbath. Seven cases of Sabbath healings are recorded: (1) the demoniac in the synagogue at Capernaum (Mark 1:21-28; Luke 4:31-37). (2) Peter's mother-in-law (Mark 1:29-31; Luke 4:38-39). No adverse reaction to these is recorded. (3) The man with the withered hand (Mark 3:1-6; Matthew 12:9-14; Luke 6:6-11). (4) The cripple at the pool of Bethesda (John 5:1-18). (5) The blind man sent to wash in the pool of Siloam (John 9:1-41). (6) The woman bent and crippled by a spirit for eighteen years (Luke 13:10-17). (7) The man suffering from dropsy (Luke 14:1-6). Also relevant is Jesus' response to critics of His Sabbath healings in John 7:14-24.

Jesus highlighted the social dimension of the fourth commandment in His defense of His disciples regarding the grain fields incident. The Greek verb *peino* in Matthew 12:1, translated "hungry," suggests the disciples were famished, not merely feeling peckish. Jesus regards the disciples' action as an act of mercy (which His citing Hosea 6:6 confirms). And as Lord of the Sabbath, Jesus has authority to declare His disciples "guiltless" (Matthew 12:5).

Jesus' stance on the Sabbath is of momentous Christological import. His declaration that "The Son of Man is lord even of the Sabbath" (Mark 2:28) articulates a claim to sovereignty over the Sabbath and also, by implication, a claim to self-identify with the Creator-God of Genesis 1:1-2:3, who demonstrated His Lordship over the seventh day of Genesis 2:2 by blessing it and making it holy. A link between the title "lord of the Sabbath" and the Genesis creation account is confirmed by the accompanying saying (recorded only by Mark): "'The Sabbath was made for man, not man for the Sabbath.'" (v. 27). The Greek verb translated "was made" is *ginomai*, "which might be compared with other references signifying 'to come into existence' and referring to God's creative act, and thus relate to the institution of primordial Sabbath."[26] The saying "implicitly refers to Genesis 1:26-2:2 (man created before the Sabbath, not vice versa)."[27] The suggestion that, in citing ceremonial lawbreaking – by David and by the priests (1 Samuel 21:1-6; Numbers 28:9-10) – in defense of His disciples, Jesus may, in effect, have been classifying the Sabbath law as of a similar ceremonial character to the regulations forbidding non-priests to eat consecrated bread and permitting priests to work in the temple on the Sabbath,[28] is less than convincing. It's more likely that in Mark 2:25-28, Jesus was affirming superiority of the Sabbath over the ceremonial regulations alluded to. At the same time, amazingly the Lord of the Sabbath humbled Himself to live under the law (Galatians 4:4; cf. Philippians 2:7-8), which specifies people's duties to God and to others. So we find Jesus sanctifying His Sabbaths by regularly worshipping God in the synagogue (Luke 4:16) and repeatedly healing the sick.

---

[26] L. Doering, "Sabbath Laws in the New Testament Gospels," in *The New Testament and Rabbinic Literature*, eds. R. Bieringer, F. Garcia Martinez, D. Pollefeyt, P.J. Thomson (Boston / Leiden: Brill, 2010), 217.

[27] S.O. Back, "Jesus and the Sabbath," *Handbook for the Study of the Historical Jesus* (E-Book), eds. T. Holmen and E. Porter, (Brill, 2010), 2603; cf. H. Weiss [A], "The Sabbath in the Synoptic Gospels," *Journal of Biblical Literature* 110, no 2 (1991): 319.

[28] D. A. Carson, "Jesus and the Sabbath in the Four Gospels," in Carson, *From Sabbath to Lord's Day*, 68-9.

Before healing the man with a withered hand (Matthew 12:9-14), Jesus responded to the question of the Pharisees – who on this occasion were joined by the scribes (Luke 6:7) and the Herodians (Mark 3:6) – by declaring, "It is lawful to do good on the Sabbath" (Matthew 12:12). (This declaration is rendered as a question in Mark 3:4 and Luke 6:9.) In this incident, by word and act, Jesus was expanding and deepening the social focus of the fourth commandment, for healing on the Sabbath is an example of benefiting the other (e.g., family members, servants, immigrants, and even animals), which the commandment envisages. Jesus understood the commandment to provide time for doing good to the sick, the disabled, and the disadvantaged. Luke points out that it was the man's *right* hand that was withered, which in all probability rendered him unable to do manual work. In restoring the man's ability to work for a livelihood, Jesus was indeed fulfilling the Sabbath commandment, for it mandates work as well as rest (Exodus 20:9).

In the case of the crippled woman in a synagogue (Luke 13:10-17), Jesus' healing demonstrated His power over the spirit world. The woman's affliction was caused by demonic oppression of her body rather than by "demon possession" of her personality. While the other Sabbath healings indicate Jesus' Messianic *authority* over the Sabbath, in this case He took the opportunity on a Sabbath to affirm the original *meaning* of the Sabbath as "the consecration of creation to its good and proper end."[29]

Whether Jesus deliberately chose the Sabbath as a day particularly suited to healing is not clear in the Synoptics. But His "violations of Sabbath law as then understood seem to be programmatic, flowing out of the alternative paradigm which Jesus taught: the Sabbath was a day for works of compassion. This change did not mean that the Sabbath was abrogated; rather, it was subordinated to deeds of compassion rather than to the [Pharisaic] quest for holiness."[30]

Turning to the fourth Gospel, the first Sabbath miracle to be recorded – the healing of the cripple at the pool of Bethesda – is in chapter 5. Some authorities, for example, E. Lohse, interpret John's account of Jesus as an acknowledgment that Jesus was indeed abrogating the Sabbath.[31] Jesus'

---

[29] E. Earle Ellis, *The Gospel of Luke: New Century Bible* (London: Thomas Nelson, 1966), 184-86.

[30] M.J. Borg, *Conflict, Holiness, and Politics in the Teachings of Jesus* (Harrisburg: Trinity Press International, 1984, 1989), 162.

[31] E.g., E. Lohse, "*šabbātôn*" in *Theological Dictionary of the New Testament*, Vol VII, eds. G. Kittel, G. Friedrich, (Grand Rapids: Eerdmans, 1974). Cf. A contrary view: H. Weiss [B], "The Sabbath in the Fourth Gospel," *Journal of Biblical Literature* 110,

defense of this Sabbath healing prompted the Jewish leaders to conclude, rightly, that He was calling God His Father and making Himself equal with God (v. 18). The rationale of Jesus' defense rests on the assumption that God works on the Sabbath as sustainer and judge of the world (a doctrine the rabbis accepted). Therefore, Jesus' assertion that He, too, was working on the Sabbath by sustaining life is clearly a claim to deity and led His critics to conclude not only that His action was unlawful, but also that His words were blasphemous. Jesus' action is in line with the exegesis noted above of God's rest in Genesis 2:2 as His reigning over creation. Lohse's assertion that John 5:18 demonstrates that Jesus abolished the Sabbath is open to serious question. The participle "was breaking" translates the Greek verb *luō*, "to loose," which sometimes can mean "to abrogate" or "to dissolve," as, for example, in Matthew 5:19. But here the imperfect tense suggests customary action rather than a definitive one-off act; hence most English versions render *luō* in this instance as "breaking" in the sense of "infringing."

In summary, the four Gospels reveal three motifs behind Jesus' Sabbath behavior. First, there is an ethical motif: the Sabbath is a day for doing good (Matthew 12:12). Second, there is a redemptive / eschatological motif: a healing is a liberation from the bond of Satan (Luke 13:16). Third, there is a messianic motif: the authority of Jesus is comparable to that of David (Mark 2:25-26), and even of God (John 5:17).[32]

Our survey of Jesus' Sabbath healings makes it reasonable to come to the following conclusions:

- Jesus expands and sharpens the Sabbath's eschatological focus.[33]
- "None of the sayings of Jesus can plausibly be construed as an attempt to abrogate the Sabbath."[34]
- The Sabbath signifies not only the creation rest of God, but also God's sovereign working in the cosmos and history.
- The fact that two out of the three healing miracles recorded in John's Gospel involve a Sabbath controversy suggests that Sabbath observance may have been an issue in the communities for whom the fourth Gospel was initially written.[35]

---

no. 2, (1991): 319: [In this incident] "Jesus did not abolish the Sabbath, but rather established the eschatological Sabbath."
[32] Cf. Back, 2601.
[33] Weiss [B], 319.
[34] Back, 2617.
[35] Weiss 1991, 311.

New Testament: The Early Church

Turning from the ministry of Jesus to the life and witness of the apostolic church, we find that the seventh-day Sabbath appears not to have been generally observed and that Paul frowned on attempts by some Jewish Christians to impose it on Gentile sisters and brothers.[36] From a very early stage, the church recognized the special significance of "the first day" and observed it as a day for corporate worship.[37] Richard Bauckham thinks Christian Sunday worship originated in the primitive Palestinian church.

> "There is no trace whatever of any controversy as to whether Christians should worship on Sunday, and no record of any Christian group that did not worship on Sunday. This universality is most easily explained if Sunday worship was already the Christian custom before the Gentile mission. It is very difficult otherwise to see how such a practice could have been imposed universally and leave no hint of dissent and disagreement. It seems hardly likely that Paul would have begun this novel practice in the course of his Gentile mission ... The conclusion seems irresistible that all of the early missionaries simply exported the practice of the Palestinian churches."[38]

Luke refers to Christians meeting on "the first day of the week" in Troas (Acts 20:7), while Paul appears to have taught the Galatian and the Corinthian believers to meet on "the first day" (1 Corinthians 16:1-2). Some forty years later John, on the Island of Patmos, tells us he received his visions on "the Lord's day" (Revelation 1:10-11), with the intention that they would be read in the worship meetings of the churches.[39] The title "the Lord's Day" would become universally used as the church grew rapidly in the second, third, and succeeding centuries.

It is significant that predominantly Gentile churches adopted the seven-day week, which was determined by the Sabbath and unknown in the ancient world outside Jewry. It is difficult to understand why the apostles retained the week if the sabbatic principle of one day in seven sanctified to the Lord had been abrogated. On the other hand, both the adoption of the seven-day week and the practice of meeting on the first day makes sense if both the sabbatic principle and the seven-day week were regarded as creation ordinances.

---

[36] Galatians 4:10; Romans 14:5-6; Colossians 2:16-17.
[37] Mark 16:2; John 20:12, 19; Acts 20:7; 1 Corinthians 16:2.
[38] R.J. Bauckham, "The Lord's Day," 236.
[39] Bauckham, 242.

The choice of the first day was not merely a matter of convenience, for its later designation as "the Lord's Day" marked it as the day to celebrate Christ's resurrection.[40] Additionally, Paul's reference in 1 Corinthians 16:1-2 to taking a collection on the first day for the famine-stricken Judean Christians indicates that the day also focused on caring for others – a striking correspondence with Jesus' use of the Sabbath. This very early practice of meeting on the first day provides today's churches with a warrant to do likewise. There is no indication that the early Christians rested from work on the first day. However, sabbatical rest would have been virtually impossible in a pagan everyday work week. Significantly, the meeting in Troas was held in the evening; according to Pliny's *Epistle*, written at the end of the first century, Christians met before dawn and again (presumably after work) in the evening.[41] This may have been the common practice among the churches.

It is important to take seriously what Paul says to the Galatians and to the Romans about the observation of days (Galatians 4:10; Romans 14:5-6) and to the Colossians about the observation of the Sabbath (Colossians 2:16). These references are wider than the weekly Sabbath, for they include celebration of "days and months and seasons and years" by the Galatian churches (Galatians 4:10) and in Colossae, "a festival or a new moon or a Sabbath" (Colossians 2:16). Paul sees such observances as "a shadow of the things to come." Now that Christ, the "reality" to which they point, had come, they had served their purpose and were obsolete. Commentators are almost certainly correct in regarding the seventh-day Sabbath to be included in Paul's classification of obsolescence. A key point in understanding Paul's thinking is the distinction made between voluntary observance by Jewish Christians – which is a matter of indifference (Romans 14:5-6) – and enforced observance upon Gentile Christians as a condition of salvation – which is "a different gospel" (Galatians 1:6).

The typology of the Sabbath, which Paul mentions briefly in Colossians 2:16, receives fuller treatment in Hebrews 3:7-4:13. It is widely recognized that the writer of Hebrews was addressing his community from an eschatological perspective. The church was living in a time of fulfilment inaugurated by Christ "in these last days" (1:2), "at the end of the ages" (9:26), but not yet consummated by His return (9:28) and His rule over the world to come (2:5-9). Both these realities are symbolized in the Sabbath motif: its initial fulfilment in Christ's first coming and its ultimate fulfilment in the "Sabbath rest" (*sabbatismos*) that remains for the people of God (4:9) at

---

[40] Bauckham, 240.
[41] Referenced in Bauckham, 239.

Christ's Parousia (9:28). Therefore, like the kingdom of God in the Gospels, the ultimate Sabbath rest to which the weekly Sabbath points has come in Christ's advent, death, and resurrection but will not fully come until His Parousia. Until then the Sabbath retains its typological significance.

Hebrews 4:9 is the only occurrence of *sabbatismos* in the NT, and it may have been coined by the writer.[42] In the Septuagint, the cognate verb *sabbatizo* is used of Sabbath observance (cf. Exodus 16:30; Leviticus 23:32; 26:34-5; 2 Chronicles 36:21), which corresponds with its use elsewhere in extant Greek literature to denote observance or celebration of the Sabbath.[43] This semantic background may suggest translating *sabbatismos* as a "Sabbath-keeping," but most commentators prefer "Sabbath rest." According to Lincoln, New Covenant believers discharge this duty of Sabbath observance by exercising faith, while for Beckwith and Stott, the sabbatic principle has been incorporated into the Lord's Day, which is regarded as a day of rest and worship.[44]

The thinking and practice of the NT church can be summarized in four observations. First, the church adopted the seven-day week from the Jews. Second, the church observed one day in seven – the first day – later called "the Lord's Day." Third, what we know of the churches' activities on this day corresponds strikingly with the two foci of worship and service featured both in the fourth commandment and in Jesus' Sabbath observance. Fourth, the typology of the Sabbath pointing to the consummation of God's purpose for His people is affirmed in the Letter to the Hebrews.

Where shall we go with the fourth commandment?

In this section we will summarize the main findings of our study of the commandment and then explore whether it continues to have relevance in church and society today.

Main Findings:

1. The Sabbath is a divinely created institution built into the fabric of the universe.
2. God resting on the seventh day of creation symbolizes taking up His rule over the newly created cosmos.

---

[42] P. Ellingworth, *The Epistle to the Hebrews: Epworth Commentaries* (London: Epworth Press, 1991), 35.
[43] Lincoln [A], 213.
[44] Beckwith and Stott, 12; Cf. P. K. Jewett, *The Lord's Day* (Grand Rapids: Eerdmans, 1972), 119-20.

3. The Sabbath shares the unique status of the Decalogue.[45]
4. An implication of Jesus declaring Himself to be Lord of the Sabbath (Mark 2:27) is that the paraphernalia attached to it in the Mosaic Covenant are now passé under the New Covenant.[46]
5. Jesus' Sabbath-keeping observed the twin foci of the fourth commandment (worship of God and service to neighbor).
6. Jesus warns against weaponizing the Sabbath to make moralistic judgments of others.
7. The early church worshiped on the first day from a very early stage and later called it "the Lord's Day."
8. The Sabbath's role as a type of salvation awaits complete fulfilment at the Parousia.
9. The Sabbath continues to claim validation in the lifestyle of the people of God throughout the interim between the *coming* of the kingdom of God in Christ's advent and its *consummation* at His Parousia.

However, a degree of ambiguity remains.[47] The New Testament lacks any express warrant either to directly follow Sabbath customs of a previous era or to abolish the Sabbath. There is no directive to rest, or even to meet, on the first day. Paul seems to be open to those who consider "all days alike" (Romans 14:5). On the other hand, Jesus claims to be the Lord of the Sabbath and the NT church calendar reflects the seven-day week. The Westminster Confession (1.6) helps us here, for it indicates that where the counsel of God is not expressly set down in Scripture, it may be deduced from Scripture by good and necessary consequence. In utilizing this Westminster hermeneutic and interpreting the above findings holistically, I conclude that the Lord's Day enjoys the status of the Christian Sabbath, as duly modified in light of the considerations specified above.

---

[45] Wright, 2021, 358.
[46] Wright, 2021, 358.
[47] Editor's note: One of the causes this ambiguity is the use of different calendars in various times and places. Though at some times in history some nations either did not observe weeks (only observing months and years) or had weeks ranging in length from five to ten days, today most of the world follows a seven-day week. What is still widely different among countries and cultures is which day is the final day of the week. In the Americas and large parts of Asia, Saturday is the last day of the week. Much of Europe legally regards Sunday as the seventh day of the week, whereas some Arabic-speaking countries regard Friday as the seventh day of the week. Some churches follow a calendar from a previous era in their region's history or from another part of the world. TJ

Some Strategic Directions

Finally, I want to suggest seven strategic steps we might take to discover Sabbath-keeping as a catalyst for God's shalom.[48] These steps are:

1. *The Lord.* Enjoy Sunday as His day! In resting on the seventh day, God initiated His sovereignty over creation and history. In rising on the first day, He demonstrated His power to turn the world upside down.
2. *The Church.* Discover worshiping with God's people on the Lord's Day to be a delight, and help to portray the church as a "contrast society" from the listless boredom of worldly values.
3. *The Self.* Become time-rich rather than time-poor. Overcome the tyranny of the urgent. Drop out of the rat race to rest in the Lord and on His promises. "In an age that has lost its soul, Sabbath-keeping offers the possibility of gaining it back."[49] Read stirring testimonies of the blessings of Sabbath-keeping.[50]
4. *The Environment.* Allow the Sabbath to remind you that God is the Creator of the natural world and has appointed you to care for it. Pray for sincere attempts to reduce toxic emissions, to utilize natural resources responsibly, and to preserve threatened animal species.
5. *The Culture.* Keep Sabbath to find new strength to speak truth to power in the form of governments and business corporations which idolize greed, exploit the poor and vulnerable, usurp others, and practice deceit.
6. *The Economy.* Each Sabbath ask God in His sovereignty to moderate today's market pressures which generate felt needs and desires, leaving people rest-less, inadequate, and unfulfilled.
7. *The Parousia.* Explain your Sabbath-keeping to others by pointing to the promise of the "Lord of the Sabbath" to return and establish an eternal Sabbath in the new heavens and the new earth.

May all of us be in the Spirit every Lord's Day! (cf. Revelation 1:10).

---

[48] For a fuller treatment of practical Sabbath keeping today, see F. MacDonald, "What about a School of Sabbatics," *The Monthly Record of the Free Church of Scotland*, June 2008.
[49] M. J. Dawn, *Keeping the Sabbath Wholly* (Grand Rapids: Eerdmans, 1989), 50.
[50] For example, Dawn, *Keeping*; E. H. Peterson: "Confessions of a Former Sabbath Breaker," *Christianity Today*, September 2, 1988; "The Pastor's Sabbath," *CT Online*, May 19, 2004; M. Buchanan, *The Rest of God: Restoring Your Soul by Restoring Sabbath* (Nashville: Thomas Nelson, 2006).

The Fifth Commandment:

"PARENTS ARE VALLEYS FOR QUENCHING THE FIRES OF LIFE"[1]

John P. Wilson, Australia

I love my mum and have fond memories of my father, but have I honored them as God requires? I'm not sure. Clearly the Bible takes obedience to parents seriously, but have I? My father revered his parents and learned life values from their example, but did he honor them as God requires? He was not sure that he did. He would have liked to have been a better son.

The fifth commandment is a word from God that is weighted heavily toward that which I cannot fulfill and holds out a promise that, on first glance, I don't expect to receive: by obeying Mum, I don't expect to add a year to my life. It's a commandment difficult to obey.

My obedience to Mum and Dad waxed and waned. At times obedience came by threat of the strap, at other times through fear of the frown of displeasure. Only later did I see the importance of honoring them as God would have me do.

Romans 1:28-32 contains a notable list of types of wickedness that reveal a depraved mind, enumerating characteristic offenses committed by people who don't acknowledge God. While upon first reading we expect to read what we see there, namely, people who are "full of envy, murder, strife, deceit, maliciousness" (v. 29), there is one offense that is out of place, and that is "disobedient to parents" (v. 30).

That phrase strikes me as odd, at least in this regard: it is easy to say we are not murderers or filled with malice. We might even assert we are not "gossips, slanderers, haters of God, insolent, haughty, boastful" (vv. 29-30), but who has never disobeyed his parents?

However, as much as the fifth commandment addresses my relationship to my parents, if this is our only consideration, we have a reductionist view of the commandments. Their purview is much wider than merely family life. We need discernment to adopt them in their proper breadth.

---

[1] From a Malawian proverb – explained later in the chapter.

Locating the fifth commandment – which table?

There is an old tradition of inscribing all the words of the Decalogue on the front wall of churches – behind the preacher, always decoratively painted, often with a scrolled banner above or below. Reading these helpfully satisfied this young mind during unintelligible sermons or insufferably long pastoral prayers. I remember that in my own church, and then also observed when visiting churches while on holiday, the Ten Commandments were invariably split into two columns, mostly five and five, sometimes four and six.

Is there a division in the Decalogue? If there are two tables of the law, on which table does the fifth commandment sit? While agreeing that there is no necessity to make a division at all, because Jesus makes two summary laws from the ten (Matthew 22:37-40), it is tempting for us to divide them.

When Moses came down from Mount Sinai with two stone tablets (Exodus 31:18), we do not necessarily conclude this was the Decalogue split between them. Rather, many insist that these were two copies of the Ten Commandments, in a similar manner that was expected when establishing covenants in the ancient Near East: the two tablets of the law were copies of the same laws. "This was typical for covenants in the ancient Near East. You'd have one for each party. You couldn't just throw it onto a copy machine, so you had to bang it out on two different pieces of stone. One copy went into the ark of the covenant for the Lord, but the other was for them to remember."[2]

If, for purposes of learning and application, we follow the tradition of dividing the Decalogue into two tablets, should we identify the fifth commandment as the first commandment of the second division or the last commandment of the first division? Many view it as the first commandment of the second division. John Currid[3] classifies the first four commandments as "vertical commands" and the second six as "horizontal commands." The Westminster Confession of Faith (chapter 19) does likewise, as does John Calvin. However, I wonder if a possible 50:50 split is helpful to consider as well.

While it is mathematically appealing to consider the two tables of law with five on each, it is also appealing theologically, because the first five commandments concern our obligation to God and to authorities higher than ourselves, while the second five relate to our responsibility toward one another as equals.

---

[2] E.g., Kevin DeYoung, *The 10 Commandments* (Wheaton: Crossway, 2018), 79.
[3] John D. Currid, *A Study Commentary on Exodus*, Vol. 2, EP study commentary series (Great Britain: Evangelical Press, 2001), 35, 44.

Recognizing that the weight of literature on this subject promotes a 40:60 split, and for good reason, the vertical dimension of this commandment lends itself to thinking of a 50:50 split. Even if that position cannot be defended sufficiently, we do well to give greater attention to the upward dimension so that we are not limiting our application of the fifth commandment to the realm of mothers and fathers in the home.

On balance, I suggest that the fifth commandment belongs with the first four. Each contains the phrase "the LORD your God," thus making them all about our gratitude to God for His blessing and our response to God for who He is. W. H. Gispen summarizes, "In the Fifth Commandment the Lord makes the question of honouring the parents His business, as was naturally the case in the first four commandments, which dealt with His service, His name, and His day."[4]

Commandment number five is like the hinge on a door, leading from the first four to the last five, because both the vertical and horizontal are present in it.

Reading the text

The fifth commandment is recorded in Exodus 20 and then repeated by Moses in Deuteronomy 5. It is referenced twice more in Scripture – first by Jesus in Matthew 15:4 (cf. Mark 7:10) and then by Paul in Ephesians 6.

These are the two Hebrew scriptural texts. The extra words in Deuteronomy 5, beyond those found in Exodus 20, are underlined:

Exodus 20:12
Honor (*kabod*) your father (*av*) and your mother (*am*), that your days may be long in the land that the LORD your God is giving you.

Deuteronomy 5:16
Honor (*kabod*) your father (*av*) and your mother (*am*), <u>as the LORD your God commanded you</u>, that your days may be long, and <u>that it may go well with you</u> in the land that the LORD your God is giving you.

The additions in the Deuteronomic version first remind us of the source of this command (i.e., words from God); they also add a second blessing, promising not only a long life, but also a flourishing life. Long life is not a blessing without flourishing (i.e., doing well), so this second version simply spells out and makes explicit what is implicit in the original Exodus version.

---

[4] Willem Hendrik Gispen, *Exodus*, trans. Ed van der Maas, Bible Student's Commentary (Grand Rapids: Zondervan, 1982), 197.

It is right to take the Exodus text as our primary reference, because the other texts refer back to it either expressly or by implication. For example, the Deuteronomy passage points back to the Mt. Sinai event, with the additional words "as the LORD your God has commanded you."

Understanding the words *Honoring parents*

The key verb is "honor." We are to honor two persons in particular: our father and our mother. In the Pentateuch, the word *honor* comes from the verb (*kabod*), meaning "to be heavy or of weight." In this context, this means "to consider important, to give honor to (your father and your mother)." Walter Kaiser says this includes "prizing them highly," "showing affection for them," "revering them."[5]

Kaiser's view is underscored by the choice of Hebrew vocabulary. Through God's purposeful authorship of Scripture, the *Piel* form of the verb *kabod* was used in Exodus 20. The simpler *Qal* form (e.g., Isaiah 24:20) appears in other passages of Scripture, but here in the Commandments, it is *Piel*, which intensifies the verb and heightens the sense of honor we are to give to our parents (and, by extension, to all in higher authority).

This view is further underscored by the commentary on the laws of God in Leviticus. In the elaboration of the Ten Commandments, Leviticus 19:3 says parents are to be "feared" (*yr'*): "Every one of you shall revere (*yr'*) his mother and his father ..."

Mark Rooker says: "The use of the verb *yr'* 'fear/awe' is conceptually related to 'honour.' This association emphasizes the importance of this command, as the root *yr'* (fear) is commonly used to express one's response to God" (Deuteronomy 28:58).[6]

This same Hebrew word appears elsewhere in the text of Exodus to refer to Pharaoh's unyielding or hardened heart (7:14 and 10:1). What it suggests is that a child must not take his parents lightly or his responsibility toward them flippantly.

Calvin's application of honor is threefold: let it be seen as "reverence, obedience, and gratefulness."[7] Calvin continues to explain that the principle of the fifth commandment is clearly part of natural law. "[God] has

---

[5] Walter C Kaiser Jr, *Exodus*, The Expositor's Bible Commentary, Vol. 2, Frank Gaebelein Gen. Ed. (Grand Rapids: Zondervan, 1990), 424.

[6] Mark F. Rooker, *The Ten Commandments: Ethics for the Twenty-first Century*, (Nashville: B&H Publishing, 2010), 107.

[7] John Calvin, *Institutes of the Christian Religion*, ed. John T. McNeill, trans. Ford Lewis Battles (Philadelphia: Westminster Press, 1960), 2.8.36.

expressly bidden us to reverence our parents, who have brought us into this life. Nature itself ought in a way to teach us this. Those who abusively or stubbornly violate parental authority are monsters, not men!"

Longer than for childhood

Honoring parents is not restricted to minors. It certainly is most applicable for young children in the home, which is why Paul includes his reference to it in Ephesians immediately after addressing the husband and the wife; he then places the fifth commandment in the context of fathers not exasperating their children (Ephesians 6:4). While the application of this commandment to the relation between fathers and small children is self-evident, this does not make the fifth commandment different from the other nine, which are more obviously and immediately addressed to the adult nation of Israel. Gregory Goswell asks rhetorically: "Is this the one commandment out of the ten with a 'sunset clause,' so that when a person reaches 18 or 21 years it no longer applies?"[8]

Broader application than parents

There's a wider application here than to the parent-child relationship. It is not a commandment addressed out of the blue only to children. As Albert Mohler writes, "This is not children's church in the middle of the Ten Commandments."[9] Rather, these are all words delivered to an adult covenant community in Israel, with lasting application for the church of all eras and for the covenant faithful of all ages.

It is not only immediate biological parents whom God has in view, for the Bible also uses the names for father and mother for those who have authority over others. Some examples:

> Genesis 45:8: Joseph declared, when appointed head of Pharaoh's household and ruler over Egypt, that he had been made a "father" (*av*) to Pharaoh.
>
> Judges 5:7: In Deborah and Barak's song, she is described as a "mother" (*am*) in Israel.
>
> 2 Kings 2:12: Elisha cried out upon seeing the prophet Elijah ascend into heaven: "My father, my father!" (*avi, avi*).

---

[8] Gregory R. Goswell, *The Fifth Commandment*, in *Love Rules*, (Melbourne: Church and Nation Committee, PCV, 2004), 50

[9] R. Albert Mohler Jr, *Words from the Fire* (Chicago: Moody, 2009), 96.

Alongside application within family life, honoring one's parents is described in Scripture as analogous to honoring God. According to the prophet Jeremiah, God refers to Himself as the father of Israel, and, inversely in Isaiah, God refers to Israel as His sons and daughters. According to the prophet Malachi, God calls for this same honor.

In application, we should understand that this commandment applies to all who are in proper authority over us. For our benefit, God has set hierarchies for the human race to live at its best and to flourish, and we do best if we honor and obey those whom God has placed over us.[10] There's a caveat, of course, in that those in authority are supposed to represent God to us; if their rule deteriorates into godlessness, obedience to those in authority is thereby qualified.

The promise

1. The obvious difficulty

Though not without difficulty in application, it's a matter of relief and joy to find a promised blessing attached to the fifth commandment. Paul reminds us (Ephesians 6) that it's the first commandment with a promise, so we should take notice of it and rejoice. By "first" we are not ignoring the words attached to the second commandment regarding God's "steadfast love to thousands of those who love me and keep my commandments." However, these words are more a reflection on the character of God than a promise for us.[11]

What is the New Testament application of this? Obedience to the fifth commandment is connected with the promise of a long life. But how? At first glance, it seems to create a merit system for living longer, but can that be true? If so, how are we to think of dear saints of God who have died young, some tragically so? Alternatively, what do we make of careless sons and daughters who have disrespected or even hated their parents but have lived into their nineties?

2. Literal (or personal) reference

According to Exodus 21:17, dishonoring parents by striking or cursing them was punishable by death. In Deuteronomy (21:18-21), a procedure is

---

[10] E.g., 1 Timothy 5:17, to church elders; Ephesians 5:22, wives to husbands within a Christian marriage; 1 Peter 2:13-14, to duly elected civil rulers.

[11] John R. W. Stott, *God's New Society - the Message of Ephesians* in The Bible Speaks Today series (Illinois: IVP, 1980), 240.

described for parents to bring a persistently disobedient son to the city elders for death by stoning. Thus, the clause "your days may be long" could have had an immediate interpretation: so that you are not put to death under the judicial law of the Old Testament.

3. Covenantal reference

The Israelites associated keeping the fifth commandment with the ability of the nation of Israel to remain in the land to which God was leading them. When teaching the fifth commandment and even reflecting on Paul's quotation of it, we must consider the immediate context of when and where it was declared as our guide. The promise should be read with covenantal interpretation.

To some extent, the promise attached to this commandment stands over all the commandments. The way that ancient Israel was to exist successfully with any degree of longevity in such a hostile land surrounded by such an anti-theistic culture was to adopt a lifestyle measured and controlled by the Decalogue. The promise of a long life in the land and of lives well-lived refers primarily to the land of Canaan and to the people of Israel.

There is, of course, a general application today in the sense that the Decalogue, including this commandment, remains God's best blueprint for the best life, long or short. The reference to the "land" in both Exodus and Deuteronomy refers to the "land of promise" – and is to be read in light of the covenant. It is using covenant language and refers to Canaan as the land specifically promised to the people of Israel. The New Testament application is the same, but the specific location has a higher focus: as children of Abraham by faith in Christ, it's not our earthly life that is the focus, but rather our "land of promise" – eternal life in heaven, our ultimate resting place.

Even if the "land of promise" for us as New Testament believers is primarily eternal, this does not reduce the specific and earthly duties of this commandment. Jesus teaches that those who do not honor their parents in very practical ways are rejecting the commandment of God (Mark 7:9-13).

Applying this to our lives

Culture – the way we are raised and particularly our own parental training in the early years – inevitably influences how we understand words and apply them to our lives. The way we value (or ignore) our parents, home, and family life is going to influence how we apply the fifth commandment. There are differences in the world's cultures, between east and west, north and south, and it is worth reflecting on these.

Reflections from African culture

Having lived in Africa and engaged with many fellow pastors there, I observe how this commandment has been highly embraced in African culture with its traditional practices: honor, fear, and respect for parents are always extended beyond biological parents to all elderly people in the community.

Non-Christian African culture

Honoring parents has been so highly regarded that it became a part of initiation teachings during the very harsh three-week boyhood-to-manhood ceremonies. Believing that parents were custodians of all the knowledge and wisdom required for a successful life and also provided security from vices that would lead to premature death, young people owed this obligation to parents and to the elderly. The practice was driven from a humanistic perspective, as traditional practice ordered by mankind for a healthy community. The elders of the village tied respect for parents to a healthy community and therefore to a long life.

African traditional practice embraced this commandment and rigorously imposed it on the youth as a rule for right living and as a prerequisite for longer life. There is a sense in which it has been easier for an African to obey the fifth commandment. Many people in Africa naturally venerate and revere their ancestors. It is in the mind of many African children to give respect to and to obey any elderly person.

The fifth commandment suits the African context especially, as it gives sense to the existence of an individual, family blessings, and long life. The father is always considered the head of any family, and the mother anchors many teachings in a family. She is a teacher of children, a protector, who plays a crucial role in the continuation of life. Children who are disobedient bring shame to the mother; the father's head lowers whenever a child misbehaves. This is very embarrassing to the family. On the other hand, many Africans believe that obedient children bring joy to the parents and give assurance of long life. A cultural awareness of the principles articulated in this commandment provides a key for obedience to the parents and for prosperity of the individuals as well as of the family. This all depends on the understanding of cultural teachings; in this case, culture and biblical teachings agree to some degree.

The weakness is simply that some would quickly abandon the practice upon their independence from the hands that bound them. Regrettably, however, with the emergence of the demand for human rights and the invasion of other cultures into African culture, honoring parents from the humanistic perspective has been grossly eroded. What seem to be the days of enlightenment today have destroyed a valuable practice.

Coming of the gospel in Africa

With the coming of the Christian gospel, discovering this fifth commandment as the law of God enhanced the need to obey because it comes from the Creator who holds and sustains life. The Christian perspective of the commandment is our only hope because honor to parents is ultimately derived from honor to God, who holds life and human destiny, rather than merely from traditional culture. The biblical understanding of this commandment seems to be our only hope for the future, because it is anchored in Him who transcends human cultures and traditional practices. This understanding helps our youth discern the practice that honors God regardless of cultural changes.

Malawi[12]

A Malawian will say, "Akulu-Akulu ndi M'dambo modzimila moto." It means parents or elderly people are valleys for quenching the fires of life. I learned this proverb from traditional Malawian culture as the reason for honoring our parents, who have knowledge and wisdom from God to pass on to their youth, and it fits with biblical teaching,

Zambia

As much as the fifth commandment was very significant and unique in the lives of the Israelites, it is also uniquely significant in Zambian lives. In Zambia, children have an obligation to honor their parents. In a Zambian worldview, family connections create strength for each member and can at some point mean survival during a crisis. The fifth commandment provides a framework for unity within the community or society, and on the other hand, it provides support to one another or to individuals. Zambians use an analogy to explain the fifth commandment; honoring parents forms a platform for children to learn or be taught by their parents, since parents are responsible for the upbringing of their children. From a Zambian pastor:

---

[12] From former Secretary-General CCAP Central Africa, Rev Colin L M'bawa.

Another critical teaching that we can learn from the Fifth Commandment has to do with identity. Identity is very critical from the Zambian perspective as everyone wants a sense of belonging either to a clan or tribe. This commandment therefore charges children to the responsibility of honouring and respecting their parents which falls within the parameters of covenant obligations. In the reality of Zambia, the Fifth Commandment communicates to children that life is about community, and for children to advance in wisdom, there must be a parent to teach them and transmit that wisdom for the sake of the future community. Parents are regarded as the bank of wisdom where children can go and withdraw. Children's highest wisdom is that they honour their parents and their relationship with God becomes relevant. Zambian honouring of parents goes beyond individualism and the egos of the community. In other words, it goes beyond death whilst focussing its emphasis on family and community.[13]

Reflections from Indian culture

Having lived in India and engaged with many fellow pastors there, I have observed how this commandment has been highly embraced in Indian culture with its traditional practices.

Non-Christian Indian culture

While the culture in India is incredibly diverse, there is a consensus that honoring parents is a virtue. In a context where the familial relationship is esteemed above individual autonomy, the fifth commandment resonates well with the cultural (natural) hierarchy of a family. Honoring parents, therefore, is seen as necessary for the proper functioning and well-being of the family system.

In many ways, the fifth commandment is the one with which Indians have the least problems. I can think of them struggling with the other nine but not with this one, because culturally and traditionally, parents are generally respected in all Indian societies, Christian and non-Christian. In some religious systems, such as Hinduism, Sikhism, Jainism, and Buddhism, they verge on literal worship of parents (not simply "honor"). It is not uncommon to see professionally qualified Indians from these backgrounds bow low and touch the feet of their parents (and such special consideration is given to mothers that they are equated with God).

In some societies, it is not uncommon for young people to stand when older persons, especially parents, enter the room (compare Job 29:8). The

---

[13] Former General Secretary, CCAP Zambia Synod, Rev. Maleka Rabson Kabandama

usual response of parents when children show this respect is to bless them by placing their hands on the heads of the children. Such respect is also shown for the extended family, including all in-laws.

Coming of the gospel in India

Even in evangelical Christian communities, this traditional cultural background shapes the understanding and the application of the fifth commandment within the evangelical churches in India. In general, the commandment is understood as a requirement for children (adult offspring as well) to submit to the authority of parents. This understanding implies that parents, especially the father, provide for the present and future needs of their offspring. Parents' efforts in raising children, establishing relationships in society, and accumulating wealth are seen as investments for the welfare of the family. Thus, honoring parents is closely associated with the prosperity of future generations. Rebellion against the authority of the parents forfeits the blessing of the parents.

Thankfully, most Christian societies in India have retained these cultural practices with slight modifications. For example, touching one's feet is substituted with folding hands (a very solemn gesture). This is reciprocated by both parties. In terms of the application of the fifth commandment, among other things, adult sons and daughters seek the blessings of their parents in major decisions of life (e.g., choosing a trade and a marriage partner). Adult children honor their parents by taking care of them in old age. Concerning the understanding of the fifth commandment, one of the challenges for Christians in India is to maintain the balance between the individuality of a person and the collective identity of the family. Has this changed in any Indian Christian communities? Yes, in urban contexts and where Indian Christians have been exposed to Western values, traditional values are fast disappearing. It's sad.

Best blueprint for all nations

Culture shifts and new sub-cultures emerge, but God's Word endures forever (Isaiah 40:8).

There's something here for the whole world. God the Creator knows what we need and how any and every society works best. Honoring our parents in the home is the precursor to honoring those duly appointed to authority in our societies. It is no accident that one mirrors the other. Respect and order in the family provide stable patterning for society. This is why a totalitarian regime will make a huge effort to disrupt the family and destroy order in the home to create state dependency in its place. Civilizations, societies, and cultures flourish best and work cohesively where there is respect and order in the home.

Even the promise attached to the commandment has this in mind. During the time of Exodus, God ruled over the nation Israel as His church (i.e., Israel was both nation and church). The covenant blessings were tied to their life in the promised land. Hence, the promises "it may go well with you" (Deuteronomy 5) and "your days may be long in the land" (Deuteronomy 5 and Exodus 20) ought to be applied, not locatively and individually, but spiritually and more generally, in the church today:

1. "... it may go well with you ..." – People who flourish and achieve the best of human endeavour are those who listen to God's words and live by them.
2. "... you may live long in the land ..." – Social stability and cohesion such that a society generally lasts longer when it is built upon and as it maintains the tenets of respect and honor for those in authority. The long life promised does not apply to every individual but broadly to the society that honors God and loves others according to His words.

The sweeping nature of the Decalogue is unmistakable from reading the book of Deuteronomy. There is a view of Deuteronomy that sees chapters 12 through 26 as exposition of the Ten Commandments, with, for example, Deuteronomy 16:18-18:22 referenced to the fifth. If this is right, it shows the wide-ranging application of the commandments to cover every conceivable area of life.

There's a sense in which the parental relationship is the prototype of all relationships – it certainly shapes all other relationships. In our families, while we are young, we learn how to obey, to understand what respect is, what proper authority looks like, and how protection feels. It is there that we first learn what honoring *any* authority looks like and why such authority structure matters. Without such early lessons, we are likely not to honor anyone. As Augustine said, "If anyone fails to honour his parents, is there anyone he will spare?"[14]

This is confirmed by the explanations of Exodus 20:12 in the Westminster Larger and Shorter Catechisms, which apply the fifth commandment to all social relations, whether "superiors, inferiors, or equals."[15] As Paul implies in his letters, the fifth commandment undergirds, instructs, and

---

[14] Quoted in Philip Graham Ryken, *Exodus: Saved for God's Glory*, Preaching the Word (Wheaton, IL: Crossway, 2005), 602.
[15] Shorter Catechism, Q. 64.

directs how husbands relate to wives, wives to husbands, children to parents, parents to children, masters to slaves, and slaves to masters (Ephesians 5:21-6:9) and then, even more broadly, how we as citizens relate to government (Romans 13) and how we as Christians relate to each other in the church (1 Corinthians 12). It is as if the whole of life can be viewed as the outworking of the fifth commandment.[16]

The need for grace

To return to where I commenced: "I love my mum, and have fond memories of my father, but have I honored them as God requires? I'm not sure." In fact, I'm sure of this: I could not and cannot obey this commandment other than with the grace of Christ in my heart. Honoring requires subjection to the authority God has placed over me and against which I naturally rebel.

The fall of man and the subsequent depravity of the human heart without Christ mean that I have inherently acquired a disposition of pride and such self-importance that longs for honor myself and will only bear subjection or compliance grudgingly. Added to this dilemma is the conclusion we have reached, that the fifth commandment is the basis for all-of-life recognition of proper authority.

Only a regenerate heart can cope with this – and with any of God's commandments. Only fleeing to Christ, the perfect Man, and falling at the foot of His cross can bring about in us the radical change of heart and will required to begin the joyful life of obedience to Him whose pathway is the best and whose wisdom for our happiness and flourishing is beyond question.

---

[16] Shorter Catechism, Q. 65.

The Sixth Commandment:

YOU SHALL NOT MURDER – CRYING OUT FOR THE OUTCAST

Leah Farish, United States

The terse and thunderous sixth commandment can be translated "No murder." It is the first commandment we see broken after Adam and Eve were banished from the Garden: their son Cain slew his brother, Abel, doubtless stunning Adam and Eve when they saw half the birthed population of the world destroyed, eliciting the declaration from God Himself, "The voice of your brother's blood is crying out to me from the ground" (Genesis 4:10).

With the two words "no murder," we are prohibited from all kinds of taking of innocent life – suicide, unjust war, slavery, recklessness, and violence. It would be impossible to address issues such as the death penalty, contraception, human trafficking, or euthanasia in this space; I will focus on the issue of abortion, speaking partly from my experience as an American civil rights and adoption lawyer for about twenty-five years.

Unborn children are the only invisible people in the world. As such, they need extra discernment and care from the rest of us. Their hiddenness has not interfered with efforts to kill them throughout history, and it should not keep Christians from protecting them. Humans don't just "attain" the image of God or "evolve" it; we are "created" in that image (Genesis 1:27), thus bearing value and dignity even in the womb.

The Westminster Larger Catechism asks what duties are required in the sixth commandment and provides a well-considered, traditional Protestant answer in ways that call us toward protection of the unborn:

> The duties required in the sixth commandment are all careful studies, and lawful endeavors, to preserve the life of ourselves and others by resisting all thoughts and purposes, subduing all passions, and avoiding all occasions, temptations, and practices, which tend to the unjust taking away the life of any; by just defense thereof against violence, patient bearing of the hand of God, quietness of mind, cheerfulness of spirit; a sober use of meat, drink, physic, sleep, labor, and recreations; by charitable thoughts, love, compassion, meekness, gentleness, kindness; peaceable, mild and courteous speeches and behavior; forbearance, readiness to be reconciled, patient

bearing and forgiving of injuries, and requiting good for evil; comforting and succoring the distressed and protecting and defending the innocent.[1]

Ample warrant beyond catechisms exists for Christians globally to oppose abortion, primarily due to scriptural teaching, but also due to church tradition and the lives of many prominent Christians, reason, and natural consequences of the practice. First, I will present these foundations upon which evangelicals have based their opposition and then consider ways the church should engage the issue in the future.

I. Our brother's blood cries out to us from Scripture.

While abortion is not treated by name in Scripture, many kinds of passages speak to believers about the sacredness of life in the womb.

Commandment

> Give justice to the weak and the fatherless; maintain the right of the afflicted and the destitute. Rescue the weak and the needy; deliver them from the hand of the wicked (Psalm 82:3-4).

No one could be weaker than an infant in the womb. What is justice for such a child? At least, to give that one a voice; at most, to rescue him or her from risk of extinction and provide help to the pregnant mother who, in her own weakness, may not see a way forward.

Narrative

> And when Elizabeth heard the greeting of Mary, the baby leaped in her womb. And Elizabeth was filled with the Holy Spirit, and she exclaimed with a loud cry, "Blessed are you among women, and blessed is the fruit of your womb! And why is this granted to me that the mother of my Lord should come to me? For behold, when the sound of your greeting came to my ears, the baby in my womb leaped for joy." (Luke 1:41-44).

Here we have four persons: Mary, the mother of Christ, and her cousin Elizabeth, pregnant with John the Baptist. Meditation on this scene reveals not only the human life of the infants but also the spiritual forces coursing between them. We observe that an unborn baby can receive a "blessing,"

---

[1] The Westminster Larger Catechism, https://prts.edu/wp-content/uploads/2013/09/Larger_Catechism.pdf, Q 135.

that he has a "mother" (not just a biological host), and that a pregnant woman can be "filled" with the Holy Spirit – implying that the baby within her would be filled as well, else she would not be truly filled.

We also see that one unborn boy can perceive the presence of another one – though these are obviously exceptional beings, and one cannot conclude too much about ordinary babies (but is there such a baby?) from this monumental story.

Finally, Elizabeth calls Mary's baby her Lord, recognizing not just a spiritual being but a *sovereign* one, even before He is born. Clement of Alexandria (ca. 200), in his *Prophetic Eclogues*, connected many of the dots in this story and "laid the groundwork for subsequent theological links between abortion and the Incarnation."[2]

Prayer

> For you formed my inward parts; you knitted me together in my mother's womb. ... My frame was not hidden from you, when I was being made in secret, intricately woven in the depths of the earth. Your eyes saw my unformed substance; in your book were written, every one of them, the days that were formed for me, when as yet there was none of them (Psalm 139:13, 15-16; see also Jeremiah 1:5 and Psalm 51:5).

Millennia before genetics told us that a fetus is human from conception, this psalm suggests the knitting or weaving process that we identify as the formation of strands of DNA in a new individual. It calls the days and arc of the lifetime that "are not as though they were," as Paul would say (cf. Romans 4:17 [NIV]). It also personalizes the tiniest embryo, referring to it as "I" and making its formation part of the psalmist's biography. The eye of the designer is on the person *ab initio*.

Law

> When men strive together and hit a pregnant woman, so that her children come out, but there is no harm, the one who hit her shall surely be fined, as the woman's husband shall impose on him, and he shall pay as the judges determine. But if there is harm, then you shall pay life for life, eye for eye, tooth for tooth, hand for hand, foot for foot, burn for burn, wound for wound, stripe for stripe (Exodus 21:22-25).

---

[2] Michael J. Gorman, *Abortion and the Early Church* (Eugene, Oregon: Wipf and Stock Publishers, 1982), 52.

This decree has been incorrectly interpreted to mean that an unborn child is treated like property, with the "coming out" of a (presumably dead or maimed) fetus being distinguished from the "harm" that calls for a life for a life. This is a wrongheaded reading for several reasons. First, "come out" does not mean "die." The Hebrew word is used dozens of times in the Old Testament to mean literally "going forth, parting ways"; thus we have a scenario where a woman has a premature *birth*.

If that is all that happens, without other "harm" involved, a mere fine is fair, since premature birth is somewhat undesirable, but things may turn out all right. But if *other harm* happens – either to the mother or to the baby, it is not specified – proportional consequences, including the death penalty, are contemplated. If death of the mother or baby were contemplated, that would be covered by the statutes on murder. Furthermore, the Exodus passage only involves two men fighting, possibly even unaware of a woman's pregnancy, and does not address an intentional abortion procedure, so that the accidental nature of the offense, whatever it is, may make a lesser punishment appropriate.

Of late, a few abortion proponents have cited Numbers 5:27's NIV translation – an unusual rendering.[3] It decrees that a woman suspected of adultery should be made to drink something which, if she has been unfaithful, will make her abdomen "swell and her womb will miscarry." The word for "womb" is usually translated, even in the NIV, as "hip" or "thigh," as in the passage where Jacob wrestles the angel and is touched in his "hip" (Genesis 32:25). Elsewhere the NIV translates it as "shaft," as in the shaft of a candlestick (Exodus 25:31; 37:17; Numbers 8:4). The word for "miscarry" is translated in most other English Bibles as "rot" or "shrivel." The logic of the argument is garbled anyway: the abdomen only swells due to the supernatural manifestation of guilt; a pregnant abdomen is not necessarily involved. An adulterous woman is not automatically pregnant, so the prescribed procedure is oddly matched to the problem if the verse describes an abortion procedure.

Other passages

There are other passages not commonly marshalled for the pro-life cause but which have implications for the topic.

---

[3] Leah Hickman, "Translation Abuse," *World*, April 10, 2021, https://world.wng.org/2021/03/translation_abuse.

A.) Deuteronomy 30:4 (and Nehemiah 1:9): If your outcasts are in the uttermost parts of heaven, from there the LORD your God will gather you, and from there he will take you.

These unusual verses are part of a promise of reward if God's people repent and obey Him. However, the mention of an outcast "in heaven" is mysterious; one might expect it to say "hell" or "the wilderness." What does "heaven" mean here? The Hebrew word is used elsewhere for the place where God is sitting on His throne, where multitudes are worshipping Him (1 Kings 22:19). It is a place of supernatural power (Daniel 4:35). Nehemiah 9:6 uses the word thus: "You have made *heaven*, the *heaven* of *heavens*, with all their host, the earth and all that is on it, the seas ... and the host of *heaven* worships you" (emphasis added). *Certainly, an aborted baby is an outcast, perhaps the ultimate outcast.*

In various ancient civilizations in which Jews dwelled, abortion, infanticide, child sacrifice, and abandonment of unwanted babies were commonplace.[4] Early readers of the Hebrew Scriptures might think of such children as the outcast in Deuteronomy 30:4, possibly having encountered their little bodies along the road or in lonesome areas. It might not be theologically sound to take comfort from this verse when thinking of the eternal destiny of children. Or it might be.

Regardless, we are meant to have mercy on outcasts (Isaiah 16:3; Zephaniah 3:19). In many societies, unwed mothers are outcasts. Shaming and honor killings or banishments of various kinds still occur in some Muslim countries when a woman becomes pregnant outside of societal norms. In Western nations, the woman may be cast out from her relationship with the baby's father or from her family of origin. True accounts, such as *Expecting Adam*[5] and *Subverted*[6], detail the chilly reception pregnant women experience in academia and in "progressive" workplaces. By contrast, kingdom ethics, or "marks of the reign of God," David Gushee's phrase, constitute seven guideposts in decision-making: deliverance, peace, justice,

---

[4] Ezekiel 16:20-21, Henry B. Smith, Jr., "Canaanite Child Sacrifice, Abortion, and the Bible," *Journal of Ministry and Theology* 7, no. 2, Feb. 17, 2003, 90-125, https://bible archaeology.org/images/Child-Sacrifice-and-Abortion/4---Canaanite-Child-Sacri fice---Smith-90-125.pdf, and Paolo Xella, "'Tophet': an Overall Interpretation", in P. Xella (ed.), *The Tophet in the Ancient Mediterranean* (SEL 29-30, 2012-13), Verona 2013, 259-281, https://www.academia.edu/8556951/_Tophet_an_Overall_Inter pretation_in_P_Xella_ed_The_Tophet_in_the_Ancient_Mediterranean_SEL_29_ 30_2012_13_Verona_2013_259_281.

[5] Martha Beck, *Expecting Adam* (New York: Three Rivers Press, 2011).

[6] Sue Ellen Browder, *Subverted* (San Francisco: Ignatius Press, 2015), 51, quoting Betty Friedan, *Life So Far* (New York City: Simon and Shuster, 2006).

healing, inclusion in community, joy, and God's presence.[7] These point *away* from abortion, child abuse, and cruelty to any kind of outcast.

B.) 1 Corinthians 6:19: Or do you not know that your body is a temple of the Holy Spirit within you, whom you have from God? You are not your own ...

Such a temple is not rightly destroyed by another. Furthermore, if even *I* am not my own, certainly my baby, who has a separate body, is not my own to do with as I please.

C.) Leviticus 17:11: For the life of the flesh is in the blood ...

An embryo's own blood cells start developing approximately three weeks after conception; the unborn child can have a different blood type from that of his or her mother. A week or two later, the tiny heart begins to beat. Until genetics made clear that even a fertilized egg is a separate human, perhaps this verse could have been used to justify "abortion" of a fetus without a separate blood supply, because it might not be considered a separate "life." But now it reminds us that even at five weeks' gestation, a separate, innocent life would be taken by removing the tissue.

D.) "What therefore God has joined together, let not man separate" (Matthew 19:6; Mark 10:9).

While Jesus said this in the context of marriage, it is indisputable that a baby in the womb, although a separate human, is joined together with the woman so closely that separating them in an untimely or negligent fashion may kill one or both of them. There were times as I was in court representing a birth mother to relinquish her child that I felt haunted by this warning. God says, "... let not man separate," but He makes an exception for divorce, "Because of your hardness of heart" (Matthew 19:8). Does that suggest there are possible exceptions for "no abortion"? It's a tenuous argument, but perhaps allowances for abortion for incest, rape, or to save the life of the mother can be found in these shadows.

E.) Isaiah 58:7's command is "... when you see the naked, to cover him, and not hide yourself from your own flesh ..."

How does a woman "hide [herself] from [her] own flesh"? Could it involve certain kinds of contraception? Abortion? Abandonment? Do others violate the command when a nurse leaves an infant to die because he or she survived an attempted abortion, when a doctor mails a prescription

---

[7] David P. Gushee and Glen H. Stassen, *Kingdom Ethics,* 2d ed. (Grand Rapids, Michigan: William B. Eerdmans, 2016), 19.

for an abortifacient to a teen in crisis, when a father shrugs off the child he has engendered, when taxpayers pay for the poor in other countries to be taught to abort unwanted babies? When youth ignore the elderly or when parents sell their children into slavery, they are also hiding themselves from their own flesh.

F.) In 2 Samuel 11, Bathsheba conceived a child with David while she was married to Uriah. David immediately acted to conceal the adultery by first attempting to get Uriah back into bed with Bathsheba, but when that did not work, by having Uriah, a valued soldier in David's army, killed. David did not seem to have entertained the notion of covering up his indiscretion by having the telltale pregnancy ended.

G.) Additional passages include God's creating mankind in God's image (Genesis 1:27), Eve's acknowledgement of God's hand in bringing forth children: "I have gotten a man with the help of the LORD" (Genesis 4:1); Job's recognition of the sovereign Creator (Job 10:11-12); the prophet's proclamation of divine work in the womb (Isaiah 44:2); children characterized as gifts from the Lord (Psalm 127:3), the eighth commandment, "You shall not steal," which could be applied to the taking of a life that is not one's own (Exodus 20:15); and the Golden Rule, "So whatever you wish that others would do to you, do also to them, for this is the Law and the Prophets" (Matthew 7:12).

II. Our brothers' and sisters' consciences cry out.

While pre-Christian Judaism had varied views about accidental or therapeutic abortions, they were "united [against] deliberate abortion ... The Jewish abhorrence of deliberate bloodshed and its respect for life, including that of the unborn, formed a natural foundation for the Christian writings on abortion."[8] This was in contrast to the pagan world, which considered factors as varied as the mother's age, "deformity" of the child, preference of a wealthy mother, burden on poor families, the state's or father's desire (or not) for children, overpopulation concerns, and more.[9]

The church was imperfect. Some Christian leaders, then as now, grappled with whether the stage of fetal development or level of homicidal intent of the parents made a difference in culpability.[10] Little in the

---

[8] Gorman, *Abortion and the Early Church*, 45.
[9] Gorman, *Abortion and the Early Church*, 22-32.
[10] Zubin Mistry, "Alienated from the Womb," PhD dissertation (London: University College, 2011), 89. https://discovery.ucl.ac.uk/id/eprint/1317777/1/1317777.pdf.

documents suggests empathy for women who ended their pregnancies. Men and women within the church furtively procured abortions knowing it was contrary to church dogma. But even with "deficiencies" such as these, "the early Christian attitude toward abortion stands as a unique ethical position in the history of the world."[11] Therefore, let us listen to a few voices from church history.

The Didache (ca. 70-100) and *The Epistle of Barnabas* (ca. 70-130) are early Greek Christian treatises that speak of abortion, with prohibition "almost on a par with the Decalogue itself."[12] A bit later, a Syrian source warned, Decalogue-style, "Thou shalt not slay thy child by causing abortion ..."[13]

A church father from ca. 350, Methodius of Olympus, appealed to an uncertain earlier text that portrayed aborted children as saying of those who abort, "'Thou, O Lord, didst not grudgingly deny us the light that is common (to all) but these have exposed us to death, despising thy commandment.'"[14] The Apocalypse of Peter, "held in great esteem by the early church," graphically described the judgment awaiting unrepentant people such as blasphemers, the cold-hearted wealthy, homosexuals, and "those who procured abortions."[15]

Athenagoras, Tertullian, Minucius Felix, Origen, Jerome, Nicholas Cabasilas, Basil of Caesarea, and others opposed abortion in the first 600 years of Christian thought.[16] Chrysostom accused fathers of aborted children at least equally with mothers (whom he called "injured"), saying, "[E]ven if the daring deed be hers, yet the causing of it is thine."[17] In the sixth century, Procopius sneered at Justinian for "lying with" his wife, who "practiced infanticide time and again by voluntary abortions."[18]

---

[11] Gorman, *Abortion and the Early Church*, 94.

[12] Gorman, *Abortion and the Early Church*, 50.

[13] Gorman, *Abortion and the Early Church*, 69, citing *Apostolic Constitutions* 7.3 (circa 380), which goes on to say, "For every thing that is shaped, and hath received a soul from God, if it be slain, shall be avenged ..."

[14] Edgar Hennecke and Wilhelm Schneemelcher, eds., *New Testament Apocrypha*, vol. 2 (Philadelphia: Westminster Press, 1963-65), 675.

[15] Hennecke and Schneemelcher, 675.

[16] Gorman, *Abortion and the Early Church*, 34-75, and John Saward, *Redeemer in the Womb* (San Francisco: Ignatius Press, 1993), 8-13.

[17] John Chrysostom, "Homily 24 on the Epistle to the Romans," trans. J.B. Morris & W.H. Simcox, *NPNF* 11 (1889), 520. https://www.fivesolas.church/chrysostom-on-abortion. And see Mistry, *Alienated from the Womb*, 68-9, 77, 93 as well re: the early church addressing men's role in the issue.

[18] Mistry, *Alienated from the Womb*, 219, quoting *Secret History* X.3 (and cf. IX.19, XVII.16), ed. and trans. H.B. Dewing (Cambridge, Mass.: 1935), 121, 109, 203.

For early believers, "Abortion was never simply apprehended through a sealed moral doctrine, but was also a theological, political, moral and social sign ... [and in the medieval church] condemnation of abortion was integrated into broader attempts to forge Christian communities."[19]

The African Augustine[20] and the Italian Thomas Aquinas[21] wondered whether the fetus might be "ensouled" at some time after conception, but it is hard to imagine them clinging to that theory if they had known about DNA.[22]

In the eighth century and beyond through medieval Europe, pastoral concern was mostly expressed in "penitentials," works focusing on the prescribed length of time for exclusion from the sacraments of a woman who had aborted.[23]

With the pastorate restricted to males for most of church history, one wonders how the teachings would have differed in a feminine voice. Regarding one ninth-century bishop, Hincmar of Rheims: "In his rebuttal of the accusation of abortion, Hincmar made an intriguing point about social epistemology. After he had outlined his main arguments from scripture, he stressed that 'we do not want to reveal to those acquainted with or suggest to those unacquainted with the virginal secrets of girls and women, which we do not know by experience.'"[24]

Caesarius of Arles preached in the sixth-century Gallic church that "Women who could not rear their children were to hand them over to others for rearing rather than abort them ... [but] we can only guess at the social structures, if any, which would have made his injunction to offer up children for adoption a seriously proffered alternative to abortion."[25] Monasteries and

---

[19] Gorman, *Abortion and the Early Church*, 53-4. Mistry, *Alienated from the Womb*, 236-7, points out that early medieval views on abortion inextricably connected murder with illicit sex.
[20] Augustine of Hippo, *Questions on Exodus by Augustine of Hippo*, Ch. 21, Question 80, Patristic Bible Commentary, https://sites.google.com/site/aquinasstudybible/home/exodus/questions-on-exodus-by-augustine-of-hippo.
[21] David Albert Jones, *The Soul of the Embryo* (London: Continuum, 2004), 124, 140.
[22] We are so influenced by modern technology and medicine. We must beware of superimposing modern understanding of genetic identity and, as Mistry says, of "modern distinctions between abortion and contraception" on ancient peoples (*Alienated from the Womb*, 236-7).
[23] Gorman, *Abortion and the Early Church*, 66, and Mistry, *Alienated from the Womb*, 103, 129.
[24] Mistry, *Alienated from the Womb*, 230.
[25] Mistry, 67-8. Caesarius said, "Presuming upon your kindness, I give this advice to all your daughters, in accord with my fatherly solicitude: that no woman take medicine for purposes of abortion, or kill her children after they are conceived or born. ... let her nurse them or give them to others for support." The familial language may

convents raised some children, and the Christian community was known from the beginning to be kind to orphans, but we lack records of consistent placement of unwanted children in any planned setting.[26]

Ninth-century Abbot Regino was aware of the attempt to conceal "concupiscence" "through a single deadly potion": "[S]o that the crime is not twinned, that is of adultery and homicide, we advise that each priest publicly announces to his people that, if any woman, corrupted in secret, should conceive and give birth, she should by no means kill her son or daughter at the devil's prompting, but, by whichever means prevails, she should have the child carried before the doors of the church and left there, so that on the next day the child can be brought before the priest to be raised and nourished by one of the faithful; and thereby she will avoid being guilty of homicide ..."[27]

John Calvin continued the tradition of condemning abortion, saying, "The fetus, though enclosed in the womb of its mother, is already a human being and it is a most monstrous crime to rob it of the life which it has not yet begun to enjoy. If it seems more horrible to kill a man in his own house than in a field, because a man's house is his place of most secure refuge, it ought surely to be deemed more atrocious to destroy a fetus in the womb before it has come to light."[28]

Martin Luther found much to protest in papal doctrine, but apparently he took no issue with it regarding abortion. Trained as an Augustinian monk, he would have studied Peter Lombard's sermon series called The Book of Sentences, which denounced abortion.[29]

---

contemplate extended family as the likely support. (Saint Caesarius of Arles, *Sermons*, Volume 1, Sermon 19.5 [Washington, D.C., Catholic University of America Press, 2010] 102. See also his Sermon 51.4) https://books.google.com/books?id=0pWzRdNohzgC&pg=PA98&source=gbs_toc_r&cad=3#v=onepage&q&f=false.

[26] Mistry, 68.

[27] Mistry, *Alienated from the Womb*, 238, footnote 10, which cites Regino of Prüm. *De synodalibus causis*. II.68, Ed. and trans. W. Hartmann. *Das Sendhandbuch des Regino von Prüm* (Darmstadt: Wissenschaftliche Buchgesellschaft, 2004), 284. "Regino of Prüm's early tenth-century episcopal handbook has often been conceived of as a conduit of Christian moral tradition to the real business of high medieval canonical and scholastic thought on abortion." Mistry, 233.

[28] John Calvin, *Commentary on the Pentateuch*, cited in Randy Alcorn, *Abortion*, Part 11, LifeFacts, LifeSiteNews.com, https://www.lifesitenews.com/resources/abortion/pro-life-101-the-ultimate-guide-to-why-abortion-is-wrong-and-how-to-fight-for-life/part-11-but-the-bible-doesnt-say-anything-about-abortion#_ednref12.

[29] *Encyclopedia.com*, Abortion: III. Religious Traditions: C. Protestant Perspectives, https://www.encyclopedia.com/science/encyclopedias-almanacs-transcripts-and-maps/abortion-iii-religious-traditions-c-protestant-perspectives.

In Europe and colonial America, whippings and executions followed evidence that the accused, male or female, had undergone or forced an abortion or infanticide - done most commonly to cover an illicit encounter such as impregnating a servant or relative and more often punished if there had been "quickening" of the fetus.[30] Thereafter, until Roe v. Wade, which legalized abortion in the U.S. in 1973, abortion was a criminal offense in most places in the West.

The American Temperance and Suffragist movement, one of the first female-led social movements, occasionally addressed abortion. Elizabeth Cady Stanton wrote that "[I]t is degrading to women that we should treat our children as property to be disposed of as we see fit."[31] In 1875 Susan B. Anthony called "abortion and infanticides ... scandals and outrages."[32] Even American feminist activist Betty Friedan said in 2000, "Ideologically, I was never for abortion. Motherhood is a value to me, and even today abortion is not."[33] Sue Ellen Browder documents how a radical element of feminism hijacked the National Organization for Women at a pivotal meeting in 1967, overcoming objections to abortion from many of the participants.[34]

Meanwhile, late nineteenth- and twentieth-century Christian leaders as varied as Dwight Moody, Karl Barth, Dietrich Bonhoeffer, Mother Teresa, Billy Graham, Beth Moore, Francis Schaeffer, Jim Wallis, and Kay Arthur opposed abortion before and after its legalization in many countries.

How much should legalization figure in an in-house theological discussion? As a professor, I recall my occasional challenge to Christian college students: "You think legalization doesn't affect your moral compass – How many of you are bothered by Sabbath-breaking?" *Of course,* legalization shapes Christians' consciences (although it shouldn't). Otherwise, there wouldn't be so much diabolical enthusiasm for legalizing anything that violates God's laws.

---

[30] Marvin Olasky, "Did Colonial America Have Abortions? Yes, but ..." *World*, January 17, 2015, https://world.wng.org/2015/01/did_colonial_america_have_abortions_yes_but. See also Cornelia Hughes Dayton, "Taking the Trade," *William and Mary Quarterly* 48, no. 1 (Jan. 1991): 19-49, (19).

[31] Marjorie Dannenfelser, "The Suffragettes Would Not Agree with Feminists Today on Abortion," *Time*, November 4, 2015, https://time.com/4093214/suffragettes-abortion/.

[32] Ken Burns and Paul Barnes, "Social Purity," *Not for Ourselves Alone: The Story of Elizabeth Cady Stanton and Anthony B. Anthony,* 2021, https://www.pbs.org/kenburns/not-for-ourselves-alone/social-purity/. And See Aileen S. Kraditor, *Up from the Pedestal*, (New York City: HarperCollins, 1968), 159.

[33] Sue Ellen Browder, *Subverted* (San Francisco: Ignatius Press, 2015), 51, quoting Betty Friedan, *Life So Far* (New York City: Simon and Schuster, 2006), 200.

[34] Sue Ellen Browder, *Subverted*, 65-70.

On the other hand, legalization frees people to discuss topics candidly; it puts advocacy on the level ground of persuasion on the merits of the activity, not merely on the side of "law and order." It was only after the U.S. Supreme Court ruled in *Roe v. Wade* that American evangelicals found their voice on abortion. And now that most nations allow various abortion rights, we can examine the effects of abortion on abortive women and the broader society.

The church is not unanimous on the issue, but most evangelicals are pro-life.[35] Ninety-four percent of Americans who say they are at least fairly certain that God exists also believe that abortion should be illegal in all or most cases.[36] For 91% of those who say religion is very or somewhat important in their lives, abortion should be illegal in all or most cases.[37] Among people who believe in outlawing abortion in all or most cases, 53% attend religious services at least once per week; of those who believe it should be legal in all or most cases, 22% attend at least once per week.[38]

Today, nearly 50 years since *Roe*, evangelicals can and should vigorously debate the assumptions and the consequences of abortion laws guided by their heritage of biblical wisdom, making themselves available for open discussion and offering practical compassion toward those who have aborted or who feel that they need it.

We will inevitably be confronted with hard cases, provoking us to make exceptions to the "no murder" rule: What should happen when the pregnancy resulted from rape or incest or when it threatens the life of the mother? Can one be pro-life and support the death penalty? Compassion and humility demand that I take much more space than is possible to discuss these matters, so I will refer the curious reader to other sources and merely note that, as Presbyterians Protecting Life says, "... [J]ustice

---

[35] Pew Research Center, "Views about abortion by religious group," *Religious Landscape Study*, https://www.pewforum.org/religious-landscape-study/views-about-abortion/.

[36] Pew Research Center, "Belief in God by views about abortion," *Religious Landscape Study*, https://www.pewforum.org/religious-landscape-study/views-about-abortion/.

[37] Pew Research Center, "Importance of religion in one's life by views about abortion," *Religious Landscape Study*, https://www.pewforum.org/religious-landscape-study/views-about-abortion/.

[38] Pew Research Center, "Attendance at religious services by views about abortion," *Religious Landscape Study*, https://www.pewforum.org/religious-landscape-study/views-about-abortion/.

understands that the baby is innocent."[39] A recent study from the United Kingdom found that between 1968 and 2011, only 0.006% of abortions were performed to save the life of the mother.[40]

III. We must cry out to touch the consciences of others.

We can touch consciences both by our arguments and by our actions.

A. Arguments

Legally, *Roe v. Wade* and other early abortion legalization have not worn well, and the twenty-first century calls for a reset for several reasons.

1. Twentieth-century laws rested on assumptions about viability and acceptance, but medical advances have been made that are increasingly making those laws obsolete. Assumptions about other factors, such as genetics, and about the danger of global population growth that operated in the 1970s are also outdated. U.S.-influenced policies oriented to population control and concealment of rape in countries like India, Indonesia, and post-WWII Japan and the Philippines are being overturned by those nations.[41]
2. Workplaces and schools are much more open to pregnant women now, leave for maternity and paternity is mandated in most nations, and discrimination against pregnant women is legally forbidden in most places. Social stigma against single motherhood in most Western nations is almost nonexistent.
3. Unintended consequences of legalized abortion include disproportionate killing of babies:
    - of color (in 2018, non-Hispanic whites, though about 61% of the population in the U.S., aborted 57,000; blacks, 40,000, though about 12% of population; Hispanics, about 34,000, though about

---

[39] Mark Atkinson, "Hard cases: Rape and Incest," https://www.ppl.org/tough-questions-rape-and-incest. He observes that in such cases, "The loathing she feels for those who violated her is turned against herself. ... Abortion is a second trauma."
[40] Martha E. Leatherman, "What about the Life of the Mother?" https://www.ppl.org/what-about-the-life-of-the-mother. And hear Dr. Byron Calhoun, "Abortion Is Never Medically Necessary," *Explicitly Pro-Life* (podcast) Ep. 95, https://player.fm/series/explicitly-pro-life/abortion-is-never-medically-necessary-dr-byron-calhoun-obgyn-episode-95.
[41] Jason Morgan, "Tokyo Pro-Life March," Asia Times, July 26, 2018. https://asiatimes.com/2018/07/tokyo-pro-life-march-and-asias-dark-history-of-eugenics/.

17% of the population).[42] (In twentieth-century America, "... [A]bortions found legislative support partly because supporters used eugenic rhetoric and arguments for population control to promote them."[43])

- who are female ("Gender-selective abortion has become a worldwide reality. For example, there are about 91.8 girls born in India for every 100 males.")[44] In China, abortion of girl babies has resulted in an excess of 30 million bachelors.[45]
- born to poor families ("Childbearing by low-income women is stigmatized in the media and in policy arenas."[46])

---

[42] In 2018, nonHispanic whites in U.S. 57,000 though about 61% of the population; blacks 40,000 though about 12% of population, Hispanics about 34,000 though about 17%, (at 6 weeks or less of gestation; for other stages, see "Table 13, Reported abortions" in Kortsmit K, Jatlaoui TC, Mandel MG, et al. Abortion Surveillance – United States, 2018. (MMWR Surveill Summ 2020; 69, No. SS-7):1–29. DOI: http://dx.doi.org/10.15585/mmwr.ss6907a1external icon.

[43] Johanna Schoen, *Choice and Coercion: Birth Control, Sterilization, and Abortion in Public Health and Welfare* (Chapel Hill: University of North Carolina Press, 2005), 3. And see "Cancel Culture Comes for Planned Parenthood," (no author) https://www.humancoalition.org/2020/08/05/cancel-culture-comes-for-planned-parenthood/ about the founder of Planned Parenthood and her attitudes toward blacks and "defectives." And hear Ryan Bomberger, "The Abortion Movement's History of Racism," Explicitly Pro-Life (podcast), Ep. 71, https://podcasts.apple.com/us/podcast/abortion-movements-history-racism-ryan-bomberger-episode/id1460746245?i=1000490082030.

[44] Tara C. Jatlaoui, Maegan Boutot, Michele Mandel, et al. "Abortion Surveillance – United States, 2015,"*Morbidity and Mortality Weekly Report (MMWR) Surveillance Summaries*, 67, no. SS-13 (2018):1–45. DOI: http://dx.doi.org/10.15585/mmwr.ss6713a1. And see Fengqing Chao, Patrick Gerland, Alex Cook, and Leontine Alkema, "Systematic assessment of the sex ratio at birth for all countries and estimation of national imbalances and regional reference levels," *Proceedings of the National Academy of Sciences of the United States of America*, https://www.pnas.org/content/116/19/9303, and Alliance Defending Freedom International, "Vanishing Girls," https://adfinternational.org/campaign/vanishinggirls/.

[45] "How China's one-child policy led to forced abortions," *Fresh Air*, National Public Radio, Feb. 1, 2016, https://www.npr.org/2016/02/01/465124337/how-chinas-one-child-policy-led-to-forced-abortions-30-million-bachelors.

[46] Roberta A. Downing, Thomas A. LaVeist, and Heather E. Bullock, "Intersections of Ethnicity and Social Class in Provider Advice Regarding Reproductive Health," *American Journal of Public Health* 97, no. 10 (2007):1803–1807. Doi: https://doi.org/10.2105/AJPH.2006.092585.

- babies with abnormalities – technology has increased screening for fetal disorders, "with abortion as the implicit option."[47]
4. Further, women in the West have been freed from "shame" about aborting, so fathers are allowed to pressure them to do so. "[A]bortion often is the coercive method men use to free themselves for responsibility to women."[48] Only when it is legal can men (and media celebrities, politicians, and nonprofits) openly pressure their girlfriends, daughters, and even wives to abort.
5. Conversely, as women have been given the sole decision about aborting, willing fathers have been rendered legally impotent to save their children's lives. Along with grandparents and siblings, men are shut out, tearing the fabric of the family.
6. Abortion often leaves women with lasting damage. *Gonzales v. Carhart* recognizes the pain women may feel after aborting.[49] Correlations with breast cancer, anxiety, depression, and eating disorders have been identified.[50]
7. Developed nations where abortion is legal are falling below replacement level (2.1 children per woman) in population. France, with the highest birth rate in Europe, only has a rate of 1.9; Italy is at 1.3; Norway is 1.6; South Korea is 1.0; by contrast, in countries where abortion is restricted (and stigmatized), such as Afghanistan and Somalia, the rates are 3.5 and 6.1, respectively. Abortion is by no means the single culprit, but it contributes to the problem.[51] In 2016, China abandoned its "one-child policy" to avoid colliding with

---

[47] Troy Duster, *Backdoor to Eugenics*. 2nd ed. (New York, NY: Routledge; 2003), 89 And regarding women over 40, see Tara C. Jatlaoui, Maegan Boutot, Michele Mandel, et al. *Abortion Surveillance - United States* (2015) https://pubmed.ncbi.nlm.nih.gov/30462632/.

[48] Stanley Hauerwas, *A Community of Character*, (Notre Dame, IN: University of Notre Dame Press, 1981), 201.

[49] 550 U.S. 124 (2007): "Whether to have an abortion requires a difficult and painful moral decision. ... While we find no reliable data to measure the phenomenon, it seems unexceptionable to conclude some women come to regret their choice to abort the infant life they once created and sustained. ... Severe depression and loss of esteem can follow" (citations omitted).

[50] Save the Storks, "Abortion's Effect on Physical and Mental Health," American Association of Christian Counselors, September 8, 2020, https://www.aacc.net/2020/09/08/abortions-effects-on-physical-and-mental-health/. And see https://www.silentnomoreawareness.org/index.aspx.

[51] "Total Fertility Rate 2021," *World Population Review*, https://worldpopulationreview.com/country-rankings/total-fertility-rate.

a lack of workers for its elderly and to end forced abortions for urban couples banned from having too many children.⁵²

8. Life becomes cheap where babies are not protected. Christian ethicists are not surprised when right-to-die legislation succeeds permissive abortion laws and when child abuse actually increases after abortion legalization. The promise of legalizers worldwide has been that child abuse and spousal abuse would decrease with abortion access. Now that we have had a few decades to observe outcomes, it is demonstrable that this has not happened.

B. Actions

We cannot look to laws to guide our actions. We must be guided by Scripture, by the Holy Spirit, and by our best traditions, such as the Westminster Larger Catechism,⁵³ referenced at the outset of this article. I will highlight some phrases from it for application.

Q. 135. What are the duties required in the sixth commandment?

A. ... avoiding all occasions, temptations, and practices, which tend to the unjust taking away the life of any.*

* At a minimum, those of us who have the means must ensure that worldwide, no woman aborts because she fears she will not have the means to support a child. As Sam Logan, Associate International Director of World Reformed Fellowship, has said, "Every child experiencing food insecurity ... is being imperiled by violations of [the sixth] commandment."⁵⁴ The safety nets for women in crisis are thicker and wider than ever in history, and they are growing. Governments and NGOs, including the resources of churches, provide most of these nets. This is something to celebrate.

... by charitable thoughts, love, compassion, meekness, gentleness, kindness;** peaceable, mild and courteous speech ... patient bearing and forgiving of injuries ...

** Gentle and kind *engagement* must be the hallmark of evangelicals' conduct toward women (and men) who are facing an abortion decision and toward those regretting such a decision. We first must be *relevant* by

---

[52] "How China's one-child policy led to forced abortions," *Fresh Air*, NPR, Feb. 1, 2016.
[53] Puritan Reformed Theological Seminary, The Westminster Larger Catechism, 1648. https://prts.edu/wp-content/uploads/2013/09/Larger_Catechism.pdf.
[54] Samuel Logan, "Being COMPREHENSIVELY 'Pro-Life,'" *Sloganwrf's Blog*, Dec. 10, 2020, https://scottishsamlogan.com/2020/12/10/being-comprehensively-pro-life/.

making the church a safe place to talk about the issues involved. A woman considering abortion, who is in community with Christians, should know that they will minister to her – and to any child – regardless of her decision, and commitment by the community to minister will make the gravity of the decision clear to all parties.

According to a 2015 survey, of 1,038 American women who had terminated a pregnancy, Christians were the most likely to agree with the statement "Churches are a safe place to talk about pregnancy options."[55] Sadly, however, of self-identified evangelicals among them, 51% said the church had no influence on their decision.[56] Of all respondents, 36% were attending a Christian church one or more times weekly at the time of their first abortion and 11% at the time of their second abortion.[57] Yet 51% said churches are prepared to provide support to women who choose to keep a child. This is a fairly encouraging statistic, given that churches must be very discreet about helping individuals in these situations and cannot trumpet their "achievements" in dissuading people from abortion or giving help to the needy.[58]

Respondents of all types said that the most influential on their abortion decision had been the baby's father (38%), another family member (19%), a medical professional (26%), and a sermon at a local church (1%).[59] Care Net's Making Life Disciples is a curriculum for churches, guiding them in giving gentle and kind guidance.[60] Podcasts reach many women who wouldn't listen to sermons.[61]

… comforting and succoring the distressed and protecting and defending the innocent.***

*** Most abortions caused by pressure from men or family members, which (abortions) are among the most unjust, are apparently not procured as a last resort from poverty but from shame or fear that a birth will spell lost opportunity or reputation for the woman. Furthermore, as an

---

[55] LifeWay Research, "Study of women who have had an abortion and their views on church," CareNet, Slide 80. https://6992fcbe-7b09-4360-9322-392d758e07b8.filesusr.com/ugd/76dd10_7f4c164496eb47278386b95679fd27e1.pdf.
[56] LifeWay Research, Slide 69.
[57] LifeWay Research, Slide 9.
[58] LifeWay Research, Slide 26.
[59] LifeWay Research, Slide 15.
[60] https://www.care-net.org/why-making-life-disciples. And see resources at Life Matters Worldwide, https://www.lifemattersww.org/CHURCHES/Resources.
[61] Help, Hope, and Healing, "8 Pro-Life Podcasts," https://helphopeandhealing.org/2019/10/18/8-pro-life-podcasts-to-add-to-your-playlist/.

attorney, I spent years handling American birth-mother relinquishments, and poverty was never the mother's stated reason for placing a child for adoption (which is, admittedly, not the same as abortion). In such a hearing, it is mandatory to ask the mother if she is aware of services and resources that will be available should she decide to keep the child; often the judge will personally inquire, even after the attorney has established that the woman knows this. The most common reason is that this is not "the right time in my life to have a baby" – due, e.g., to school or work aspirations, to not having a good living/family situation for the child, to the emotional state of the mother.

Worldwide, factors inducing women to abort include unmarried status of the mother, adultery, ambiguous paternity, mother's poor health, lactation of the mother, consent of the father, death of the father, rape, incest, and other varieties of illegal union.[62] The church must find ways to support women who have been involved with "illegal unions" but without compromising biblical standards for sex and marriage. I have found it is helpful to speak in terms of a "third way" that neither inflicts Bronze-Age punishments nor abandons reverence for marriage. Most people of good will are ready to walk this balanced "narrow way."

"Protecting and defending the innocent" relates to all infants, particularly to those with medical problems. Technology has made it possible to identify certain health issues, such as Down syndrome, in the womb,[63] occasioning more abortions.[64] But advances have also enabled us to treat children's problems before delivery, made it safer to carry babies to term, and reduced chances of the dilemma of abortion vs. a mother's safety. And approximately 78% of *undecided* women who view their baby *in utero* on ultrasound choose not to abort.[65] While some

---

[62] R.N. Shain, "A cross-cultural history of abortion," *Clinical Obstetrics and Gynaecology* 13, no. 1 (1986): 1-17. https://pubmed.ncbi.nlm.nih.gov/3519038/.

[63] Claire Chretien, "Iceland kills 100% of babies with Down syndrome," *LifeSiteNews*, August 15, 2017, https://www.lifesitenews.com/news/new-report-iceland-aborts-100-of-babies-with-down-syndrome.

[64] Julian Quinones, Arijeta Lajka, "What kind of society do you want to live in?" *CBS News*, August 14, 2017, 4:00 p.m.

[65] Adam Cohen, "The Next Abortion Battleground: Fetal Heartbeats," *Time Ideas*, October 17, 2011, https://ideas.time.com/2011/10/17/the-next-abortion-battleground-fetal-heartbeats/, and Mary Gatter, Katrina Kimport, Diana Greene Foster, Tracy A. Weitz, Ushma D. Upadhyay, "Relationship between ultrasound viewing and proceeding to abortion," *Obstetrics and Gynecology*, 123, no. 1, (2014):81-87 https://pubmed.ncbi.nlm.nih.gov/24463667/. On the other hand, it appears that most aborting women who know their baby is a human life still choose it. CareCast, "New PBS Documentary Reveals Why Women Are Having Abortions,"

questionable research is being done on "womb transplants," might it be possible someday to remove an unwanted fetus and "transplant" it in another womb?[66]

Q. 136. What are the sins forbidden in the sixth commandment?

A. ... all excessive passions, distracting cares ... and ... immoderate use of meat, drink, labor, ["physic," or drugs/medicine in Q/A 135] ... and recreations.****

**** In my legal experience, most *relinquishing* women had not only not intended a pregnancy but had never intended to pursue a lifetime with the man who engendered the child. The women usually expressed a low opinion of the father, and many of them did not know, could not remember, or were not sure with whom, of multiple men, they had conceived the child. Some saw relinquishment as a way to end any connection with the father. Often the mother or the father was abusing a substance when conception occurred. It is not judgmental to be realistic about "distracting cares" and "recreations" that lead to unwanted pregnancies. The evangelical church needs to teach a more compelling theology of the body that includes sexual purity and, urgently, clear teaching about drug abuse, which is exploding in the U.S. and is virtually never mentioned in church. The isolation and immediate gratification provided by media must be fought at home and at church.

Of course, distracting cares and temptations include the hardships of living in poverty. In nations with few safety nets, the church must battle hunger, provide medical care, and help exhausted women with children they were pressured to bear.[67]

... all taking away the life of ourselves, or of others, except in case of public justice, lawful war, or necessary defense; the neglecting or withdrawing the lawful and necessary means of preservation of life; sinful anger, hatred, envy, desire of revenge ... provoking words, oppression *****,

---

    https://soundcloud.com/carecast/carecast-new-pbs-documentary-reveals-why-women-are-having-abortions.

[66] Paige Comstock Cunningham, "Womb Transplant Babies: A Preliminary Exploration of Recent Biomedical Advances," *Center for Bioethics and Human Dignity*, December 31, 2014, https://cbhd.org/content/womb-transplant-babies.

[67] WorldVision, Operation Blessing, Compassion International, and other organizations at http://chosenforlifeministries.org/orphan-care-resources show mercy in a variety of nations. (Orphans are mentioned, because in some countries, abandoned children are formally or informally designated as "orphans.")

quarreling, striking, wounding, and whatsoever else tends to the destruction of the life of any.

*****In many places, women have become more violent and abusive since abortion was legalized.[68] Women are oppressed in some situations, and they are oppressors in some situations; sometimes they are both.

C. Strategies in light of current opposition

The effort to promote abortion worldwide is becoming sophisticated, well-funded, crucially connected to technological advances, and punitive to opponents. One should keep some developments in mind.

Secularists tend to operate on the "wholesale" level, seeking massive grants to provide abortions, bullying small nations to accept abortion to receive other benefits, and churning out school curricula and counselors who will steer youngsters toward abortion. Christians tend to operate on the "retail" level, rejoicing over one heart changed, over one baby born and placed for adoption after months of nurturing a woman who was "abortion-minded." This is legitimate celebration, but meanwhile thousands are being lost. We need to think on a larger scale without losing compassion for the individual. We rightly regard one "I-regret-my-abortion" story as a trophy,[69] but even here, others are beginning to counter with stories boasting about their abortions.

Working on a bigger scale means engagement at the United Nations level, lending support to courageous nations resisting the blandishments of abortion proponents. Excellent, lonely work is being done by C-Fam on this.[70] American Christians who have been voting for candidates regardless of their stance on abortion because they think that candidate cannot do much, that it is all up to the Supreme Court, are mistaken. Elected officials decide funding and our stance vis-à-vis other nations. If, with *Dobbs v. Jackson Women's Health Organization* likely to be ruled on in early summer 2022, the United State Supreme Court gives abortion interdiction to the states, that will simply split pro-life efforts over dozens of battlegrounds.

---

[68] Zur Institute, *Female Batterers, Male Victims*, https://www.zurinstitute.com/clinical-updates/female-batterers/, CPT Sheila R. Adams, MSW; LTC Dexter R. Freeman, DSW, "Women Who Are Violent," *Military Medicine* 167, no. 6, (2002):445. https://academic.oup.com/milmed/article-pdf/167/6/445/24217129/milmed-167-6-445.pdf.

[69] Savethestorks.com and silentnomoreawareness.org furnish these. See also https://www.rachelsvineyard.org and https://www.lifeperspectives.com.

[70] Center for Family and Human Rights, https://c-fam.org.

Silencing of pro-life advocacy has become vicious, with tech-censorship of voices such as lifesitenews.com, physical attacks on prolife protesters with impunity – some of which I have personally observed – and lawsuits against clinic protesters, crisis pregnancy centers, and journalists.[71] Project Veritas and Judicial Watch, bravely investigating trafficking-type activity in body parts of fetuses, have been assailed with obstruction and retaliation. Evangelical law firms such as Alliance Defending Freedom and American Center for Law and Justice (ACLJ) need funding to continue fighting court battles in many countries.

Abortion is increasingly easier to access due to telemedicine and "abortion by mail," whereby patients receive abortifacients without visiting a clinic.[72] This makes abortion decisions more private than before. Online presence of the prolife position is thus more needed than ever. Good work is being done at heartbeatinternational.org, which furnishes an interactive directory to locate pregnancy help centers for any geographic location provided.[73] Other groups (some highlighting the use of aborted fetal tissue in medicines) who make valuable contributions worldwide include Doctors for Life International https://www.doctorsforlife.co.za/; Center for Bioethics and Human Dignity https://cbhd.org/category/issues/reproductive-ethics; Cornwall Alliance https://cornwallalliance.org/a-call-to-protect-the-unborn-and-the-pro-life-movement/; Christian Medical / Dental Associations https://cmda.org/standards-4-life/; Lifeinternational.com; and Population Research Institute https://www.pop.org/.

Evangelical Protestants need allies, and they will find them among, e.g., Catholics and Orthodox (hli.org, priestsforlife.org, thomasmore.org, oclife.org, orthodoxprolife.org);[74] Muslims (www.prolifemuslims.com); and feminists of various faiths or none (feministsforlife.org). The Institute on Religion and Democracy can help with navigating mainline denominational strategies (https://theird.org). Co-belligerents give us an opportunity to build relationships with people of good will but with differing vocabularies and methods.

---

[71] "Life Legal Cases to Watch," https://lifelegaldefensefoundation.org/life-legal-cases-to-watch/.
[72] The number of medical abortions is approaching that of surgical abortions in the U.S. Katherine Kortsmit, Tara c. Jatlaoui, Michele G. Mandel, et al. "Abortion Surveillance – United States, 2018," *Morbidity and Mortality Weekly Report (MMWR) Surveillance Summaries* 69, no. SS-7 (2020): 1-29. http://dx.doi.org/10.15585/mmwr.ss6907a1external icon.
[73] Heartbeatinternational.org. See also ppl.org, optionline.org, and lifeonbelay.org.
[74] For a fuller list, see "Pro-Life organizations," https://www.ewtn.com/catholicism/library/prolife-organizations-9557.

New strategies, such as media aimed at young audiences;[75] SafeHaven Baby Boxes, allowing women to anonymously leave unwanted infants;[76] and Reprotection, which holds abortionists to statutory medical standards, are interesting efforts. Holistic, community approaches are emerging through groups such as Sister India and Life on Belay.

If the U.S. Supreme Court overturns *Roe v. Wade*, the likely result will be to give the issue to the fifty states, diffusing funding and energy, and reminding the world that abortion is ultimately a matter of conscience and culture. Romans 13 teaches that government "bears the sword" to punish evil, but the verse just before this chapter division is Romans 12:21: "Do not be overcome by evil, but overcome evil with good." Regardless of the law, the job for evangelicals is not to punish with the sword, but to overcome with good.

IV. Conclusion

In 2 Samuel 14:14, we read, "We must all die; we are like water spilled on the ground, which cannot be gathered up again. But God will not take away life, and he devises means so that the banished one will not remain an outcast." Evangelicals have the joy and mandate to work with God as He sovereignly "devises means" to help the outcast.

---

[75] Students for Life, "Top 10 Pro-Life Podcasts," https://studentsforlife.org/2020/03/17/top-10-pro-life-podcasts-to-check-out/. Most pro-life podcasts are less than two years old. See also https://twitter.com/ProLifeAction , https://twitter.com/prolifecampaign, PragerU, "Do College Students Support Abortion or Life?" https://www.youtube.com/watch?v=kYFjD1VjHnc. Some are even using humor – https://twitter.com/prolifememetics, Babylon Bee, "Update: 3,000 New Deaths Today but Enough about Abortion," April 2, 2020, https://babylonbee.com/news/breaking-3000-new-deaths-today-but-thats-enough-about-abortion.

[76] Shbb.org. Justice Amy Coney Barrett's mention of safe haven laws (as a possibly significant protection from prosecution for women who leave their unwanted babies with other adults) was an interesting feature of oral arguments on American abortion in *Dobbs v. Jackson Women's Health Organization*, Dec. 1, 2021, https://www.oyez.org/cases/2021/19-1392.

God Hates Murder More Than You Hate Murder

Thomas K. Johnson, United States and Czech Republic

> This is a revised version of a sermon preached at the International Church of Prague, Czech Republic, on September 23, 2018. Dr. Johnson preached a sermon with a similar title and outline on November 10, 1991, at Hope Evangelical Church (PCA), in Iowa City, Iowa, USA.
>
> **Deuteronomy 5:17:** *You shall not murder*
>
> **Genesis 4:1-10:** *Now Adam knew Eve his wife, and she conceived and bore Cain, saying, "I have gotten a man with the help of the Lord." And again, she bore his brother Abel. Now Abel was a keeper of sheep, and Cain a worker of the ground. In the course of time Cain brought to the Lord an offering of the fruit of the ground, and Abel also brought of the firstborn of his flock and of their fat portions. And the Lord had regard for Abel and his offering, but for Cain and his offering he had no regard. So Cain was very angry, and his face fell. The Lord said to Cain, "Why are you angry, and why has your face fallen? If you do well, will you not be accepted? And if you do not do well, sin is crouching at the door. Its desire is contrary to you, but you must rule over it."*

Cain spoke to Abel his brother. And when they were in the field, Cain rose up against his brother Abel and killed him. Then the Lord said to Cain, "Where is Abel your brother?" He said, "I do not know; am I my brother's keeper?" And the Lord said, "What have you done? The voice of your brother's blood is crying to me from the ground."

> **Luke 10:30-35:** *Jesus replied, "A man was going down from Jerusalem to Jericho, and he fell among robbers, who stripped him and beat him and departed, leaving him half dead. Now by chance a priest was going down that road, and when he saw him he passed by on the other side. So likewise a Levite, when he came to the place and saw him, passed by on the other side. But a Samaritan, as he journeyed, came to where he was, and when he saw him, he had compassion. He went to him and bound up his wounds, pouring on oil and wine. Then he set him on his own animal and brought him to an inn and took care of him. And the next day he took out two denarii and gave them to the innkeeper, saying, 'Take care of him, and whatever more you spend, I will repay you when I come back.'"*

One of the first mass murders on an American university occurred 1 km. (1100 yards) from our church, about a week before I was scheduled to preach a sermon on the commandment, "You shall not murder." On Friday afternoon, November 1, 1991, Gang Lu attended a meeting of the plasma physics research group at the University of Iowa, where he was finishing a Ph.D. He pulled out a .38 revolver, an old-fashioned pistol, and began shooting people in the head. This was so unexpected that other people in the room first thought it was a Halloween joke. Nothing like this had happened before. Five of the people he shot died, and one was reduced to a wheel chair. He then went to his room and killed himself with his own gun.

Shock spread across our small university town. It was normally a peaceful and tolerant place. Some saw our town as an outpost of civilization and enlightenment in the midst of countless miles of Iowa corn fields. How could this happen?!! In a few days the shock turned into outrage, really burning anger.

In the following week I studied this commandment and listened to the reactions of people in the community. Then I decided in my sermon to emphasize the theme, "God hates murder more than you hate murder." I still have vivid memories of the intense feelings expressed in our church and across the city.

Today most of us do not live in a small town where murder is rare. We live in a global village where murder is the order of the day. When I read the news or watch it on TV, one of the questions in my mind is "Who today is claiming to do something great by murdering ordinary people?" As citizens of the global village, what should *we* say about this commandment?

There is something we must note by way of definition. The commandment refers to one individual killing another individual. It is not referring to matters such as capital punishment or participation in a just war. Occasionally believers read this commandment and think it rules out being a police officer or serving in the military because those roles might require them to use deadly force. But the same Old Testament books that give us this commandment also prescribe capital punishment in certain very rare situations, and it gave rules for enforcing the law and fighting a war without losing our humanity. The biblical respect for human life should lead us to see any taking of human life as tragic – but perhaps as necessary in carefully defined and hopefully rare circumstances.

As we look carefully at this commandment, I would like to point out *two assumptions* and then *two implications* of the commandment.

The first assumption in this commandment is that we have a murderous potential deep within ourselves. To put it differently there is a bit of Cain in all of us. The possibility of committing murder, or of having murderous thoughts, is not only something that afflicts other people. It is in each of us.

When we look at Cain, we see that his murder of Abel was not an expression of momentary frustration. It was a planned, calculated act. He led his brother out into the fields, away from other family members, away from civilization, where no one would stop him.

While listening to the news reports about the murders over 30 years ago, it seemed that the reporters had a hard time accepting the fact of a premeditated, carefully planned murder. A momentary act of frustration was something the reporters could comprehend, but not a planned, calculated murder. Because we are naïve about human nature, we are reluctant to admit that a brilliant young scientist, with a promising career ahead of him, could carefully plan to kill his professors and university leaders. It feels too painful to confess this truth about human nature, but there it is. Ouch! That is the kind of people we are; this potential remains true of us, even if we are talented and highly educated.

Think back to Cain and Abel: It is valuable to notice that from very early times in human history people were making a clear distinction between killing a person and killing an animal (in this case for religious worship), despite the obvious physical similarities between humans and animals and the similarity in the process of killing humans and animals. It is also valuable to notice that this early murder of a man was an expression of anger at God. Cain was angry at God because God had not accepted his sacrifice; it was very difficult for Cain to directly attack God, but it was not so difficult to attack someone who was a mirror image of God and who seemed to be a friend of God. The background of this earliest murder was *religious frustration*: hostility toward God can be misdirected toward people.

There was something wrong with Cain's worship, his sacrifice, that made it unacceptable to God, even if we do not know exactly *what* was wrong with his worship. Cain knew there was something deficient in his worship; he was not at peace with God. But Abel's worship was accepted by God, leaving Cain frustrated at the deepest level of his soul. And this religious frustration led to murder.

I study religiously motivated violence for my job as a human rights theorist. There are two common paths through which religion leads to violence, even deadly violence, in our day. The first of these pathways to religiously motivated violence is most commonly found in some Islamic movements, though it is also possible in other religions. Within some varieties of Islam, it is difficult for people to be certain they will go to Paradise when they die. This uncertainty weighs heavily on the souls of many. A few varieties of Islam resolve this problem by saying that if you die during a religious war, a jihad, then you can have certainty of going to Paradise. Therefore, some people take on suicide missions in what they perceive to be a religious war. It is their ticket to Paradise, as they see it, though I would call it dysfunctional religion.

Another pathway from religion to violence in our day is a particular type of religious nationalism. Some types of religious nationalism do not lead to repression or violence. For example, John Adams, the second President of the United States, famously said, "We have no government armed with power capable of contending with human passions unbridled by ... morality and religion ... Our Constitution was made only for a moral and religious people."[1] When Adams said this, he was probably assuming that "religion" usually meant some type of Christianity, but the political principle he articulated can also apply to some other religions. Adams thought healthy religion would help us restrain our Cain-like passions and thereby contribute to nation-building. This is a constructive religious nationalism.

There is also another type of religious nationalism that claims that to be a good citizen in our society, and to have rights in our society, one must belong to the right religion. And if one does not belong to the right religion, one does not have rights. Such people without rights may be treated inhumanly, whether turned into slaves, driven away, or killed. Such dysfunctional religious nationalism turns our Cain-like passions into a political principle.

We see this problem when Hindu nationalists say, "India is for Hindus," meaning Christians and Muslims do not belong in India and may be attacked, killed, or driven out of the country. I have a good friend from India, a brilliant scientist, whose father converted from Hinduism to Christianity. Because of their Christian faith, this family and their church in India have suffered repeated attacks for many years. Cain-like anger has become a destructive type of Hindu religious nationalism, leading to death and destruction.

We also see this problem in how the Rohingya people have been treated in Myanmar. This is now described at the highest levels as genocide and a crime against humanity. These normal people were killed or driven away, with horrible suffering, largely because they are a Muslim minority and not Buddhists. This is dysfunctional Buddhist nationalism that cannot imagine that people of another religion can be good citizens of their country. I see it as Cain-like anger turned into a political ideology.[2]

We who read or write a book such as this have to be careful about Christian nationalism. We can recognize that John Adams has something to teach

---

[1] John Adams, "Speech to the Massachusetts Militia," October 11, 1798, spelling modernized; https://founders.archives.gov/documents/Adams/99-02-02-3102.

[2] See the addendum to this chapter about religious frustration and human rights.

us, but at the same time we must confess that Christians have sometimes acted and sounded too much like Islamicist jihadists. We must never think or say that only people of our religion have normal human rights or can be good citizens of our country, regardless of which country we call home.

The relationship of faith to peace or violence is especially true on an individual level. People who are at peace with God, and know they are at peace with God, will not have the desire to murder someone. Of course, you will get angry with people from time to time. We all do. But true peace with God will overshadow and restrain anger. If you or a friend are deeply angry, to the point of almost wanting to murder someone, come back to the question of religious frustration. Peace with God by faith in Jesus Christ, and knowing we have this peace, is the way to solve the murderous potential inside of us.

The second assumption of this commandment is that human beings are created in the image of God. The image of God is the relationship or dialogue each person has with God. Even if a person's relationship with God is negative, even to the extent that the person claims to be an atheist, their relationship with God is what makes them human. To equip us for this relationship, God gave us our rational capacity, our moral sense, our creative abilities, and our need for human relationships.

In connection with this commandment, we must see that the image of God has to do with how God sees a person. Whatever abilities or capacities a person may or may not have, God sees the person as valuable because God is speaking to that person. Each human life belongs to God because each person is in a discussion with God, even if that discussion is a heated argument right now. Any attack on a person is an attack on a friend or enemy of God, and God loves his enemies. We could say an attack on a person is an attack on God reflected through the other person.

This is the tie between false worship and murder. True worship of God leads to honoring his image in other people, both God's friends and his enemies. False worship dishonors God, and it leads to dishonoring people in his image. Any assault on a person is also an assault on God, and any assault on God leads to assaults on people.

It is terribly important that people of the Bible talk about the image of God, because, I believe, modern secularism is without any basis or reason to believe in human value or dignity. Let me give you two examples of non-Christian philosophers who write about these things who do not have a sufficient basis for human dignity.

Michael Tooley is a philosopher who defends a prochoice stance on abortion. He writes that the only being who has a right to life is the one who has a desire for continued life. He points out that the unborn, as well as young children, have no concept of, and therefore no desire for continued life. He thinks, rather consistently, that it is morally allowed to kill young children. I am afraid to hear what he would say about those who are senile or unconscious.

Peter Singer is one of the leading animal rights philosophers. He claims that the capacity to feel pain gives a being a right not to be assaulted. Since many animals, such as chimpanzees, cows, sheep, and rats have a capacity to feel pain, they have a moral right to life and protection equal to human beings. To think otherwise is to be guilty of "species-ism," which is similar to racism in his mind.

I mention Tooley and Singer to show the vast gulf between Christian and nonbelieving views of human dignity. In the providence of God, I studied some of the atheist philosophers who write about human dignity during the time when my mother-in-law was in decline because of Alzheimer's disease. According to the definitions of some of these authors, the life of this dear woman, the mother of my wife, may no longer have had any value or dignity because she no longer had normal human abilities. Yet our family saw her as a daughter of God, even when she could no longer respond to us.[3] God had created her in his own image, and God had spoken to her in creation and redemption.

The nonbelieving world is struggling to find any good reason to believe in human dignity, any good explanation of why people have rights and where those rights come from. If you lose God, you also lose human dignity. Nonbelieving writers on the topic tend to apply the murder commandment to animals, or else not apply it to some groups of people. In the Christian view, the command not to murder is firmly based on the claim that human beings are created in the image of God.

This is the second assumption of this commandment. Now the two implications of this commandment.

The first implication is that we must deal with murderous attitudes in ourselves. In Matthew 5:21, Jesus says, "You have heard that it was said to the people long ago, 'Do not murder, and anyone who murders will be subject to judgment.' But I tell you that anyone who is angry with his brother will be subject to judgment. Again, anyone who says to his brother, 'Racca,' is answerable to the Sanhedrin. But anyone who says, 'You fool!' will be in danger of the fire of hell."

---

[3] For more on this topic see Thomas K. Johnson, "Is Human Dignity Earned? Or is Human Dignity a Gift?" https://www.academia.edu/45429707/Is_Human_Dignity_Earned_or_Is_Human_Dignity_a_Gift.

Apparently, there were people in Jesus' day who wanted to use a philosophical trick to limit the application of the commandment to the physical act of murder. But Jesus says the commandment always has applied to words and thoughts as well. Destructive words and angry thoughts, in God's view of things, are similar to murder.

We must be precise here. It is possible to be angry without sin. Jesus became angry without sin. Yet very often anger is the occasion of sin. In some situations, anger is the only right response. This is true when we are witnesses of terrible injustice. Some of the prophets of ancient Israel sound angry. Most of us are angry about injustice far too seldom.

Most of us can, I believe, tell the difference between good anger and bad anger. But let me just mention a few things that are indicators of sinful anger. Are you angry very often? If you are, you need to deal with it. Do you get angry without a reason or for a very slight reason? That is a problem. Do you stay angry for a long time or bear a grudge against a person for a long time? Are you unwilling to forgive? Does anger make you get out of control? Do you express your anger in inappropriate ways?

Not all anger is sinful. But very often anger is the occasion of sin. When angry, we must be very careful not to commit something like murder or slander. If you are angry too much or too often, ask for help. A pastor or counselor may be what you need. And ask yourself, is your anger really religious frustration? Is the cure for your anger a new awareness of peace with God?

Many years ago I was very angry about something that someone did to me. As I realized the level of my anger, I decided to go for a walk in a park. While I was walking, I thought about a few people I had met who were always angry, so much that their anger became, in my perception, their defining characteristic. Soon I knew that I faced a decision, to forgive or to become a chronically angry person. It was not easy, but in view of God's forgiveness in Christ, I was able to let go of my anger so that I was not destroyed by anger.

A second implication of this commandment is that we must try to protect human life. This commandment, like several, is stated in the negative, assuming intelligent readers will figure out the positive demand of God. That demand of God is that we attempt to protect the lives of people created in God's image.

One of the greatest stories in the Bible to this effect is the story of the Good Samaritan. A traveler on foot is robbed and mugged, left along the road half-dead. The next two travelers simply pass by, but the third traveler, at considerable risk and expense, stops, applies first aid, puts the injured man on his donkey, and carries him to safety. And that becomes the model for us – self-sacrificing love to protect people, even people from an ethnic group we are supposed to hate.

This is the reason why believers trained in health care so often go out of their way to help people who would not otherwise be helped. That is why Christians led in abolishing the slave trade and slavery. That is why some believers hid Jews from the Nazis. That is why Christians have helped refugees and have set up shelters and rescue missions for the homeless, the alcoholics, and drug addicts. That is why Christians should be so concerned about abortion and infanticide. It is widely known and recognized in the US that when there is a terrible hurricane or another natural disaster, the emergency money comes mostly from the government, but much of the emergency help will come through the churches.

Our faith gives us a way of seeing things, and that way of seeing things leads to action. If we believe God created us in his image, if we believe he gave us the Ten Commandments, then we must each do what we can to protect human life. This will require responding in love to the needs God brings to our attention.

There is one very recent problem I would like to mention. In caring for a friend or relative who is ill to the point of death, we may sometimes wonder if God wants us to use every possible medical resource, or if there is a point at which it is right to allow an illness to take its course, which may lead to death. My opinion is this – because our lives belong to God, it is wrong to commit suicide, wrong to help someone commit suicide, and wrong to practice any active euthanasia. On the other hand, because every life belongs to God, if you have reached the point where medical resources no longer can restore a degree of health, it is okay to allow an illness to take its course, provided love and care is shown to the end. In this situation, we should continue to pray for the person and even ask God if He might be willing to restore the person's health. The Lord gives life that we must respect; the Lord also takes life at his good time.

In some ways my topic this morning is rather gloomy – murder, sin, and death. But remember where I started. God hates murder too, far more than we hate murder.

Come back to Gang Lu, the mass murderer in Iowa more than 30 years ago, and ask the question, "Did he know that what he was planning to do was wrong?" Without knowing much of his personal story I would guess he was not very familiar with the Bible. He had probably never read the story of Cain and Abel, and maybe he had not read the Ten Commandments. He might have known the story of the Good Samaritan, since that is more widely known. Did he know his plans were evil?

I think the answer is yes and no at the same time. There are important truths that all people know about right and wrong because we all live in God's world, but some would prefer not to know so much.

People can convince themselves they do not know something when they really know it. They suppress this knowledge, perhaps replacing proper moral knowledge with anger, dysfunctional religion, or a horrible ideology.

So let us more fully imitate God as people who hate murder, who love people made in the image of God, and who talk about complete forgiveness in Christ as the antidote, the solution, for the murderous anger that so easily rises within us.

Addendum: Religious Frustration and Human Rights[4]

It is easy for the observer to notice that various types of religious frustration contribute to different types of human rights abuses. Frequently an entire people group has been persecuted because of its beliefs, whether that people group is Jewish, Christian, Hindu, Muslim, or whatever. The presence of an articulated religious system makes a people into a distinct target for people who have all sorts of hostilities and frustrations. Think of these persecuted people as being represented by Abel; their number is massive. The persecution of a religious group is rarely purely religious. Such persecutions are often mixed with ethnic hatred, economic envy, personal grudges, nationalistic zeal, and a range of other dark motives. The people committing the crimes are often broadly frustrated with life. And the well-identified religious community, religious institution, or religious leader becomes the target for violence or discrimination. Frustration with life turns into aggression toward a person or group who might be close to God. Those represented by Abel are murdered too often.

There are also those religiously frustrated people represented by Cain. Their religion or religion substitute (such as Communism, National Socialism, and various other political ideologies) makes some people or the entire movement hostile toward others and may also provide some explanation why another group of people should be hindered or destroyed. These religions or religious/political ideologies have within their doctrine and ethics certain ideas, claims, examples, or principles that explain why all other people or certain other people should be repressed, expelled, or killed. Sometimes the despised or second-class hu-mans are identified by race, sometimes by religion, or sometimes by social class. These religions and ideologies can be grouped together as giving organized expression to internal religious frustrations, similar to those of Cain. Their religion has

---

[4] This is adapted from Thomas K. Johnson, *Human Rights: A Christian Primer,* 2nd edition (Bonn: VKW 2016), 46-48; https://www.academia.edu/36884876/Human_Rights_A_Christian_Primer.

not provided peace with God, with themselves, or with other people. The observable results around the world are gruesome.

It is for good reason that freedom of religion is sometimes de-scribed as the "first freedom" or the "mother of human rights." The society that has learned how to protect a very extensive freedom of religion is also learning how to manage its own religious frustrations which are the root cause of many other abuses of human rights. And once those religious frustrations are largely managed, it is much easier to take steps to protect the full range of human rights. Biblical realism about human nature lets us see that protecting the freedom of religion will often also lead to the practical protection of a wide range of other human rights and the flourishing of society very broadly. Of course, real freedom of religion is both individual and collective; this means both individuals and whole communities must be allowed to give full expression to their faith.[5]

Having a deep religious need is close to the center of what makes us human; if God created us in the reflection or image of his heart and mind, it is only natural that one of our deepest drives or instincts will be for a relationship with God. When Augustine prayed, "Our hearts are restless until they find their rest in you," he was not only confessing his own desire for God.[6] He was describing a central element of what makes us human. Even though he did not believe in God, philosopher Ludwig Feuerbach claimed that what makes people human is the fact that they are religious. "Religion has its basis in the essential difference between man and the brute – the brutes have no religion." (The word "brute" meant animal.)[7] Protecting religious freedom is very close to protecting the mystery or essence of humanness.

---

[5] Real freedom of religion must include such matters as freedom of speech that arise from a person's or a community's basic beliefs, e.g., freedom to educate one's children in light of one's faith, freedom to gather with fellow believers, freedom to own or rent suitable buildings or facilities for such activities. Real freedom of religion contains within it real freedom of speech, freedom of the press, freedom of assembly, freedom to travel, and freedom of education.

[6] This the opening line in the famous *Confessions* of Saint Augustine (354-430), bishop of Hippo, which is in today's Algeria. This valuable book is available in various English translations and in many other languages.

[7] Ludwig Feuerbach (1804-1872) was a German atheist philosopher of religion. Some of his ideas were later adopted by Karl Marx and by Sigmund Freud, making him one of the important sources of modern European atheism. Very ironically, some of his central ideas were in his book *The Essence of Christianity*, which is an attack on Christian belief. The quotation is the opening statement of this book, which is available in various editions and languages; it is also included in many anthologies of Western philosophy.

The Seventh Commandment:

YOU SHALL NOT COMMIT ADULTERY

Diane Langberg, United States

> The commands of the Lord are radiant, giving light to the eyes ...
> More to be desired are they than gold, ...
> sweeter also than honey and drippings of the honeycomb.
> (Psalm 19:8b[NIV], 10[ESV])

Every word that proceeds out of the mouth of our God is a gift. His law is an expression of love for His covenant people. Old Testament Scriptures contain many types of law, but that which concerns us here are the Ten Commandments – the Decalogue – sometimes simply called the "ten words." As tempting as it may be to see the Decalogue as ten rules or requirements that we must obey in hopes of meeting God's stringent demands, such thinking would lead us to miss the wisdom and riches of our God and to ignore the good news that Christ is our righteousness. As we will see, the law was birthed by a God whose love for His people is beyond measure.

As a clinical psychologist, I have had many conversations with broken and suffering people, many of them damaged, oppressed, and violated by others, often having harmed themselves as well. Their understanding of God and His law is clouded with confusion, fear, and pain. Rather than seeing God's law as radiant and desirable, as the psalmist did, they ignore the Decalogue, twist it, or even reject it outright. For these people, the commandments of a loving God are heard not as emanating from the eternal love of the Father, but as arbitrary and demanding rules regarding human behavior declared by a God whom they consider unsafe. They do not understand that the Eternal Heart of Love seeks the perfection – never the harm – of every broken human being.

The Ten Commandments are in fact given by a loving God who desires the humans He created to flourish and in turn to bless others. When the confused or despairing see the image of God in the lives of those who name the name of Christ, they can learn more accurately to perceive who God is and who they are. We, the people of God, are called to reflect His true image to others in our messed-up world, by the power of the Holy Spirit. Our view of the law – and indeed our very lives – will be shaped by our relationship with God in Christ. So first we need to ponder the law in the light of Jesus Christ, the Word incarnate.

The Decalogue is a divine self-revelation; each commandment shows us a facet of our covenant God, connected by strands of love to the first commandment. God begins by reminding us who He is and what He has done for His people. "I am the LORD your God, who brought you out of the land of Egypt, out of the house of slavery" (Deuteronomy 5:6). Then follows the command, "You shall have no other gods before me."

"Quite rightly ... Martin Luther emphasized the manner in which all other commandments relate to the first," observes Christian ethicist Gilbert Meilaender. "To have no other gods – to love and trust God above all else – enables a person to keep the other commandments."[1]

The subject of this chapter is a single law, the seventh[2] commandment, which states, "You shall not commit adultery." This is usually understood as a stand-alone rule which simply forbids having sexual intercourse with anyone to whom you are not married. When adultery occurs, it tends to be regarded as a limited, concrete "mistake" and is dealt with accordingly in some churches. Yet if we are to understand this facet of God's multifaceted law, we must simultaneously focus on the whole. James 2:10 says, "For whoever keeps the whole law but fails in one point has become accountable for all of it."

The Big Picture

Considering the weight of all of the commandments enables us to see more clearly the meaning of the prohibition on adultery. The first commandment says God shall be our first love. Breaking *any* of these laws causes us to break the first commandment and constitutes unfaithfulness, breaking the Eternal Heart of Love. We are to worship God alone and to have no other gods before Him. When we disobey His commandments, we put another – e.g., ourselves, a person, our work, or an institution – in God's place in our lives. To break the seventh commandment is to break the first.

We are to love and serve God with all we have, all we are, and all we do, *so that His likeness will be seen in us*. Reformed theologian John Calvin wrote, "For God has so depicted his character in the law that if any man carries

---

[1] Gilbert Meilaender, *Thy Will Be Done* (Grand Rapids: Baker Academic, Division of Baker Publishing Group, 2020), xi.

[2] Lutheran and Roman Catholic traditions number the Ten Commandments slightly differently and consider this the sixth commandment.

out in deeds whatever is enjoined there, he will express the image of God, as it were, in his own life."[3] God created humankind to bear His image. To love God is to reflect His character. Loving God means He is the One you crave; He alone satisfies your deepest longing; He is the One you relentlessly serve; He is first among your loves.

All other relationships, including marriage, are to grow out of the primary relationship with God and are subservient to it. To love Him means to live a life full of the Spirit of God, manifesting His fruit, demonstrating the character of Christ to all who enter your world or your mind. Worship shapes our character.

God created male and female as an expression of His divine image. To bear His character is to love your neighbor. And loving your neighbor includes loving faithfulness to your spouse. For a married couple, the unity of their relationship produces God-imaging fruit – in the possibility of offspring certainly – but also in character and in conduct. The commandment against adultery guards and protects that in-the-flesh unity. Any unfaithfulness in a marriage distorts and mars the image of God as well as breaks the commandment against adultery, a violation of love and communion.

Ransomed humanity is the instrument through which the character of our God is revealed. Marriage is one of those mirrors. The marriage relationship is to be characterized by the wisdom and kindness of God and by the fruit of His Spirit, which includes love, faithfulness, and self-control (Galatians 5:22-23). To see such love relationally, in the flesh, is to see the Father's love.

What Is Adultery?

A brief look at the origin of the word adultery exposes the depth of the commandment against adultery. The English word comes from the Latin *adulterare*, which means "to corrupt, to debase, or to make impure." Adultery in a marriage includes unfaithfulness, falseness, and disloyalty. It severs the one-flesh union and violates the law of love to both God and spouse.

In contrast, consider some of what Scripture tells us about the character of our God.

> "Know therefore that the Lord your God is God; the faithful God ..." (Deuteronomy 7:9).

---

[3] John Calvin, *Institutes of the Christian Religion Volume XX*, ed. John T. McNeill, trans. Ford Lewis Battles, Library of Christian Classics 20 (Philadelphia: Westminster Press 1977), 2.8.51.

"The steadfast love of the LORD never ceases;
his mercies never come to an end;
they are new every morning;
great is your faithfulness"
(Lamentations 3:22-23).

"Trust in him at all times, O people; pour out your heart before him;
God is a refuge for us"
(Psalm 62:8).

"... he who promised is faithful"
(Hebrews 10:23b).

Any unfaithfulness in a marriage relationship – on any level – is unlike our Lord Jesus, whose faithfulness is unremitting. He said, "I *always* do the things that are pleasing to [the Father]" (John 8:29; emphasis added).

The Many Faces of Adultery

I have worked for almost fifty years with clients who have experienced trauma. I have seen countless incidents of all sorts of adultery. For the most part, the body of Christ defines adultery as occurring in a marriage when one spouse is having or has had a sexual relationship with someone outside the marriage. That is indeed adultery. It does great damage, not only to both husband and wife, but can impact offspring for generations. But adultery has other faces as well. One of them is trauma.

I began my work as a psychologist in the early 1970s. There were no books, no training, and no understanding of trauma or of some of its many causes. The impact of war, domestic violence, sexual abuse, and rape were poorly understood. What I heard from my clients were experiences of evil and suffering unlike anything I had ever imagined – evil perpetrated in "Christian" homes by "Christian" people.

A young woman sat down in my office, pulled her hair over her face, and said, "My father used to do weird things to me." I had no idea what she meant. She taught me, and I learned. Her well-respected father was in church leadership. He was also sexually abusing his daughter. I saw many women who had suffered from chronic, often sadistic, abuse at the hands of so-called Christian fathers, grandfathers, uncles, and teachers. The father of an adolescent girl I was counseling was escorted from my office in handcuffs because he had been sexually abusing my adolescent client.

I discovered that a nine-year-old foster child who had been sexually molested, removed from her birth home, and placed with a "Christian" family, was abused there as well. A woman married to a well-respected Christian businessman and church elder tentatively began to describe the violence in her home to me. One day she stood up in my office to lift her skirts and show me the bruises on her legs from being beaten with a bat because she had displeased him. I worked with wives whose husbands spent hours each night glued to the computer staring at pornography involving women, men, or children – and sometimes trafficking them. I found myself plunged into unspeakable sufferings and evil *in Christendom* before I was thirty years old.

Some years later, I was called into the murky waters where shepherds were victimizing their sheep; missionaries raped the nationals they had gone to serve; pastors abused their power to feed their own desires with the women in their pews. Many so-called Christian institutions and organizations I encountered systematically closed ranks to protect the abuser rather than the victim. I saw evil hidden and ignored rather than exposed to the piercing light of our God. Rather than caring for the sheep, shepherds and churches had become predators.

I sat with a "Christian" leader who battered his wife black and blue, repeatedly twisted the truth, and told me I was young, after all, and did not yet understand that sometimes "a little force was necessary to accomplish God's will in the home." I made a phone call to a pastor about a woman in his church whose life was in danger. That pastor sent her right back home to her abuser, because that is, after all, "where women belong." She was horrifically beaten and required long-term hospitalization.

I met with a young girl who was being sexually abused by her youth pastor. The church leaders helped him move away so he could continue his "dynamic" ministry elsewhere: "We wouldn't want a little mistake to destroy such a gifted man, would we, Diane?" I worked with pastors and missionaries addicted to pornography, who had sex with the women they were called to shepherd; some solicited prostitutes; others preferred little boys.

Are the perpetrators of these atrocities guilty of adultery? Are they unfaithful, full of deceit and disloyalty? I believe that they are.

Commenting on Genesis 9:6, Calvin wrote,

> Men are indeed unworthy of God's care, if respect be had only to themselves. But since they bear the image of God engraven on them, he deems himself violated in their person. Thus, although they have nothing of their own by which they obtain the favor of God, he looks upon his own gifts in them, and is thereby excited to love and to care for them. This doctrine, however, is to be carefully observed that *no one can be injurious to his brother without*

wounding God himself. Were this doctrine deeply fixed in our minds, we should be much more reluctant than we are to inflict injuries.[4] (emphasis added)

Statistics

Consider the following statistics:

- Thirty percent of women have experienced physical or sexual intimate-partner violence.[5]
- Forty-two percent of those women report an injury.[6]
- Thirty-eight percent of the murders of women are committed by an intimate partner.[7]
- Covid-19 increased the risk factors, and access to services is limited.[8]
- Financial abuse occurs in 99% of domestic violence cases.[9]
- Women in poverty experience domestic violence at two times the rate of those who are not in poverty[10]
- Women account for 49% of human-trafficking victims globally.[11]
- Two hundred million women and girls have undergone female genital mutilation.[12]
- Fifteen million teen girls have experienced forced sex.[13]
- Less than 40% of women who experience violence seek help.[14]

---

[4] John Calvin, *Commentaries on the First Book of Moses Called Genesis, Volume 1* (Grand Rapids: Christian Classics Ethereal Library), accessed May 24, 2021, https://ccel.org/ccel/calvin/calcom01/calcom01.xv.i.html.

[5] "Violence against women," World Health Organization, March 9, 2021, https://www.who.int/news-room/fact-sheets/detail/violence-against-women.

[6] "Violence against women."

[7] "Violence against women."

[8] "Violence against women."

[9] "Financial Abuse Fact Sheet," *National Network to End Domestic Violence*, July 2019, https://nnedv.org/wp-content/uploads/2019/07/Library_EJ_Financial_Abuse_Fact_Sheet.pdf.

[10] "Financial Abuse Fact Sheet."

[11] "Facts and figures: Ending violence against women," *UN Women*, March, 2021, https://www.unwomen.org/en/what-we-do/ending-violence-against-women/facts-and-figures.

[12] "Facts and figures."

[13] "Facts and figures."

[14] "Facts and figures."

- Three out of four children who are two-to-four years of age suffer violence by parents.[15]
- One in five women is sexually abused as a child.[16]
- One in five to one in eight males report some kind of sexual assault.[17]
- Five-to-ten percent of boys are raped in their lifetime.[18]
- More than 90% of disabled men and women will experience sexual abuse.[19]
- Eighty-three percent of pastors have counseled an abused woman; eight percent have felt equipped to respond.[20]
- Ninety-five percent of church women report never hearing a sermon against abuse of any kind.[21]
- Consumption of pornography is at an all-time high. Accessibility, affordability, and anonymity put adult content right at our fingertips.[22] The American Psychological Association (APA) estimates that 50-99% of men and 30-86% of women have viewed porn.[23]

Shocking as they are, the statistics noted above do not merely reflect the secular world. They reflect the *Christian* world as well. I sit with many victims whose abusers name the name of Christ. Not only do they call themselves Christian, but they use the name of our Lord to justify their adulterous ways.

To abuse is to use wrongly, treating someone or something in a harmful or injurious way. To call ourselves Christian, whether we refer to a Christian person, a Christian home, a Christian friend, a Christian leader, or a Christian church, we are claiming to be people or organizations who are committed to the teachings of Jesus Christ – people who follow Jesus Christ and bear His likeness. To be a Christian or to be in a Christian environment

---

[15] "Child maltreatment," World Health Organization, June 8, 2020, https://www.who.int/news-room/fact-sheets/detail/child-maltreatment.
[16] "Child maltreatment."
[17] "Male Survivors of Sexual Violence," Michigan Resource Center on Domestic and Sexual Violence, accessed April 19, 2021, https://www.michigan.gov/documents/datingviolence/DHS-DatingViolence-MaleSurvivors_198439_7.pdf.
[18] "Male Survivors."
[19] "Male Survivors."
[20] Elaine Storkey, *Scars Against Humanity* (Downers Grove: InterVarsity Press, 2018), 210.
[21] Storkey, 210.
[22] Kirsten Weir, "Is pornography addictive?" *Monitor on Psychology*, April 2014, http://www.apa.org/monitor/2014/04/pornography.
[23] Weir, "Is pornography addictive?"

and to perpetrate, condone, or ignore abuse is a hideous, in fact, a hellish oxymoron. Abuse is unfaithfulness to God. It is adultery. It is sin.

Such people use the name of Christ to sanction drawing a veil over evil. Oftentimes that cover-up is carried out, or at least supported, by those who say they are protecting both God's name and His church. In all these places, in all these ways, we Christians are an adulterous people. We have abandoned love and obedience to our God for other gods. Unfaithfulness, impurity of any description, is the destruction of love.

The Word Made Flesh

How are we to respond to these devastating and ungodly situations? How are we as individuals who name Christ as our Head and collectively constitute His body here on earth to see clearly and walk with humility in the light of exposure by the seventh commandment? According to Paul, love does not behave unbecomingly or unfaithfully (1 Corinthians 13:5). Would love tolerate the sexual abuse of a child or an adult? Would love call the battering of a spouse physically or verbally ugly and unseemly? Would love ignore pouring pornography into a mind and heart? Would Eternal Love call the abandonment of those tossed aside, their cries ignored, unfaithfulness?

We, God's covenant people, have broken the law of love and the heart of the God of love. We have been unfaithful; we have acted in unworthy ways; we have profaned the name of our Lord. Our unfaithfulness to God spills out and pollutes all of our other relationships. It is His purpose that our growing fidelity to Him should instead spill out into every aspect of our lives. Where it does not, our infidelity to God is exposed.

"And the Word became flesh and dwelt among us, and we have seen his glory, ... full of grace and truth" (John 1:14). Our Forerunner, the Lord Jesus Christ, has gone before us and demonstrated in the flesh what faithfulness looks like. Jesus' relationship to humanity was and is rooted in His faithful relationship to the Father. To be like Him means that how I behave toward my spouse pleases God. Faithfulness is how I respond to corrupt or negligent leadership. Who I am with the sick, the slow, the weak, and the helpless brings joy to the heart of the Father. The way that I am with all humanity demonstrates the love of the Father. Eternal love of the Father was supreme in Jesus Christ – all other relationships were subservient to that love. The love of His Father was the root of all Jesus' loves and was expressed in loving service to all He met. Love of others, in word and deed, is the fruit of an unwavering love of God.

In Matthew 22 we learn of an encounter between Jesus and a Pharisee lawyer who wanted to know what the great, underlying commandment was. He said, "Teacher, which is the great commandment in the Law?" Jesus replied, "You shall love the LORD your God with all your heart and with all your soul and with all your mind. *This* is the great and first commandment" (vv. 37-38; emphasis added).

Any failure of obedience to this command is a failure of all the commandments. And coming out of the first commandment is a second, "You shall love your neighbor as yourself" (Matthew 22:39). The character formed through obedience to the first and greatest commandment is demonstrated in conduct. If you love God, that love will show itself in love to your neighbor – your spouse, your children, the vulnerable, the hungry, and the abused. To fail to love your neighbor is to fail to love our God. In contrast, to witness that love in another life is to see the Father. We reflect our Lord – the Word made flesh. We become the instrument through which wisdom and kindness and faithfulness are revealed.

John gives us two characteristics by which we might recognize God in the flesh. How am I to assess myself or another? John first says, "God is light, and in him is no darkness at all. If we say we have fellowship with him while we walk in darkness, we lie and do not practice the truth. But if we walk in the light, as he is in the light, we have fellowship ..." (1 John 1:5-7). Darkness conceals and despises, distorting, hiding, and disturbing vision so that things appear other than they really are. Darkness varnishes over blemishes. We use it to hide ourselves from ourselves, from others, and from God. In God there is no darkness. In our God there is no adultery, no unfaithfulness.

John also says that we know that we know Him because we keep His commandments. Our conduct in life reveals to us and to others whether our words, promises, and fidelity are true. To say we know Jesus and to disobey is to lie. Our words may promise fidelity, but if our lives do not match our words, we have committed adultery. We have failed to walk in the light.

To say I know the God of light and then pour corruption into my mind through pornography is to walk in darkness. To exploit those under my care, to feed off them in some fashion – to feed my pocketbook, my lust, my position, or my status is to walk in darkness. To fail to protect the little ones from wolves, or to fail to care for those wounded by wolves in our midst, is to lie and to fail the One who is Truth – all such unfaithfulness is adulterous.

The second characteristic is that God is love. Again, John said, "By this we know that we love the children of God, when we love God and obey his commandments. For this is the love of God, that we keep his commandments" (1 John 5:2-3). Our love of God is manifest in our love, first to the

Father and then to others. Does infidelity to our marriage vows reflect the Father's love? Is love of the Father seen in our verbal and physical battering and rage in the home? Is the love of the Father evident in using power to bully and then to self-protect and deny the truth of wrongdoing? Is the love of the Father seen in seeking out and feeding on pornography? Are these things unfaithfulness? Are they adulterous?

"Little children, let us not love in word or talk but in deed and in truth. By this we shall know that we are of the truth ... because we keep his commandments and do what pleases him" (1 John 3:18-19, 22).

The Body of Christ

Our human relationships are meant to be illustrations of how the Head of the church and His body live together, united by one overarching goal. That goal is giving glory to God. Paul says, "Now you are the body of Christ and individually members of it" (1 Corinthians 12:27). My individual life is meant to be a manifestation in the flesh of the character of my Lord. Like Christ, we are each to be an instrument through whom wisdom, kindness, and love are revealed. In marriage, our love for each other is to be an in-the-flesh picture of the mutual love between God and His Son. Our faithfulness to God and to each other means there is no room for harshness, demeaning, neglect, or crushing or abusive behavior.

Like marriage, the body of Christ is also to be a living picture of the character of our God. The church's love of the Father and its obedience to Him mean that when we see the church, we see the Father. To fail to reveal the Father is unfaithfulness to Him and to each other. It is adultery.

My father was a pilot in the Air Force for many years. He dropped paratroopers over Normandy in World War II. He was a bright, gifted, and athletic man. When he was 42 years old, he was diagnosed with a neurological disorder no one could name. He had to leave the life he had built and loved and retire much earlier than he had planned. For the next 32 years, we watched his body deteriorate until he could no longer tie his shoes or pick something up off the floor; eventually he lacked the coordination required to walk. He knew very well how to do all those things, but his body would not follow his head. His body either refused or did the task in a twisted manner. I learned many things from my father. One is a truth based on watching his deterioration and uncooperative body. The principle is this: A body that does not follow its head is a very sick body.

When we, the body of Christ, refuse to follow our Head in any way, we are a sick body. To cover up sin in the corporate body is to walk in darkness. To fail to protect and care for victims of abuse is to walk in darkness.

We – the body of Christ – become a den of robbers, a safe place for those who steal. We are to love God with everything we are and have, so that love is visible in marriage and in the body that is the church. The God we are to make real in our flesh so all can see is a faithful God. Adultery of any kind is a failure of love for our God and a failure to make His image visible in our flesh.

Called to Unadulterated Love

Many years ago, I took my first speaking engagement in another country. I had been asked to speak about abuse in a country that had no books on the topic and had never heard it discussed. A group of Christians asked me to teach them about the topic and how to respond. I did not speak the language. I was in a country that was strange to me, with no language skill to deliver critical new information to my audience. Obviously, I needed a translator. I had never had one before.

The experience of having one's words translated in real time requires a great deal of trust. The translator must listen accurately and speak truly. He must know two languages well. He must know how to communicate both the words and the heart of the one for whom he speaks. The speaker must relinquish a measure of control and trust that the translator will take what is presented and accurately deliver it, so the speaker is not misrepresented. The reputation of the speaker is in the hands of the translator. The relationship the speaker has with individuals in the audience is in the hands of the translator.

Is this not something like our lives as the representatives of God in this world? Our lives and mouths are to communicate the words of God and the heart of God to the world. We must listen to Him accurately and speak truthfully. We must know the language of heaven and the language of earth. We represent Him, and He has entrusted us with His reputation in this world. As Oswald Chambers puts it in *My Utmost for His Highest*, "The reputation of God is at stake in your bodily life." Others know Christ and experience Him through our lives and our words. I left Brazil with a longing to translate the person and work of Christ well. His reputation may be in our hands.

I longed for my translator to understand the topic, my compassion for those who have been sexually abused, and my love for the people. I wanted those in the audience to hear from me that there is hope for healing in Jesus Christ. I wanted them to hear truth about abuse. I wanted them to get an accurate set of facts. Their lives and the lives of many others would be impacted by what the translator spoke to them. Is this not a glimmer into the heart of our God? Does He not long for us as His translators to represent His truths and His heart as well?

God, who has loved us and bought us with His blood, has called us to translate His great love and truth to this world. It is not simply a verbal exercise. It is a whole-life exercise. Both our character and our conduct, along with our words, are to communicate who God is accurately and lovingly, as did His Son Jesus Christ. We do great damage to that wonderful name when our translation is false. *"And the Word became flesh and dwelt among us, and we have seen his glory, ... full of grace and truth. ... the only God, who is at the Father's side, he has made him known"* (John 1:14,18).

How Shall We Respond?

God is faithful, and He calls us to be faithful. But adultery is rampant among God's people. It is often not recognized as such. In excusing individuals, covering up unfaithfulness and lies, and protecting our reputations and institutions, we deceive ourselves; we deceive others; we have forgotten our God and have grieved Him deeply. God suffers when His people are unfaithful. To say "I love God" and to hate, to dismiss, to abuse, or to feed on or to crush another is to lie. There are many precious people, loved by our God, who are suffering greatly because we who call ourselves the body of Christ have loved ourselves more than we love the Lamb who was slain. Jesus made His stance very clear when He spoke to the religious leaders: "Woe to you, ... hypocrites! For you shut the kingdom of heaven in people's faces" (Matthew 23:13). Where we are unfaithful, where we are adulterous, we follow the way of the Pharisees.

Our hearts, thoughts, conduct, and longings all reveal whom or what we love. Given our standard – likeness to Christ – and our own unfaithfulness as humans, what is the God of light and love calling us to do? If we humble ourselves before our faithful God, He will indeed search us and help us see our places and patterns of unfaithfulness, of adultery.

First, we must individually pray with David, the king whom God had appointed for His people and who had himself committed adultery. We must ask the Light of the World to show us who we are and where we are unfaithful to Him. With David we must say, "O Lord, you have searched me and known me! ... you discern my thoughts from afar ... You ... are acquainted with all my ways ... Search me, O God, and know my heart! Try me and know my thoughts! And see if there be any grievous way in me ..." (Psalm 139:1-3; 23-24a).

Go to Him and ask, "Where does my heart stray from you, God? What is my primary concern, my first love? Is it myself, my reputation, my status, my comfort? Where am I unfaithful to You because I love something else more?

"Where does my mind stray from loving God? Thoughts of criticism and judgment? Lustful thoughts that use others to feed myself in some way? Angry thoughts – fury when I do not get my way, self-protection, hiding from the light, or misusing my power? Where does my conduct fail to reflect truth and love? Where have I made decisions based on what protects me or in ways that misuse my power? Where have I turned away from those I am meant to protect?"

God will answer. And He always calls things by their right name. When He shines His light on our failures, confession and repentance need to be our next response. The prophet Daniel, who was faithful under dire circumstances, prayed collectively on behalf of his people who were unfaithful and adulterous.

"We have sinned and done wrong and acted wickedly and rebelled, turning aside from your commandments and rules ... All Israel has transgressed your law ..." (Daniel 9:5, 11a). He went on to plead with God: "'... O Lord, make your face to shine upon your sanctuary, which is desolate ... For we do not present our pleas before you because of our righteousness, but because of your great mercy. O Lord, hear; O Lord, forgive. O Lord, pay attention and act. Delay not, for your own sake, O my God, because your city and your people are called by your name'" (Daniel 9:17b, 18b, 19). As the Lord said to Solomon, "'... if my people who are called by my name humble themselves, and pray and seek my face and turn from their wicked ways, ... I will ... heal their land" (2 Chronicles 7:14). Our hope is in the Lord.

God will hear. God will forgive. And we will come to see His commands as promises as in Christ we are empowered to walk in His ways and reveal His love to a hurting world.

May we flee from anything within us and around us that would seduce us into adulterous ways. May we be faithful to our Lord, who is our First Love.

The Eighth Commandment:

YOU SHALL NOT STEAL

Andrew McGowan, Scotland

The Ten Commandments are listed in Exodus 20 and repeated in Deuteronomy 5. The eighth commandment is found at Exodus 20:15: "You shall not steal."[1] Traditionally understood, the first table of God's law (commandments 1-4) comprises our duty toward God, and the second table of the law (commandments 5-10) comprises our duty toward other human beings. The eighth commandment, then, is part of our duty toward others. If the seventh commandment concerning adultery flows out of the holiness and purity of God, we might say that the eighth commandment flows out of the justice of God.

The Teaching of the Old Testament

The eighth commandment also occurs in Leviticus 19:11-13, which both states and elaborates on the requirements of the commandment, giving examples: "You shall not steal; you shall not deal falsely; and you shall not lie to one another. And you shall not swear by my name falsely, and so profane the name of your God: I am the LORD. You shall not oppress your neighbor or rob him; the wages of a hired servant shall not remain with you all night until the morning." It is clear from this passage that it is not simply theft (or robbery) which constitutes a breach of this commandment but also "dealing falsely," "oppressing your neighbor," and failure to pay wages on time. We shall elaborate on these later.

In the spelling out of the duties and obligations of the people of God in relation to the Ten Commandments, there is recognition that the commandments require interpretation and that there are different levels of breach with correspondingly different levels of punishment. For example, the one who kills a neighbor intentionally (murder) was to be executed, but the one who killed accidentally (manslaughter) would receive a less severe sentence (see Numbers 35). Similar to the eighth commandment, there is a recognition elsewhere of varying degrees of culpability regar-

---

[1] All Bible references are from the *English Standard Version* (ESV, 2001).

ding theft. In Proverbs 6:30-31 we read: "People do not despise a thief if he steals to satisfy his appetite when he is hungry, but if he is caught, he will pay sevenfold; he will give all the goods of his house." The stealing is wrong and will be punished, but the one who steals food when starving, in order to live, is not despised in the same way as one who steals through a desire for personal gain or to increase wealth.

In the Old Testament, the commandment is also spelled out to include such things as kidnapping, that is, to steal a person. For example, Exodus 21:16: "'Whoever steals a man and sells him, and anyone found in possession of him, shall be put to death.'" Similarly, in Deuteronomy 24:7: "'If a man is found stealing one of his brothers, of the people of Israel, and if he treats him as a slave or sells him, then that thief shall die. So you shall purge the evil from your midst.'"

The Old Testament also mentions other kinds of stealing, for example, using false measures, as we see in Deuteronomy 25:13-16: "'You shall not have in your bag two kinds of weights, a large and a small. You shall not have in your house two kinds of measures, a large and a small. A full and fair weight you shall have, a full and fair measure you shall have, that your days may be long in the land that the LORD your God is giving you. For all who do such things, all who act dishonestly, are an abomination to the LORD your God.'" We find this, too, in Amos 8:4-6: "Hear this, you who trample on the needy and bring the poor of the land to an end, saying, 'When will the new moon be over that we may sell grain? And the Sabbath, that we may offer wheat for sale, that we may make the ephah small and the shekel great and deal deceitfully with false balances, that we may buy the poor for silver and the needy for a pair of sandals and sell the chaff of the wheat?'"

The Teaching of the New Testament

If we now turn to the New Testament, we find the eighth commandment stated and spelled out in some detail. In Matthew 19:16-19, when approached by a wealthy young man, Jesus spells out the second table of the law: "And behold, a man came up to him, saying, 'Teacher, what good deed must I do to have eternal life?' And he said to him, 'Why do you ask me about what is good? There is only one who is good. If you would enter life, keep the commandments.' He said to him, 'Which ones?' And Jesus said, 'You shall not murder, You shall not commit adultery, You shall not steal, You shall not bear false witness, Honor your father and mother, and, You shall love your neighbor as yourself.'" The importance of these verses is the enduring value of the second table of the law for the Christian life. The young man assured Jesus that he had kept all of these commandments but was then challenged as to his real problem, namely, that money had become more important to him than God and was taking first place in his life. Nevertheless, Jesus began by pointing him to the commandments. The point surely is that keeping the commandments is not a literal and simplistic obedience to a few prohibitions; it is a whole life of obedience to God in everything. As is made clear in the Sermon on the Mount, the commandments go much deeper and are much more demanding than we would otherwise see. The bottom line is that if we are truly keeping the Ten Commandments, God will have first place in our lives, and we will live accordingly.

In Romans 13:8-10, Paul puts the observance of the commandments in the context of the love which believers ought to have for one another: "Owe no one anything, except to love each another, for the one who loves another has fulfilled the law. The commandments, 'You shall not commit adultery, You shall not murder, You shall not steal, You shall not covet,' and any other commandment, are summed up in this word: 'You shall love your neighbor as yourself.' Love does no wrong to a neighbor; therefore love is the fulfilling of the law."

The eighth commandment is also spelled out in Ephesians 4:28: "Let the thief no longer steal, but rather let him labor, doing honest work with his own hands, so that he may have something to share with anyone in need." Here the emphasis is on providing for oneself and for one's family through honest work and not by stealing. Here we see something of the dignity of work and the fact that work enables the Christian to help others.

Just as in the Old Testament, where there was the prohibition of kidnapping, so, in the New Testament, Paul gives a list of sins and includes slave traders in 1 Timothy 1:9-12: "... understanding this, that the law is not laid down for the just but for the lawless and disobedient, for the ungodly and sinners, for the unholy and profane, for those who strike their fathers and mothers, for murderers, the sexually immoral, men who practice homosexuality, enslavers, liars, perjurers, and whatever else is contrary to sound doctrine, in accordance with the gospel of the glory of the blessed God with which I have been entrusted."

Examples

If we take all these passages together, in both Old and New Testaments, we can say that the eighth commandment condemns stealing but includes much more. It includes dealing falsely, defrauding a neighbor, failure to pay wages on time, kidnapping, using false measures, and immoral trading practices. This enables us to see the full scope of the commandment and its application to everyday life. Reading these passages of Scripture provides an antidote to any idea that, as Christians, we have never broken the eighth commandment. We might think we have never been guilty of stealing because we have never robbed a bank or broken into someone's house and stolen from him or been guilty of shoplifting or kidnapping or of any other obvious example of stealing. In light of the Scriptures, however, we must ask some deeper questions.

Have we ever dealt falsely with someone or defrauded anyone?

I remember having lunch with some assistant ministers thirty years ago. One of them was selling a car that we knew to be in poor condition. Several of the others said that there was no obligation on the seller to point out any of the faults to a prospective buyer. The maxim seemed to be "buyer beware." Yet surely, to sell something without mentioning the defects in the product is a form of stealing, taking money under false pretences.

Charles Hodge, a nineteenth-century professor of theology at Princeton Seminary, was scathing in his critique of practices which broke the eighth commandment. He gives various examples of breaches of the commandment, including the following:

> All false pretences in matters of business; representing an article proposed for purchase or exchange to be other and better than it is. This includes a multitude of sins. Articles produced at home are sold as foreign productions, and the price asked and given is determined by this fraudulent representation. Shawls of Paris are sold as Indian; wines manufactured in this country are sold as the productions of France, Portugal, or Madeira. It is said that more Champagne wine is drunk in Russia than is made in France. More cigars are consumed in this country, under the name of Havanas, than Cuba produces. A great part of the paper made in the United States bears the stamp of London or Bristol. This kind of fraud has scarcely any limit. It does not seem to disturb any man's conscience. Worse than this is the selling things as sound and genuine, which in fact are spurious and often worthless.[2]

Have we ever failed to pay fair wages in full and on time?

There is no doubt that many people in business are willing to break commandments for a profit. For example, there are many businesses who pay

---

[2] Charles Hodge, *Systematic Theology* (Grand Rapids: Eerdmans, 1986 reprint; first edition, 1873), vol. 3, 434-435, https://www.ccel.org/ccel/h/hodge/theology3/cache/theology3.pdf.

people a pittance in sweat factories in Asia rather than paying a fair wage to people in their own town or country. Similarly, many try to avoid regulatory regimes in their own countries and engage in practices overseas which would never be allowed in their own countries. This has implications for ethical investment. Christians and churches should certainly not invest money in firms that steal by using unethical methods and by engaging in morally dubious practices. Christians should always pay a fair day's wage for a fair day's work, and that wage should be paid when it is due.

Some politically conservative writers, particularly in America, have used this commandment as an argument in favor of private property. If it is wrong to steal, then it must be right to privately own goods and property. Without denying the logic of this conclusion, it does tend to deflect the force of the commandment away from the rich and the powerful. By using the commandment in this way, to make a political point against socialist/communist views of communal ownership, it is possible to avoid the challenge which the commandment brings to business. It would be much more appropriate to ask about the implications of business practices for greed and for building up riches on earth.

Have we ever used false measures or made false claims or returns?

When the UK moved to decimal currency in February 1971 and the old shillings and pennies were phased out, prices were listed in the new decimal currency. It immediately became apparent that some unscrupulous traders had taken the opportunity to increase profits by marking up prices instead of using the precise equivalent of the old currency. There was an outcry over this and something of a backlash against the guilty parties, and rightly so. This was the equivalent of using false measures. We might note similar issues in currency transfers and in the fees charged for some financial exchanges. One does not have to use false scales to be guilty here.

Another breach of the commandment is to make false claims or returns. Selling a business while concealing the true financial picture of the company, keeping two sets of accounts, or supplying false information in business transactions all involve a breach of the commandment. It is, however, not only those in business who can be guilty in this way. Have we ever avoided paying our proper taxes by making false representations in tax returns? This involves stealing from the government and is a breach of the commandment. We might also break the commandment by stealing from an employer by not doing a fair day's work for our wages, by being lazy, or by helping ourselves to our employer's property, from stationery all the way through to computers and other goods. In all these matters, Christians should, of course, display the highest level of integrity, honesty, and diligence.

Do we value the dignity of work?

When God created Adam, Adam was not left to be idle or to lie around in the sun. He was given work to do, as we see in Genesis 2:15: "The LORD God took the man and put him in the garden of Eden to work it and keep it." In the first chapters of Genesis, we have several creation ordinances, a creation ordinance being defined as something which is part of the very fabric of the natural order as created by God. Work is one of these creation ordinances. When Adam was given work to do, therefore, God was laying out something which was essential to the nature and dignity of being human. As human beings made in the image of God, work gives us dignity and purpose to life.

It is part of the constitution of human beings that we are designed for work and to use our time positively, fruitfully, and for good purpose. It is therefore scandalous when governments develop policies which create or allow unemployment for economic benefit. By so doing, they are denying human beings the dignity and usefulness of work. On the other hand, when governments have a system of benefits and support for the employed which make it more lucrative to avoid work than to seek employment, they are also guilty of an immoral policy.

The importance of work also has a message for those who would do anything to avoid hard work. And there are those who need to be reminded that wasting time at work is stealing from an employer. On the positive side, work enables us to earn money so we can have food, clothes, accommodation, and all the other things which make life bearable and even enjoyable. Paul expressed the importance of work in 2 Thessalonians 3:10-12: "For even when we were with you, we would give you this command: If anyone is not willing to work, let him not eat. For we hear that some among you walk in idleness, not busy at work, but busybodies. Now such persons we command and encourage in the Lord Jesus Christ to do their work quietly and to earn their own living." We are not to obtain the things we need by stealing but by working.

Are we living our whole lives for God, with Him at the center?

The core problem in all decision-making concerns the centrality of God. Adam's first and primary sin was to decide that he would weigh up what

God had said and what Satan had said, and then he, Adam, would make a decision regarding whom to trust. What Adam did was to put himself at the center of all decision-making. Previously, he had lived a God-centered life: what God said, Adam accepted; what God commanded, Adam obeyed. Now he had chosen to live a self-centered life, making his own decisions and ignoring God. This led to disaster for him and for the whole human race. If God is not at the center of our lives and at the center of all decision-making, we will never be able to obey the commandments properly.

The Larger Catechism

The Westminster Larger Catechism (1647) discusses the duties required and the sins forbidden by the eighth commandment:

> Q. 141. What are the duties required in the eighth commandment?
> A. The duties required in the eighth commandment are, truth, faithfulness, and justice in contracts and commerce between man and man; restitution of goods unlawfully detained from the right owners thereof; giving and lending freely, according to our abilities, and the necessities of others; moderation of our judgments, wills, and affections concerning worldly goods; a provident care and study to get, keep, use, and dispose these things which are necessary and convenient for the sustentation of our nature, and suitable to our condition; a lawful calling, and diligence in it; frugality; avoiding unnecessary law-suits, and suretiship, or other like engagements; and an endeavour, by all just and lawful means, to procure, preserve, and further the wealth and outward estate of others, as well as our own.
>
> Q. 142. What are the sins forbidden in the eighth commandment?
> A. The sins forbidden in the eighth commandment, besides the neglect of the duties required, are, theft, robbery, man-stealing, and receiving any thing that is stolen; fraudulent dealing, false weights and measures, removing landmarks, injustice and unfaithfulness in contracts between man and man, or in matters of trust; oppression, extortion, usury, bribery, vexatious law-suits, unjust inclosures and depopulations; ingrossing commodities to enhance the price; unlawful callings, and all other unjust or sinful ways of taking or withholding from our neighbour what belongs to him, or of enriching ourselves; covetousness; inordinate prizing and affecting worldly goods; distrustful and distracting cares and studies in getting, keeping, and using them; envying at the prosperity of others; as likewise idleness, prodigality, wasteful gaming; and all other ways whereby we do unduly prejudice our own outward estate, and defrauding ourselves of the due use and comfort of that estate which God hath given us.

The answers to these two questions clearly demonstrate the scope and breadth of the commandment.

God's Anger

It is clear throughout the Scriptures that God's anger is kindled when His commandments are broken. The most striking example is in Exodus 31, when Moses' brother Aaron made a golden calf for the people to worship while Moses was still on the mountain. There are, of course, other examples, including those relating to the eighth commandment:

The Story of Achan in Joshua 7

The people of Israel under Joshua had defeated Jericho, but the people were told not to take the silver or gold for themselves; it was to go into the Lord's treasury. One of the men, Achan, disobeyed this and took some of the gold and silver for himself. The Lord was angry at this, and the next time the people went into battle, against the city of Ai, they were heavily defeated. Joshua realized what had happened, and finally Achan was discovered and punished. Achan stole, God was angry, and judgment followed.

The Story of David and Nathan in 2 Samuel 12

When David arranged to have Bathsheba's husband, Uriah, killed so he could take Bathsheba for himself, it was as if he had stolen her from her husband. When Nathan the prophet went to see David after this incident, he told him a story, which is recorded in 2 Samuel 12. It was a story of a rich man who had everything he could need, but when a visitor came, he stole the pet lamb of a poor man and served that to his visitor. David was furious at this and claimed that the man who did this deserved to die, until Nathan pointed out that he was the man! David was a thief in the eyes of God, and God was angry.

The Story of Naboth's Vineyard in 1 Kings 21

King Ahab wanted Naboth's vineyard, but Naboth refused to sell it to him since it was his ancestral land. Ahab's wife, Jezebel, assured him that she would get the vineyard for him. She arranged for Naboth to be falsely accused and stoned to death. Then Ahab took possession of the vineyard, which had effectively been stolen from Naboth. God's anger was apparent in what followed, as described in 1 Kings 21:17-19: "Then the word of the LORD came to Elijah the Tishbite, saying, 'Arise, go down to meet Ahab king of Israel, who is in Samaria; behold, he is in the vineyard of Naboth, where he has gone to take possession. And you shall say to him, "Thus says the LORD: 'Have you killed, and also taken possession?'" And you shall say to him, "Thus says the LORD: 'In the place where dogs licked up the blood of Naboth shall dogs lick your own blood.'"'" Ahab and Jezebel stole the vineyard, and judgment followed.

The Story of Judas in John 12:1-6

On one occasion when Jesus was in Bethany at the home of Mary, Martha, and Lazarus, Mary anointed His feet with an expensive perfume. We read in verses 4-6, "But Judas Iscariot, one of his disciples (he who was about to betray him), said, 'Why was this ointment not sold for three hundred denarii and given to the poor?' He said this, not because he cared about the poor, but because he was a thief, and having charge of the moneybag he used to help himself to what was put into it." Judas Iscariot was a thief as well as a traitor and duly incurred the wrath of God.

Restitution

If we steal and are conscience-stricken, we must turn to Christ without delay and find forgiveness. We must also make restitution. We see those principles clearly demonstrated in the story of Zacchaeus as recorded in Luke 19:1-10.

The story of Zacchaeus is the final incident in the long account of Jesus' journey to Jerusalem, where He was to be crucified. It is only contained in the Gospel of Luke, and it seems likely that Luke saw the story as being a summary of the gospel. As Professor Howard Marshall says, "It is a supreme example of the universality of the gospel offer to tax collectors and sinners."[3] The lessons we learn from this encounter are of the utmost importance for our understanding of salvation.

From what this passage says, we can assume that Zacchaeus was one of the leading tax men of his day, and he may well have been the general tax-farmer of Jericho. In other words, he was the government agent in Jericho, responsible to the Roman authorities for collecting taxes from all the people, and he would have had other tax collectors working under him. It is

---

[3] I. H. Marshall, *The Gospel of Luke: A Commentary on the Greek Text,* The New International Greek Testament Commentary (Grand Rapids: Eerdmans, 1978), 694.

important to note that the tax collector was not paid for his work by the Roman authorities; rather, he was expected to charge sufficient from each person to meet his quota to the government and have enough left over for his wages. This meant that he could charge whatever amount of tax he liked!

As a result of this situation, tax collectors were hated by the people. They were hated first because they were quislings working for the Romans and second, because they charged exorbitant taxes and so cheated the people. As a chief tax collector and a rich one, Zacchaeus was no doubt hated more than most. On this particular day, we can imagine Zacchaeus trying to find a vantage point to see Jesus. Like everyone else, he had heard of Jesus and was anxious to see Him. The problem was that Zacchaeus was, we are told, "small of stature," so he could not see Jesus for the crowd. You can also imagine that those in the crowd who recognized him would have taken great delight in pushing him out of the way or standing in front of him. Eventually he solved this problem by climbing up a tree so he would get a good view as Jesus passed.

Then a remarkable thing happened. Jesus came along, saw Zacchaeus, and told him that he was coming to stay at his house. We are told that when those around him saw this, they objected strongly, saying that Jesus had gone to be the guest of "a sinner." They had already forgotten Jesus' earlier rebuke, when He told them that it is the sick who need a doctor, not those who are well. Paul summed it up very well in 1 Timothy 1:15: "... Christ Jesus came into the world to save sinners."

Despite the outcry of these Jews, Jesus went to be with Zacchaeus, and a remarkable change took place in the man's life. Zacchaeus had been one of those who desired riches, but his encounter with Jesus changed all of that. When Jesus met with Zacchaeus, Zacchaeus' life was transformed, and getting more and more money was no longer the driving force in his life. The Spirit of God came into his life and changed him. He turned away from his former way of life, and he turned to God.

Zacchaeus showed his repentance by giving much of his money away. The Old Testament gives instructions as to how much should be repaid when a thief is seeking forgiveness. We are told that a thief must return what he stole plus a fifth extra. Zacchaeus did far more than this. He returned four times as much as he had taken and, on top of this, he gave half of his money to the poor. Zacchaeus was a thief who stole from his own people, but he repented and made restitution. This is the biblical pattern for everyone who steals and then realizes his sin.

Conclusion

In conclusion, we should pause to consider the grace of contentment. Stealing is the complete opposite of contentment. In Hebrews 13:5, we are told to be content with what we have, which is the way to avoid stealing. After all, theft is often the conclusion of a number of sins, including envy, greed, and covetousness. May God help each of us to be content, to keep this commandment, and to be very careful in all our dealings.

The Ninth Commandment:

YOU SHALL NOT BEAR FALSE WITNESS AGAINST YOUR NEIGHBOR

Words That Hurt and Words That Heal[1]

Samuel Logan, United States

The law of God is nothing more or less than the externalization of the very being and moral character of God. When God spoke, He was expressing who He was and is, and for this reason, obedience to the Word of God is the path of life. Thus, when we study the Decalogue, we are, in at least one sense, studying the very nature of God. When we obey these commands, we are on the path of life, reflecting God's very nature back to Him as we were created to do when He said, "Let us make man in our image, after our likeness ..." (Genesis 1:26).

But, of course, we – in Adam – did not originally obey God's word. We sinned in Adam and, in doing so, we chose the path of death. If there was to be life for God's human creation, He would have to provide that life Himself in a way consistent with His very nature. And that He did ... in Jesus. As Jesus said to Thomas, "I am the way, and the truth, and the life. No one comes to the Father except through me" (John 14:6).

Jesus is *the* way, *the only way*, back to God for sinners. No amount of obedience to the commands of the Decalogue will earn salvation for sinners. Salvation is *by grace alone through faith in Christ alone*. This is why the gospel really is *very* good news for sinners. This is also the reason why Jesus is called "the Word" in John 1 – He is the Word of salvation; He is the reason for the creation of the New Jerusalem in Revelation 21. He is *the Word of rejoicing.*

Why then should we bother with the Decalogue? Because, in our earthly lives, God deserves the worship which our being "back in His image" brings Him.[2] Obedience to the Decalogue thus accomplishes the

---

[1] Some of this material is taken from Samuel T. Logan, Jr., *The Good Name: The Power of Words That Hurt and Words That Heal* (Greensboro, N.C.: New Growth Press, 2019); used with permission.

[2] See Jonathan Edwards, *Treatise on Religious Affections*, for a full explanation.

fulfillment of the two "greatest commandments." Jesus, God Incarnate, was asked about this, and His answer is recorded in Matthew 22:37-40: "You shall love the Lord your God with all your heart and with all your soul and with all your mind. This is the great and first commandment. And a second is like it: You shall love your neighbor as yourself. On these two commandments depend all the Law and the Prophets." What it means to love the Lord my God with all my heart, soul, and mind is described in Commandments 1-4. What it means to love my neighbor as myself is described in Commandments 5-10.

Because Jesus paid the penalty which we deserved, we now have the ability and the privilege, the *joyful* privilege, of bringing to the Triune God the worship and obedience He deserves. This includes the privilege of speaking the gospel to other sinners – what a joy to realize that words we utter about Jesus might be used by the Holy Spirit to bring sinners into union with Christ. And this, in turn, is the pathway to the extraordinary eternal blessedness of Revelation 21 and 22.

In today's world (2021), the ninth commandment seems especially important. Here are some evidences for this claim:

1. Two recent issues of byFaith, the official quarterly magazine of the Presbyterian Church in America, dealt with applications of this commandment: The April 2019 issue, on the cover of which was the headline "Words That Honor God"[3] and the first issue of 2021, on the cover of which was the headline "The Power of Words"[4].
2. Ongoing secular source warnings like this continue to appear: "The Holocaust did not begin with killing; it began with words."[5]
3. "The Dangerous Speech Project," which attempts to deal with the very reality the ninth commandment forbids, has recently been created.[6]
4. Especially in a post-Covid-19 world, the trustworthiness of *words* spoken by political and scientific leaders matters a great deal to all of us on planet earth.[7]

---

[3] https://byfaithonline.com/words-that-honor-gods-word/.
[4] https://byfaithonline.com/the-power-of-words/.
[5] https://www.washingtonpost.com/news/acts-of-faith/wp/2016/11/22/the-holocaust-did-not-begin-with-killing-it-began-with-words-museum-condemns-alt-right-meeting/.
[6] https://dangerousspeech.org/guide/.
[7] See the numerous publications on this subject mentioned here: https://biologos.org/common-questions/should-we-trust-science?gclid=Cj0KCQjw1PSDBhDbARIsAPeTqreB7P_nNDpCdS0Z5TLhsZvLOyBxPkMRmD0gHDMe8W_FZ76gjDRBGCIaAu5yEALw_wcB.

Numerous other contemporary examples could be provided.[8]

Speech matters ... *greatly!*

Indeed, the source which evangelical Christians trust more than any other, the Scriptures of the Old and New Testaments, focuses extraordinary attention on the act of speaking. Beginning with Genesis 1:3, "And God *said,*" that word appears 383 times in the original of Genesis 1, the vast majority of its occurrences coming from the Hebrew *amar*. Some of the other NIV translations of *amar* include "ordered, commanded, demanded, and declared." This speaks clearly of the creative power which the original Old Testament writers ascribed to language. In the New Testament, the emphasis continues. Over and over again, when Jesus speaks, things happen: water becomes wine, the dead come to life, lepers are cleansed.

In this context, we come to the ninth commandment: "You shall not bear false *witness* against your neighbor." (emphasis added)

It is interesting here that the original Hebrew used in Exodus 20:16 places particular emphasis on the giving of *legal* evidence. It appears four times in Genesis 31; and verses 43-48, which include the dialogue between Laban and Jacob, provide a further sense of the covenantal formality suggested by this term, sometimes translated "testimony" and other times "witness."

> Then Laban answered and said to Jacob, "The daughters are my daughters, the children are my children, the flocks are my flocks, and all that you see is mine. But what can I do this day for these my daughters or for their children whom they have borne? Come now, let us make a covenant, you and I. And let it be a **witness** between you and me."
>
> So Jacob took a stone and set it up as a pillar. And Jacob said to his kinsmen, "Gather stones." And they took stones and made a heap, and they ate there by the heap. Laban called it Jegar-sahadutha, but Jacob called it Galeed.
>
> Laban said, "This heap is a **witness** between you and me today." Therefore he named it Galeed ... (emphasis added)

Further to this point are Deuteronomy 17:6 and 19:15.

---

[8] See also an article in the first 2021 issue of *Christianity Today* entitled "When a Word Is Worth a Thousand Complaints." https://www.christianitytoday.com/ct/2021/january-february/bible-translation-devil-in-details.html, and a similar article describing how Wheaton College determined to change the way it has honored alumnus and martyred missionary Jim Elliott because of one word in the plaque bearing Elliott's name. https://www.christianitytoday.com/news/2021/march/wheaton-college-missionary-plaque-jim-elliot-waorani.html.

On the evidence of two **witnesses** or of three **witnesses** the one who is to die shall be put to death; a person shall not be put to death on the evidence of one **witness**.

A single **witness** shall not suffice against a person for any crime or for any wrong in connection with any offense that he has committed. Only on the evidence of two **witnesses** or of three **witnesses** shall a charge be established. (emphasis added)

Repeatedly, the Hebrew word which the Holy Spirit inspired for these passages of Scripture contains elements of both power and legal formality.

Further, the *way* in which the commandment has been expressed suggests that what is being proscribed here is with regard to *individualistic* verbal comments about another person. There clearly is – and must be – a recognized and accepted process by means of which error can be addressed. And later in this chapter, I will provide four specific examples of what evangelical denominations have done to accomplish this. The ongoing *testimony* of Scripture has been to warn against any condemnation of a person or of a group of people that does not take into account the appropriate structure which binds all members of that group together.

Throughout the ages, evangelical Christians have codified these elements in their formal confessions. The Westminster Confession of Faith and Catechisms were written in the mid-seventeenth century and have been used by generations of Presbyterians ever since. Here is how the Larger Catechism explains what is commanded and what is prohibited by the ninth commandment.

> Q. 144. What are the duties required in the ninth commandment?
>
> A. The duties required in the ninth commandment are, the preserving and promoting of truth between man and man, and the good name of our neighbour, as well as our own; appearing and standing for the truth; and from the heart, sincerely, freely, clearly, and fully, speaking the truth, and only the truth, in matters of judgment and justice, and in all other things whatsoever; a charitable esteem of our neighbours; loving, desiring, and rejoicing in their good name; sorrowing for, and covering of their infirmities; freely acknowledging of their gifts and graces, defending their innocency; a ready receiving of a good report, and unwillingness to admit of an evil report, concerning them; discouraging tale-bearers, flatterers, and slanderers; love and care of our own good name, and defending it when need requireth; keeping of lawful promises; studying and practicing of whatsoever things are true, honest, lovely, and of good report.
>
> Q. 145. What are the sins forbidden in the ninth commandment?
>
> A. The sins forbidden in the ninth commandment are, all prejudicing the truth, and the good name of our neighbours, as well as our own, especially

in public judicature; giving false evidence, suborning false witnesses, wittingly appearing and pleading for an evil cause, out-facing and overbearing the truth; passing unjust sentence, calling evil good, and good evil; rewarding the wicked according to the work of the righteous, and the righteous according to the work of the wicked; forgery, concealing the truth, undue silence in a just cause, and holding our peace when iniquity calleth for either a reproof from ourselves, or complaint to others; speaking the truth unseasonably, or maliciously to a wrong end, or perverting it to a wrong meaning, or in doubtful or equivocal expressions, to the prejudice of truth or justice; speaking untruth, lying, slandering, backbiting, detracting, talebearing, whispering, scoffing, reviling, rash, harsh, and partial censuring; misconstructing intentions, words, and actions; flattering, vain-glorious boasting; thinking or speaking too highly or too meanly of ourselves or others; denying the gifts and graces of God; aggravating smaller faults; hiding, excusing, or extenuating of sins, when called to a free confession; unnecessary discovering of infirmities; raising false rumors, receiving and countenancing evil reports, and stopping our ears against just defense; evil suspicion; envying or grieving at the deserved credit of any, endeavoring or desiring to impair it, rejoicing in their disgrace and infamy; scornful contempt, fond admiration; breach of lawful promises; neglecting such things as are of good report, and practicing, or not avoiding ourselves, or not hindering what we can in others, such things as procure an ill name.

One does not have to be part of the Presbyterian or Reformed tradition to appreciate the force of this explanation, especially in light of the 105 different Scripture passages which the authors of the catechism cited to support their conclusions. Here are just a few of those Bible texts, well worth reading to get a sense of the force of the Bible's teaching on this topic:

O, LORD, who shall sojourn in your tent?
Who shall dwell on your holy hill?
He who walks blamelessly and does what is right
    and speaks the truth in his heart;
who does not slander with his tongue
    and does no evil to his neighbor,
    nor takes up a reproach against his friend (Psalm 15:1-3).

Therefore, having put away falsehood, and let each one of you speak the truth with his neighbor, for we are members one of another (Ephesians 4:25).

Do not speak evil against one another, brothers. The one who speaks against a brother or judges his brother, speaks evil against the law and judges the law. But if you judge the law, you are not a doer of the law but a judge (James 4:11).

These kinds of concerns are not exclusive to Presbyterians, many of whom subscribe to The Westminster Confession of Faith and Catechisms. Here are the ways in which some other evangelical Christians have described the requirements of the ninth commandment.

The Heidelberg Catechism was written in Germany in 1563 and is the central doctrinal standard of many Continental evangelicals. It says this about the ninth commandment.

> Question 112. What is required in the ninth commandment?
> That I bear false witness against no man, nor falsify any man's words; that I be no backbiter, nor slanderer; that I do not judge, nor join in condemning any man rashly, or unheard; but that I avoid all sorts of lies and deceit, as the proper works of the devil, unless I would bring down upon me the heavy wrath of God; likewise, that in judgment and all other dealings I love the truth, speak it uprightly and confess it; also that I defend and promote, as much as I am able, the honor and good character of my neighbour.

As with The Westminster Larger Catechism, careful Scripture citations are provided in support of this interpretation of the ninth commandment. Seventeen Bible passages are cited; thirteen of those are also passages cited by The Westminster Larger Catechism.

The similarity of these two historic Protestant catechisms regarding the ninth commandment should compel our attention. Indeed, this similarity is found in many other historic Christian texts. For example, The Baltimore Catechism of the Roman Catholic Church affirms that, by this commandment, "We are commanded to speak the truth in all things, but especially in what concerns the good name and honor of others." It further stipulates that this commandment "forbids lies, rash judgment, detraction, calumny, and the telling of secrets we are bound to keep," and it argues that a person breaks the commandment when "without sufficient reason, he believes something harmful to another's character" or when "without a good reason, he makes known the hidden faults of another."

The Methodist Episcopal Church states, "The ninth commandment concerns truth and man's good name." And the Baptist Catechism deals with the requirements and prohibitions of the ninth commandment in this way.

> Question 82. What is required in the ninth commandment?
> The ninth commandment requireth the maintaining and promoting of truth between man and man, and of our own and our neighbour's good name, especially in witness-bearing (Proverbs 14:5, 25; Zechariah 8:16; 3 John 12).

Question 83. What is forbidden in the ninth commandment?
The ninth commandment forbiddeth whatsoever is prejudicial to the truth, or injurious to our own or our neighbour's good name (Leviticus 19:16; 1 Samuel 17:28; Psalm 15:3).

The Orthodox Church's Catechism of St. Philaret deals with the issue in a different but powerful way.

Question 597. What is forbidden under the words false witness?
1. False witness in a court of justice; when men bear witness, inform, or complain falsely against any one.
2. False witness out of court, when men slander any one behind his back, or blame him to his face unjustly.

And questions 598 and 599 ask what may be the most challenging questions of all.

Question 598: But is it allowable to censure others when they are really to blame?
No; the gospel does not allow us to judge even of the real vices or faults of our neighbors, unless we are called by any special office to do so, for their punishment or amendment. Judge not, that ye be not judged (Matthew 7:1).

Question 599. Are not such lies allowable as involve no purpose of hurting our neighbor?
No; for they are inconsistent with love and respect for our neighbor, and unworthy of a man, much more of a Christian, who has been created for truth and love.[9]

Where did the writers of various catechisms get this idea regarding respect for the good name of a neighbor and regarding who is a neighbor? First, the Hebrew word translated *neighbor* in the ninth commandment, *re'a*, does not necessarily have specific religious denotations. Throughout the Old Testament, it seems to have a wide variety of meanings. It is used to identify a person with whom one is close, and it is occasionally used to suggest a spouse or a lover (Jeremiah 3:1; Hosea 3:1). More often, it is used in the context of general friendship (1 Samuel 30:26), but occasionally there can even be the sense of the *re'a* being an opponent (Exodus 21:18).

With this understanding of what the Bible says about our neighbor, we should not assume that the ninth commandment applies only to what we

---

[9] The online sources for these various catechisms can be found in Samuel T. Logan, Jr., *The Good Name*, 169-170.

say about other Christians. According to the totality of biblical teaching, the Scriptures seem to teach that the God-given rules about telling the truth mean that there must be no difference in how we talk to and about Christians and how we talk to and about non-Christians.

Next is the matter of the meaning of the word *name*, which is mentioned in numerous evangelical discussions of the ninth commandment. The English word *name* appears 798 times in the New International Version of the Bible, and both the Hebrew word most often translated "name" (*sem*) and the Greek word most often translated "name" (*onoma*) carry the strong connotation of "reputation" or "character." The authors of the various catechisms clearly had done their exegesis when they set out to explain the meaning of the ninth commandment.

The same can be said for John Calvin, who began his commentary on the ninth commandment with these words: "God here makes a provision for every man's character and good name, lest any should be undeservedly weighed down by calumnies and false accusations." Calvin continues, "Although God seems only to prescribe that no one, for the purpose of injuring the innocent, should go into court, and publicly testify against him, yet it is plain that the faithful are prohibited from all false accusations, and not only such as are circulated in the streets, but those which are stirred in private houses and secret corners."[10]

Recall that Adam was given the task of naming the animals. Numerous writers, both religious and secular, have commented on the way naming is a fundamental aspect of human identity. One of the most influential secular resources on this subject is Ernst Cassirer's *Language and Myth*, in which he examines "the notion that name and essence bear a necessary and internal relation to each other, that the name does not merely denote but actually is of the essence of its object, that the potency of the real thing is contained in the name."[11]

Our words have power – this is precisely what we must remember. Human words never create reality in the sense that God's words do, but they may create impressions or attitudes, and those, in turn, may affect the lives of others. The ninth commandment *requires* that we carefully consider this, especially when we speak words of judgment. Beyond what we owe our neighbors simply out of obedient charity, it is especially critical that when we talk about other professing Christians, we

---

[10] John Calvin, *Commentaries on the Last Four Books of Moses, Arranged in the Form of a Harmony*, (Grand Rapids: Baker, 1998), 3: 179-180.

[11] Ernst Cassirer, *Language and Myth* (New York, Harper and Row, 1946) Kindle Edition, Location 96.

remember that we are communicating something about the Savior whose name we and they together bear.

The book of Acts tells the origins of our specific name. It begins in Acts 10, with Peter telling a room full of Gentiles that everyone who believes in Christ receives forgiveness of sins through His name. "While Peter was still saying these things, the Holy Spirit fell on all who heard the word. And the believers from among the circumcised who had come with Peter were amazed, because the gift of the Holy Spirit was poured out even on the Gentiles" (Acts 10:44-45).

As if to emphasize the kingdom importance of those events, Peter repeated the story to Jerusalem Jews, who affirmed those conclusions and authorized a mission to Antioch to spread the word. After a year of teaching, the results were clear: "And in Antioch the disciples were first called Christians" (Acts 11:26). No longer merely "disciples," but "Christians."

Scholars have debated the precise meaning of the word "Christian" and its likely root in the Greek word *christos*, which means "anointed one." But again, it is John Calvin whose suggestions are most relevant to this study. In his commentary on Acts 11:26, Calvin writes, "But when [the disciples] began plainly to be called that which they were, the use of the name served greatly to set forth the glory of Christ, because by this means they referred all their religion to Christ alone. This was, therefore, a most excellent worship for the city of Antioch, that Christ brought forth his name thence like a standard, whereby it might be made known to all the world that there were some people whose Captain was Christ, and which did glory in his name."[12]

When we speak as Christians or speak about Christians or use that name, it reflects directly on Christ, to whom that name points. Look again at the third chapter of James: "With [the tongue] we bless our Lord and Father, and with it we curse people who are made in the likeness of God. From the same mouth come blessing and cursing. My brothers, these things ought not to be so. Does a spring pour forth from the same opening both fresh and salt water? Can a fig tree, my brothers, bear olives, or a grapevine produce figs? Neither can a salt pond yield fresh water" (James 3:9-12).

If we see figs on a tree, we know what it says about that tree. The words we use reflect powerfully on our very identity if we call ourselves Christian. If our words are nasty and divisive, those around us are likely to draw conclusions about the One whose name we claim. Also, the words we use

---

[12] John Calvin, *Commentary on The Acts of the Apostles* (Grand Rapids: Baker, 1998), 1: 472.

about other Christians are heard by non-Christians, and, rightly or wrongly, those non-Christians use our words to define Christianity. Given the power of words, this should not surprise us.

Consider what the Bible requires of Christians with what Frank Viola uncovers in his blog post "Warning: The World Is Watching How We Christians Treat One Another." Viola used Google to identify the most frequent way searchers complete the question "Why are Christians so ...?" Among the top results were the words "mean," "hypocritical," and "judgmental". There has been some pushback to his method, but there still is enough substance to his argument to help us see the relevance of concern for our neighbors' good names. Here is the essence of his argument:

> It's not uncommon for some Christians to throw verbal assaults at one another on Facebook, blogs, Twitter, and other Internet venues. As a result, the world sees people who profess to follow Jesus – the Prince of Peace – fighting, misrepresenting one another, and even "blocking" one another ... Civil disagreement and even debate, when done in the spirit of Christ, are healthy and helpful. But when disagreements descend into second-guessing motives, distortions of one another's words, mischaracterizations of one another's views, and personal attacks, then we've moved into the flesh. The net is that the name of Jesus gets tarnished in no small way.[13]

It should concern us if the words "mean" and "hypocritical" turn up frequently in that Google request and if such words as "loving" and "gracious" appear very rarely. There surely is ground for James Davidson Hunter's powerful comment, "If Christians cannot extend grace through faithful presence within the body of believers, they will not be able to extend grace to those outside."[14] In summary, when we say anything about other professed Christians, the total content of our remarks – both denotation and connotation – gets applied, whether we intend it or not, to Him whose name we share. Of course, keeping silent in the face of error or sin is absolutely wrong. No question! But how we speak is as important as that we speak, because the good name ultimately at stake is the name of Jesus Christ.

This leads to another profound teaching of the catechisms about bearing true witness. The Heidelberg Catechism cautions against "condemning anyone rashly" (question 112). The Westminster Larger Catechism argues that the ninth commandment forbids "speaking the truth unseasonably" and that the commandment also prohibits speaking the truth "maliciously

---

[13] https://frankviola.org/2013/01/14/warning/.
[14] James Hunter, *To Change the World* (Oxford, 2010), Kindle edition, location 96.

to a wrong end, or perverting it to a wrong meaning, or in doubtful or equivocal expressions" (question 145). Mere verbal accuracy is not, by itself, adequate.

Here is an example. Pastor X, as part of a sermon on the seventh commandment, spends a significant but appropriate amount of time interpreting that commandment in Exodus through Matthew 5:28, where Jesus says, "But I say to you that everyone who looks at a woman with lustful intent has already committed adultery with her in his heart." The pastor continues by asserting that, according to Jesus, he himself and probably every other man in his congregation is an adulterer. One of his opponents in the congregation later tweets that his pastor has just admitted to being an adulterer. That statement is accurate, but it clearly perverts the pastor's words to a wrong meaning.

Yet there are times when we must speak up. Leviticus 5:1 says, "If anyone sins in that he hears a public adjuration to testify, and though he is a witness, whether he has seen or come to know the matter, yet does not speak, he shall bear his iniquity." Proverbs 31:8-9 instructs us, "Open your mouth for the mute, for the rights of all who are destitute. Open your mouth, judge righteously, defend the rights of the poor and needy."

No question then: When confronted by what we understand to be sin, we must speak out. The question is, "How?" How do we make sure that all the other requirements of the ninth commandment are also followed?

Here are a few guidelines.

1. Our specific words matter.

In Matthew 12, Jesus warns that everyone will have to account for empty words he has spoken. As always, context matters. Jesus' public ministry caused both jubilation and hatred, and these produced a major confrontation in this chapter. After Jesus healed a man on the Sabbath, the crowds swarmed Him, and He healed many of them (v. 15). "Then a demon-oppressed man who was blind and mute was brought to him, and he healed him, so that the man spoke and saw. And all the people were amazed, and said, 'Can this be the Son of David?'" (vv. 22-23). Yes, of course, it could be – and it was!

Not everyone saw things this way. "But when the Pharisees heard it, they said, 'It is only by Beelzebul, the prince of demons, that this man casts out demons'" (v. 24). Jesus' response to the Pharisees concludes with this powerful statement:

"You brood of vipers! How can you speak good, when you are evil? For out of the abundance of the heart the mouth speaks. The good person out of his good treasure brings forth good, and the evil person out of his evil treasure brings forth evil. I tell you, on the day of judgment people will give account for every careless word they speak, *for by your words you will be justified, and by your words you will be condemned*" (Matthew 12:34-37; emphasis added).

No, Jesus is not repudiating the doctrine of justification by faith alone. However, He is making abundantly clear that our speech matters. Both the words and the condition of the heart in which the speech originates have huge and possibly eternal consequences. The Pharisees had first questioned Jesus about the man healed on the Sabbath, and Jesus had responded with a clear and specific answer. It is okay to ask questions. And when those questions are asked without the use of lying labels, they can be answered simply and directly. But labeling Jesus a disciple of Beelzebul crosses a line, just as our labeling a minister in good standing a heretic crosses a line.

To stay on the right side of the God-honoring line while still raising necessary questions and concerns takes work. But such work brings honor to our Lord, and nothing is more important than that.

2. Check your motive.

If we genuinely love those with whom we disagree, we will deeply desire that they come to the truth and, in that truth, find the blessings of God. The lesson of Jonah must always remain uppermost in our mind when we are conversing about or with those whom we think are wrong. Jonah seemed to detest the fact that the Ninevites to whom he preached repented in response to God's word. But to borrow from God's words to Jonah, should we not have great concern for those whom we believe are wrong? Should not our speech to and about them express not just disagreement but also loving concern? Before, during, and after we speak any words of disagreement, we need to make sure our most fundamental motive is love.

We must not bear false witness, especially when communicating about a matter on which we disagree with other Christians. We should be asking, what words can I use that are most likely to communicate truth, with a clear, ultimate purpose of leading my antagonist to the joy and blessing of the truth? If we think other people are actually Ninevites, do we speak to or about them in ways that push them toward the judgment we think they deserve? Or do we find ways of speaking which are most likely, in the power of the Holy Spirit, to attract them to the truth? This is what I believe is meant by "speaking the truth in love" (Ephesians 4:15).

Yes, it is challenging to try to speak hard things in love, but that is exactly what God did for us in Christ. And that is what He offers us the opportunity to do for others.

3. Stay on point and cast no aspersions.

The third point follows directly from the first two. We should stay on point when discussing issues and, as appropriate, discuss them vigorously. But we should never cast aspersions on the intelligence, the theological orthodoxy, or the moral standing of the professed Christians with whom we are disagreeing.

I once had occasion to comment favorably on Facebook about what has been called "Christotelic hermeneutics," an approach to biblical interpretation which suggests that we read the ultimate meaning of *all* of Scripture in terms of what the New Testament tells us about the person and work of Jesus Christ. In response to my comments, one professed Christian posted a response that my opinion should carry no weight because of my "liberal politics" and "obsequious" relationship with one of my sons. I certainly may have been wrong in my approach to Scripture. And I suppose that someone could accuse me of being liberal politically, depending on how he or she defines it. I also may very well have been a bad parent. But there was no clear and necessary connection between either of these characteristics and Christotelic hermeneutics. Perhaps there is some connection, but if there is, staying on point requires that this connection be clearly made.

Another way of saying this is to insist that in every circumstance of expressing disagreement with another Christian, we must concentrate our words on the issue and not on the character of the person who has made what we believe to be an error.

4. Remember the corporate nature of the church – both visible and invisible.

The ongoing testimony of the Scriptures has been to warn against any condemnation of a person or a group of people that does not take into account the appropriate structure which the members of that group share together. The World Reformed Fellowship is an organizational member of the World Evangelical Alliance and, therefore, WRF members are, either directly or indirectly, members of the WEA. Several WRF member churches have made powerful and official statements about this matter. Four such statements are below.

The Evangelical Presbyterian Church

Scriptural law is the basis of all ecclesiastical discipline because it is the revelation of God's holy will. Proper disciplinary principles are set forth in the Scriptures and must be followed. According to Matthew 18:15 and Galatians 6:1, these principles include instruction in the Word and the individuals' responsibility to admonish one another. If the initial admonition is rejected, then one or more witnesses must be called (Matthew 18:16). If rejection persists, then the church must act through her courts in proper order for the exercise of discipline. No charge involving a personal offense will be received unless the offended person alleges and proves to the court evidence demonstrating that he has followed the procedures required under Matthew 18:15-16 and Galatians 6:1. If anyone knows a Minister to be guilty of a private offense, he should warn him in private. But if the offense be persisted in, or become public, he should bring the case to the attention of some other Minister of the Presbytery.

The Free Church of Scotland

Discipline is part of the function of ministers and elders as those called to bear rule in the Church of Christ. It must be administered in the spirit of loving concern for the recovery of any that are "out of the way." Distress and sadness there may be, but there ought never to be a spirit of bitterness. Those who endeavour to apply discipline must always remember that the important thing is not the winning of an argument but the making safe of one who has become endangered and whose predicament also menaces the fellowship of the faithful. There is no place for a spirit of rivalry in any disciplinary process. That a spirit of meekness and fear should characterize those embarking on a disciplinary action the apostle emphasizes: "Consider thyself ... also in the flesh." No one dare indulge in a "holier than thou" attitude. The hurt of one Christian is the hurt of all and directs all to the only effective Healer, our Lord Jesus Christ.

The Presbyterian Church in America

Scriptural law is the basis of all discipline because it is the revelation of God's Holy will. Proper disciplinary principles are set forth in the Scriptures and must be followed. They are:
    a) Instruction in the Word;

> b) Individuals' responsibility to admonish one another (Matthew 18:15; Galatians 6:1);
> c) If the admonition is rejected, then the calling of one or more witnesses (Matthew 18:16);
> d) If rejection persists, then the Church must act through her court unto admonition, suspension, excommunication and deposition.
>
> Steps (a) through (d) must be followed in proper order for the exercise of discipline.

The Presbyterian Church of Australia

> Ordinarily a matter appearing to call for the exercise of discipline shall not be proceeded with formally until the Court, or a committee appointed by the Court, has in private conferred in a loving way with the alleged offender with a view to avoiding the necessity of formal process if possible. The result of this conference shall be reported to the Court in general terms bearing in mind the nature and purpose of the conference and that report shall be confidential to the Court and be kept in a record apart.

This is certainly not the only way in which the corporate nature of the church may be remembered and expressed. But it is one good way of assuring that "the good name" of one's neighbor is protected and false witness is avoided.

How might this same goal be accomplished when there is no single church or organization to which both the possible offender and the possible accuser belong? A difficult question ... as are many of the questions about faithful obedience to the various commandments.

Here is one possibility: If there is no single church or organization to which I and a person who I believe is sinning belong, I should seek out an "accountability partner," someone with whom I share fundamental biblical and theological commitments. I should ask him/her to examine the words or actions of the person that I believe are wrong and the response that I am planning, and to advise me if there is a better, more biblical way to say or do what I am considering. Having inconsistently proceeded in this way in the past, I know this approach is better than simply "blasting away," speaking without careful consideration of my words.

My point is that those who are as committed to obeying the Ten Commandments as they are to reporting on the errors and/or sins of others *will* find a way. The honor of the God who gave those commandments warrants the effort.

Because of concern for the ninth commandment, the World Reformed Fellowship sponsored a Consultation on Christian Civility in New

York City in October 2017. The full results of that Consultation provide some possible guidance toward the goal mentioned immediately above and may be found here: https://wrf.global/blog/blog-2/society/taking-stand-christian-civility.

The point of that Consultation and the basic point of this article regarding the meaning of the ninth commandment can be summarized quite briefly. That summary appears in the Sermon on the Mount, directly from the mouth of Jesus:

> So whatever you wish that others would do to you, do also to them, for this is the Law and the Prophets (Matthew 7:12).

If we always speak about others as we desire that they speak about us, we will have fulfilled the ninth commandment.

The Tenth Commandment:

YOU SHALL NOT SET YOUR DESIRE ...

Davi Charles Gomes, Brazil

I still remember how enthralled I was in my early teens with Francis Schaeffer's insight into the tenth commandment.[1] "The climax of the Ten Commandments is the Tenth Commandment," said Schaeffer. For him, the fact that it is an inward commandment, which, in a way, gets broken before breaking any of the previous nine commandments, made it the "hub of the wheel." He explained:

> Coveting is the negative side of the positive commands, "Thou shalt love the Lord, thy God, with all thy heart, and with all thy soul, and with all thy mind. ... Thou shalt love thy neighbor as thyself" (Matthew 22:37, 39).[2]

Schaeffer nailed his point for me in the example of the apostle Paul, who otherwise would consider his old self "... alive apart from the law," were it not for the conviction of breaking the tenth commandment, as he clearly states in Romans 7:7-9.

Years later, when reading J. Douma's important book on the Ten Commandments, though especially intrigued by his refinement of the idea of the tenth commandment as understood by Schaeffer (and by John Calvin, as well), the point that struck me was something else. As to the refinement, Douma suggested that the broader concept of the commandment as

---

[1] Exodus 20:17: "You shall not covet your neighbor's house; you shall not covet your neighbor's wife, or his male servant, or his female servant, or his ox, or his donkey, or anything that is your neighbor's." Deuteronomy 5:21: "And you shall not covet your neighbor's wife. And you shall not desire your neighbor's house, his field, or his male servant, or his female servant, his ox, or his donkey, or anything that is your neighbor's." *The Holy Bible*: English Standard Versio. (2016). Wheaton, IL: Crossway Bibles.

[2] F. A. Schaeffer, (1982). *True Spirituality*, in *The Complete Works of Francis A. Schaeffer: A Christian Worldview* (Vol. 3, p. 203). Westchester, IL: Crossway Books. For a more technical discussion of this point as well as of Schaeffer's point about the relationship between breaking the tenth commandment and breaking all commandments, see: J. I. Durham, (1987). *Word Biblical Commentary: Exodus* (Vol. 3, p. 298). Dallas: Word, Incorporated.

rendering "a verdict about the human heart" (which he sees as the starting point for Calvin) should actually be the point of arrival, after considering the "literal and direct meaning of the Tenth Commandment and only then move to its deeper significance."[3]

Setting Your Desires

The something else that struck me, however, was Douma's coupling of this basic idea of starting with the textual meaning with his proposal for a better translation of "covet." Following language scholar J. T. Lettinga, he proposed a better translation for the commandment, "You shall not set your desire(s) on your neighbor's house, wife, etc." He then argued:

> If we set our desire upon something, we are out to get what we desire. Thus, to set our desire upon something *already* involves forming a *plan* (recall what Calvin said [distinguishing desiring and planning to act]) ready to be put in motion as soon as opportunity arises.[4]

The notion that began to form in my mind regarding the tenth commandment is best understood with an illustration. Harry begins coveting Brad's house, wife, or car. He looks upon those objects with desire. Yet he has not moved to adultery or theft. The seventh and eighth commandments would already cover this. But the problem is not that he has simply looked at those objects as desirable. Rather, the problem is that he has "set his desires" upon those objects – the operating word is "set." The distinction may seem tenuous, but in practice, it boils down to the difference between simply observing the desirableness of something and making that something into a focus of desire. The latter involves not only an evaluation or appreciation of what belongs to another, but also an intentional "focusing upon" that at once reflects, in the words of the Westminster Larger Catechism (WLC):

> ... discontentment with our own estate; (1 Kings 21:4, Esther 5:13, 1 Corinthians 10:10) envying (Galatians 5:26, James 3:14,16) and grieving at the good of our neighbour, (Psalms 112:9-10; Nehemiah 2:10) together with all inordinate motions and affections to any thing that is his. (Romans 7:7-8, Romans 13:9, Colossians 3:5, Deuteronomy 5:21).[5]

---

[3] J. Douma, (1996). *The Ten Commandments: Manual for the Christian Life* (p. 340) Phillipsburg, NJ: P & R Publishing Co.
[4] Douma (1996) p. 341. Original emphasis.
[5] *The Westminster Larger Catechism: with Scripture Proofs.* (1996). Oak Harbor, WA: Logos Research Systems, Inc. Answer 148.

We must be very clear: envy, resentment, and wishing ill for our neighbors are not merely a preamble to breaking the commandments summed up in "love your neighbor." It is already the act of breaking it. It is also an act of breaking the commandment to "love the Lord your God."

Desire Is a Spreading Fire

When Douma claims that a "plan" is already involved in this process of "setting the desire," he is arguing that even if this imaginative planning never gets set in motion, the mere existence of this internal process already brings about practical sinful results.

Going back to the illustration of Harry and Brad, if Harry simply observes what a good wife Brad has or what a great house or company he has, he could simply give praise to God for having blessed his friend in such ways. Yet the moment Harry begins to ponder how he "wishes" he could *have* Brad's wife or house or business, something else already begins to take place. Harry would dwell on his discontentment with his own wife or possessions; he would start to imagine how he wished he had what was Brad's *and* to envision the conditions whereby he might make them his own. He would likely also begin to resent Brad for having that something that he does not have. Ultimately, he would resent God for giving Brad that which has become the object of his desire.

This final state of "coveting" involves two very problematic states of affairs. Douma sums up the first like this:

> Stated briefly, we could also say it this way: Anyone who has set his desire(s) on his neighbor's house, wife, employees or animals will not be able to keep his hands off. With premeditation he intends to strike. That is the primary meaning of the Tenth Commandment.[6]

Yet the second problem of this final condition is that, even if the "striking" never actively sees the light of day, its destructive force already has very practical consequences. This state of coveting that "lies somewhere between the disposition and the deed" allows desire to become a "spreading fire" and that which "lies brooding in the human heart" will manifest itself in very destructive ways even if the adultery or theft is never consummated.[7]

---

[6] Douma (1996), 341.
[7] Douma (1996), 343.

Harry will no longer find his own wife desirable; he might begin to hate his house, resent his job, or even foster fantasies of a new life in order to quench the dissatisfaction with what God has given him. His relationship with Brad, therefore, will be destroyed, and he will look for opportunities to repay Brad in evil ways for his blessedness. Harry's relationship with his wife will likely suffer damage, as well as his relationship to society and to his community – usually a sense of entitlement, a sinful anger, and a sense of injustice will follow.

The roots of so much destruction in the history of individuals and society are easily traced to the territory of coveting! Covetous desire rages like an all-consuming fire. This is seen from Cain's murderous rebellion against God, because he resented God's approval of Abel's offering, through Israel's murmuring in the desert as they set their desires back on the onions of Egypt. It is clear, from David's sin with Bathsheba and its murdering consequences all the way to the false prophets who teach heresy (see 2 Peter 2:1-14). Like idolatry (Colossians 3:5), coveting is also an enslaving force.

The Slavery of Covetousness

This last point about the correlation between coveting and idolatry is especially useful if we wish to add another aspect to our reflection. Just as coveting is pervasive and highly damaging on its own, setting the stage for outwardly breaking the other commandments, so also it possesses a very powerful characteristic of establishing the kind of bondage that is the antithesis of the freedom promised in the law-gospel continuum.

Perhaps a little help from John Bunyan's classic *The Pilgrim's Progress* (1678) can assist us here. Bunyan writes beautifully about Christian, who is on a pilgrimage to the Celestial City. Along the way he has many encounters, challenges, and lessons. At one point in the book, in what Bunyan called the Seventh Stage (Chapter 7), he writes of an encounter that is strikingly relevant to our topic. Christian and Hopeful, his then current traveling companion, meet up with a man called By-ends. Christian's prior traveling companion, named Faithful, has just been slain in the town of Vanity, the seat of the Vanity Fair. He was condemned in a kangaroo court, with Envy as the star witness of the prosecution and a jury made up of the following men: Mr. Blindman, Mr. No-good, Mr. Malice, Mr. Love-lust, Mr. Live-loose, Mr. Heady, Mr. High-mind, Mr. Enmity, Mr. Liar, Mr. Cruelty, Mr. Hate-light, and Mr. Implacable.

Now Christian and Hopeful cross paths with By-ends and invite him to join them on their pilgrimage. By-ends refuses, however, to tell them his name and origin (the town of Fair-speech). Christian is willing to have him as a traveling companion, but concerned with By-ends's love of convenience, he warns:

> If you will go with us, you must go against wind and tide; the which, I perceive, is against your opinion: you must also own Religion in his rags, as well as when in his silver slippers; and stand by him, too, when bound in irons, as well as when he walketh the streets with applause.[8]

Offended, By-ends responds: "You must not impose or lord it over my faith; leave it to my liberty, and let me go with you." Very concerned, Christian says he may not go "one step further" with them unless he agrees to those conditions. By-ends's answer is definite: I will then go on my own until I find companions that are okay with me, for I shall never desert my old principles, since they are harmless and profitable." At this point in Bunyan's story, the crux of the illustration comes as the narrator comments:

> Now I saw in my dream, that Christian and Hopeful forsook him, and kept their distance before him; but one of them, looking back, saw three men following Mr. By-ends; and, behold, as they came up with him, he made them a very low congee; and they also gave him a compliment. The men's names were, *Mr. Hold-the-world, Mr. Money-love,* and *Mr. Save-all,* men that Mr. By-ends had formerly been acquainted with; for in their minority they were schoolfellows, and *taught by one Mr. Gripeman, a schoolmaster in Lovegain, which is a market-town in the county of Coveting,* in the North. This Schoolmaster taught them the art of *getting, either by violence, cozenage, flattering, lying, or by putting on a guise of religion*; and these four gentlemen had attained much of the art of their master, so that they could each of them have kept such a school themselves.[9] (emphasis added)

Adding a final touch, Bunyan tells of the conversation between these old schoolfellows. Their common condemnation of Christian and Hopeful appears as a disingenuous claim of Christian Liberty on the part of Mr. Hold-the-world: "Aye, and hold you there still, good Mr. By-ends; for, for my part, I can count him but a fool, that having the liberty to keep what he has, shall be so unwise as to lose it."[10]

In short, the whole encounter should paint a vivid picture of people who will falter in their pilgrimage; thinking themselves free, but actually

---

[8] John Bunyan (1995). *The Pilgrim's Progress: From This World to That Which Is to Come.* Oak Harbor, WA: Logos Research Systems, Inc.
[9] Bunyan (1995).
[10] Note: Thanks to my father, Dr. Wadislau Martins Gomes, for the suggestion of this illustration from *The Pilgrim's Progress*.

in bondage to pragmatism, self-condescension, love of money, and grievance, they will fail to realize that their bondage began in their training in the school of Lovegain, in the county of Coveting.

This is the insidiousness of the sin condemned in the tenth commandment! It is enslaving, binding the will and the desires; yet it hides in plain sight under many cloaks. No wonder Deuteronomy makes the connection between obedience to the second commandment, coveting the gold of idols, and being enslaved: "The carved images of their gods you shall burn with fire. You shall not covet the silver or the gold that is on them or take it for yourselves, lest you be ensnared by it, for it is an abomination to the Lord your God" (Deuteronomy 7:25).

In the seventh chapter of Paul's Epistle to the Romans, cited briefly above, besides identifying coveting as the sin that, the realization of which, broke his illusion of self-righteousness apart from Christ, Paul also makes a final connection between coveting and slavery, which I believe the New International Version (NIV) captures very well. In verses 7 and 8, Paul makes clear how the tenth commandment caused him to realize his unrighteousness. Then in verses 9 through 14, he explains that the condemnation brought about by the law meant death to his self-deception but opened him up to life and to the realization of the bondage of sin:

> Once I was alive apart from the law; but when the commandment came, sin sprang to life and I died. I found that the very commandment that was intended to bring life actually brought death. For sin, seizing the opportunity afforded by the commandment, deceived me, and through the commandment put me to death. So then, the law is holy, and the commandment is holy, righteous and good. Did that which is good, then, become death to me? By no means! But in order that sin might be recognized as sin, it produced death in me through what was good, so that through the commandment sin might become utterly sinful. We know that the law is spiritual; but I am unspiritual, sold as a slave to sin.[11]

This aspect of the sinful bondage that coveting brings about is also present in the condemnation of false teachers by Peter, to which I have already referred above in passing but want to discuss now. Peter says that these false prophets are "like irrational animals, creatures of instinct, born to be caught and destroyed." They blaspheme in their ignorance and are destroyed by their own destruction; they deceive and are self-deceived (2 Peter 2:12-13). They are, says Peter, "full of adultery" and "insatiable for sin."

---

[11] *The Holy Bible*: The New International Version. (2011). (Romans 7:9-14). Grand Rapids, MI: Zondervan.

They entice and lead others to sin, they are moved by love of gain, and their lot is gloom. Peter then continues:

> For, speaking loud boasts of folly, they entice by sensual passions of the flesh those who are barely escaping from those who live in error. They promise them freedom, but they themselves are slaves of corruption. For whatever overcomes a person, to that he is enslaved.[12]

Again, sin is always bondage. The sins addressed in the tenth commandment, however, have a special ability to create a kind of bondage that flies under the radar and which can fester secretly. Nevertheless, make no mistake, secret chains cause manifest damage. As Goethe properly reminds us, "No one is more a slave than the man who thinks himself free while he is not."[13]

Freedom Now from the Bonds of Coveting

I have borrowed the title for this final heading from the first section of Schaeffer's book *True Spirituality* (1982). He calls that section "Freedom Now from the Bonds of Sin." In the WLC, we have identified discontentment, envying, "grieving at the good of our neighbour," and the "inordinate motions and affections" toward what belongs to others as such sins forbidden by the tenth commandment. The positive side of the commandment is "such a full contentment with our own condition and such a charitable frame of the whole soul toward our neighbour, as that all our inward motions and affections touching him, tend unto, and further all that good which is his."[14] Yet right after listing duties (answer 147) and prohibitions (answer 148) comes the crucial question whether any man is "able perfectly to keep the commandments of God." The answer, of course, is no:

> No man is able, either of himself (James 3:2; John 15:5; Romans 8:3) or by any grace received in this life, perfectly to keep the commandments of God (Ecclesiastes 7:20; 1 John 1:8,10; Galatians 5:17; Romans 7:18-19) but doth daily break them in thought (Genesis 6:5; 8:21), word, and deed (Romans 3:9-19; James 3:2-13).[15]

---

[12] *The Holy Bible*: English Standard Version. (2016). (2 Peter 2:12-20). Wheaton, IL: Crossway Bibles.
[13] Johann Wolfgang von Goethe, (1872), *Elective Affinities* (p. 202). Translated by Victoria C. Woodhull. Boston: W. Niles.
[14] *The Westminster Larger Catechism: with Scripture Proofs*. (1996). Answer 147. Oak Harbor, WA: Logos Research Systems, Inc.
[15] WLC. Answer 149.

The Heidelberg Catechism makes this even more stringent by making it more general: "That even the smallest inclination or thought, contrary to any of God's commandments, never rise in our hearts."[16]

How do we then, as Christians, experience the freedom from this bondage and live out our overall freedom from slavery to sin in the present age? In a way, the answer is quite simple. Because we have been made free from the condemnation for our sins through the sacrifice of Christ and have died to our old selves, we ought also to express this freedom by being sanctified on the basis of Christ's holiness and by constantly forsaking our old habits. It is a process somewhat like clipping one's toenails: they grow and must be repeatedly clipped before they cause harm. It involves ongoing hygiene of the heart until the day we take on our new flesh.

Can we, however, flesh out some helpful insights into this process I have called hygiene of the heart? I think Schaeffer may help us again here. The help comes right after he sums up how the tenth commandment helps identify the internal process that makes us all inexcusable before the law, both those who do not know Christ as an absolute condition and those who know their Savior as a knee-bending reminder of their dependence upon that sweet Savior. This is how he starts:

> This is a very central concept if we are to have any understanding or any real practice of the true Christian life or true spirituality. I can take lists that men make and I can seem to keep them, but to do that my heart does not have to be bowed. But when I come to the inward aspect of the Ten Commandments, when I come to the inward aspect of the Law of Love, if I am listening even in a poor fashion to the promptings of the Holy Spirit, I can no longer feel proud. I am brought to my knees. In this life I can never say, "I have arrived; it is finished; look at me – I am holy." When we talk of the Christian life or true spirituality, when we talk about freedom from the bonds of sin, we must be wrestling with the inward problems of not coveting against God and men, of loving God and men, and not merely some set of externals.[17]

Schaeffer explains the process in a way that is golden. He first tackles the question as to whether the tenth commandment is an indictment of desiring, to which he answers that the Bible does not categorize all desire as sin. So when does "proper desire become coveting"? His answer sets the stage:

---

[16] The Heidelberg Catechism (Question 113). In *Historic Creeds and Confessions*. (1997). (electronic ed.). Oak Harbor: Lexham Press.
[17] F. A. Schaeffer, (1982). *True Spirituality*, 204.

"Desire becomes sin when it fails to include love of God or men."[18] This leads to a proposal of two complex yet simple tests for Christians.[19]

The first test is whether I love God enough to experience contentment: "Otherwise even our natural and proper desires bring us into revolt against God." Discontentment is rebellion, a refusal to accept God's allotment to us. It stands opposite to the "thankful-heart" characteristic of those who know God, trust Him, and are grateful to Him in all things. Paul sets coveting and thankfulness as opposites in Ephesians 5:3-4:

> But sexual immorality and all impurity or covetousness must not even be named among you, as is proper among saints. Let there be no filthiness nor foolish talk nor crude joking, which are out of place, but instead let there be thanksgiving.

The second test is whether I love my neighbor "enough not to envy." This is how Schaeffer puts it:

> There is a simple test for this. Natural desires have become coveting against a fellow creature, one of our kind, a fellow man, when we have a mentality that would give us secret satisfaction at his misfortune. If a man has something, and he loses it, do we have inward pleasure, a secret satisfaction at his loss? Do not speak too quickly and say it is never so, because you will make yourself a liar.[20]

This is a powerful test, because this inner coveting, this envy of the blessings, gifts, relationships, or possessions that God has given our neighbors, cannot easily be kept inward forever and will eventually spill over into sinful external actions toward other people. We have an easier time, however, identifying the external sin we commit against our brothers in humanity than recognizing that at the root of these actions is a sinful, internal disposition. That is why, as an antidote, the Apostle Paul reminds us: "Let no one seek his own good, but the good of his neighbor" (1 Corinthians 10:24). A few chapters later, he characterizes love of neighbor in this way: "Love is patient and kind; love does not envy or boast; it is not arrogant or rude. It does not insist on its own way; it is not irritable or resentful" (1 Corinthians 13:4-5).

---

[18] F. A. Schaeffer, (1982). *True Spirituality*, 205.
[19] I am thinking here of the quote attributed to Oliver Wendell Holmes: "For the simplicity on this side of complexity, I wouldn't give you a fig. But for the simplicity on the other side of complexity, for that I would give you anything I have." See https://www.goodreads.com/author/quotes/1203736.Oliver_Wendell_Holmes_Sr_.
[20] Schaeffer (1982), 209.

Schaeffer closes this argument describing what should happen when we realize that just as ungrateful discontentment is a manifestation of covetousness toward God, so are envying and resentment of others, the opposite of loving our neighbor, the outworking of coveting:

> When we read these things and understand that failure in these areas is really coveting, a lack of love, every one of us must be upon his knees as Paul was upon his knees when he saw the commandment not to covet; it destroys any superficial view of the Christian life.[21]

Earlier in this chapter I referred to Bunyan's pilgrim. Perhaps he may help us with an appropriate closing. After Christian and Hopeful encounter the sons of the city of Coveting and after they have some interesting moral-theological debates about the inappropriateness of making choices simply in order to fulfill selfish desires, they come upon a new character called Demas. Demas invites them to come and enrich themselves by doing a small detour from their path to the Heavenly City for some digging in a silver mine. Hopeful is tempted, but Christian resists. As By-ends and his companions (the children of Coveting) arrive, however, they are also entreated by Demas and follow him. Yet Mr. By-ends, Mr. Hold-the-world, Mr. Money-love, and Mr. Save-all, together with Demas, disappear into the silver mine, never to be seen again. Christian then sings a sad song:

> By-ends and silver Demas both agree;
> One calls, the other runs, that he may be
> A sharer in his lucre: so these two
> Take up in this world, and no farther go.[22]

Right after these events, Christian and Hopeful cross a small plain and encounter a strange monument. They are puzzled for a brief moment, and then they see the inscription that opens their eyes: "Remember Lot's wife." They "both concluded that that was the pillar of salt into which Lot's wife was turned, for her looking back with a covetous heart." This leads them to the following dialogue, which illustrates quite well how discontentment and ungratefulness toward God, as well as envy and lack of love to neighbor – in sum, covetousness – are at the root of much destruction:

> Christian: Ah, my brother, this is a seasonable sight: it came opportunely to us after the invitation which Demas gave us to come over to view the hill Lucre; and had we gone over, as he desired us, and as thou wast inclined to

---

[21] Schaeffer (1982), 210.
[22] John Bunyan, (1995).

do, my brother, we had, for aught I know, been made, like this woman, a spectacle for those that shall come after to behold.

Hopeful: I am sorry that I was so foolish, and am made to wonder that I am not now as Lot's wife; for wherein was the difference betwixt her sin and mine? *She only looked back, and I had a desire to go see. Let grace be adored; and let me be ashamed that ever such a thing should be in mine heart.*

Christian: Let us take notice of what we see here, for our help from time to come. *This woman escaped one judgment, for she fell not by the destruction of Sodom; yet she was destroyed by another*, as we see: she is turned into a pillar of salt.

Hopeful: True, and she may be to us both caution and example; caution, that we should shun her sin; or a sign of what judgment will overtake such as shall not be prevented by this caution: so Korah, Dathan, and Abiram, with the two hundred and fifty men that perished in their sin (Numbers 16:31, 32), did also become a sign or example to others to beware. But above all, I muse at one thing, to wit, how Demas and his fellows can stand so confidently yonder to look for that treasure, which this woman but for looking behind her after, (for we read not that she stepped one foot out of the way,) was turned into a pillar of salt; especially since the judgment which overtook her did make her an example within sight of where they are; for they cannot choose but see her, did they but lift up their eyes.

Christian: It is a thing to be wondered at, and it argueth that their hearts are grown desperate in the case; and I cannot tell who to compare them to so fitly, as to them that pick pockets in the presence of the judge, or that will cut purses under the gallows. It is said of the men of Sodom, that they were "sinners exceedingly," because they were sinners "before the Lord," that is, in his eyesight, and notwithstanding the kindnesses that he had shown them; for the land of Sodom was now like the garden of Eden as heretofore (Genesis 13:10-13). This, therefore, provoked him the more to jealousy, and made their plague as hot as the fire of the Lord out of heaven could make it. And it is most rationally to be concluded, that such, even such as these are, that shall sin in the sight, yea, and that too in despite of such examples that are set continually before them, to caution them to the contrary, must be partakers of severest judgments.

Hopeful: Doubtless thou hast said the truth; but what a mercy is it, that neither thou, but especially I, am not made myself this example! *This ministereth occasion to us to thank God*, to fear before him, and always to remember Lot's wife.[23] (emphasis added)

---

[23] John Bunyan, (1995).

Afterword

OUR OBEDIENCE PRAISES AND DELIGHTS THE LORD

Samuel Logan, United States

After all the previous "words" about the Ten Commandments, why should there be an Afterword? Simply as a reminder of the most fundamental reason why it is so important that we obey those commandments.

Among the earliest words that the Lord is recorded as having spoken in Scripture are these which describe the creation of human beings:

> Let us make man in our image, after our likeness ... (Genesis 1:26).

And among the latest words that the Lord is recorded as having spoken in Scripture are these which describe the Lord's servants in the Celestial City:

> No longer will anything be accursed, but the throne of God and of the Lamb will be in it, and his servants will worship him. They will see his face, and his name will be on their foreheads ... (Revelation 22:3-4).

Human beings were created for the primary purpose of reflecting God's very nature back to Him. But when Eve and Adam disobeyed God by eating of the forbidden fruit, that purpose was disrupted, and it took the life and death and resurrection of God's own Son to restore that purpose:

> He [the Son] is the radiance of the glory of God and the exact imprint of his nature ... We see him, who for a while was made lower than the angels, namely Jesus, crowned with glory and honor because of the suffering of death, so that by the grace of God he might taste death for everyone. (Hebrews 1:3; 2:9).

That purpose was disrupted by man's disobedience, and it is not just Adam and Eve who are at fault. It is every human being who has *ever* violated *any* part of God's holy law, simply, and most importantly, because the law of God is nothing more or less than an *externalization* of the very being of God.

Therefore, and this is the main point of the present Afterword, obedience to God's law – the Decalogue – is important primarily because such obedience reflects God's nature and glory back to Him, which was the essential purpose of creation in the first place.

Yes, of course, God, throughout His Word, promises blessings to those who obey Him and who obey His law, which mirrors Him. But the reception of blessings by God's creatures is not – and never was – the primary purpose of the Decalogue or of any other divine laws. The primary purpose of obedience to God's law is to give God the glory which is His by right, because of who He is.

Thus, apologetic arguments that it is to man's "benefit" to obey God's law may be correct but, even if they are, such arguments are beside the point because *God – not man – is at the center of the universe which God created*. And ultimately, therefore, even if obedience to a specific divine law were shown to be contradictory to the welfare of man, such a demonstration would have absolutely no impact on the validity of that specific divine law.

There can be no question about God's love for His creation – even when human beings disobeyed the laws which are simply the manifestation of God's nature, He did not abandon that creation to its just deserts. He gave His only begotten Son to provide a way back. That is how much He loved – and loves – us.

And our love for Him is best demonstrated by both words and deeds of thankful obedience. Christians have sometimes used the language of "holy affections" to describe the proper response of the human will to the holiness of God and the beauty of the gospel of Christ. Proper affections in relation to God lead to both proper words and proper deeds.

Jonathan Edwards is pre-eminent among the theologians making this fundamental point. In his *Treatise On Religious Affections*, he states this as his fundamental thesis: "True religion, in great part, consists in holy affections," and entitles Section II of Part III this way:

> The first objective ground of gracious affections is the transcendentally excellent and amiable nature of divine things as they are in themselves, and not any conceived relation they bear to self or self-interest.

Proper affections do not arise primarily from considering what God might do for me; proper affections arise from considering the excellency of God. Edwards then applies this principle directly to the point of this Afterword:

> The exercises of true and holy love in the saints arise in another way. They do not first see that God loves *them*, and then see that He is lovely; but they

first see that He is lovely, and that Christ is excellent and glorious; their hearts are first captivated with this view ... **The saints' affections begin with God**, and self-love has a hand in these affections consequentially and secondarily only. (emphasis added)

We are to obey the commands of the Decalogue most fundamentally because this is what we were created to do – *image* the Triune God, our Creator – and such obedience is what most honors Him.

Appendices

There are some important questions in Christian ethics that were not directly addressed in the chapters of this book but which merit the attention of readers. Therefore, we have added these appendices.

Sign and Countersign: The Battle against Pornography in the Church

Daniel Weiss, United States

The Creation story in Genesis contains some of the most beautiful language of the Bible. Modern scientific man might prefer textbooks on the inner workings of astrophysics, biodiversity, and cellular functioning, but for me, poetry is the better way. Like all great poets, God's scarcity of words enhances the imagination, increasing our awe at the mystery of His creative process.

Within the poetic account of Genesis 1, one theme becomes obvious enough to draw our attention a bit closer. On each day of creation God reveals and divides, brings forth and distinguishes one element of creation from another. Light from dark, land from water, distinct lights, diversity of vegetation, winged creatures from those that swim, and a host of discreet animals to fill the land. This description of creating and separating is a profoundly simple way of describing an extraordinarily complex universe crafted to work together in harmony for God's purposes.

Using this same pattern, God creates humankind in His image and likeness – male and female. We are like the other sex, but also unlike. Genesis 2 teases this out beautifully. First, God creates *adam* from the dust of the ground and the breath of the Spirit. *Adam* is fully alive, but not complete. He is without a helper. At this point God causes *adam* to fall into *tardema*, a sleep deep enough for him to be unmade and remade into a more accurate reflection of God. He had been created; he is now also separated and reunited. As philosopher Peter Kreeft reflected, "We fit the nature of things."[1]

We can only imagine Adam's first gasp of joy as he beheld his new bride standing before him radiant and naked and pure: *At last, here is one for me.* Like the end of a great fireworks display, what happens in the creation finale almost overshadows all that came before. By God's grace we are able to see and understand the Triune nature stamped into the division of the sexes and the life-giving one-flesh union of marriage.

Would that our first parents had not fallen into sin!

---

[1] Humanum Episode 1: The Destiny of Humanity: On The Meaning of Marriage; http://www.eccefilms.com/humanum (accessed July 22, 2022).

Yet, they did, and we see throughout the Scriptures how destructive our sinful nature is and has been. More than mere disobedience, sin unleashed a violent rupture between humanity and God and God's creation, including divisions between men and women and the inner disintegration of thought, desire, and will in every human person. At once, we were separated from God, each other, and the inner harmony of our God-designed selves.

This has been the case for every generation, but a relatively recent threat is widening these divisions at alarming rates: *digital pornography*.

The Greatest Threat

Some years ago, a prominent American ministry leader called pornography the "greatest threat to the cause of Christ in the history of the world."[2] While this claim may seem absurd, at this very moment pornography has in its brutal grip hundreds of millions (perhaps billions) of people around the globe, a majority of which are likely teenagers or younger. Perhaps it's worth a deeper exploration.

As temptations go, pornography is among the most cunning and spiritually lethal, yet it is rarely addressed in the Church. One pastor told me he wouldn't talk about pornography because he preaches to the 90% of his congregation that is relatively healthy. Another pastor didn't discuss sexual issues because he was afraid that people would approach him for help, and he didn't know what to do.

While these and other Christian leaders remain silent, 41 percent of *practicing* Christian young men (13-24) and 13 percent of practicing Christian young women are worshipping pornographic idols at least monthly or more often. Concurrently, 23 percent of adult Christian men (25+) and five percent of adult Christian women are engaged in digital adultery at least monthly or more.[3] Pornography *is* in the Church and often at only slightly lower rates than the general population.

Whether we want to or not, the Church must openly address the impact of pornography if we hope to advance the Gospel in a sexually explicit culture. Both within and outside our churches, men, women, and children are

---

[2] Mark Martin, "Alarming Epidemic: 'Porn the Greatest Threat to the Cause of Christ,'" CBNnews.com, https://www1.cbn.com/cbnnews/health/2016/april/alarming-epidemic-porn-the-greatest-threat-to-the-cause-of-christ, (accessed 07/22/2022).

[3] *The Porn Phenomenon*, A Barna Report produced in partnership with Josh McDowell Ministry (2016), p. 32.

losing themselves to an addictive neural drug that is disintegrating them spiritually, emotional, relationally, and sexually before our very eyes. The harms of pornography, as they say, are hidden in plain sight.

I am among those that believe the Church holds the primary antidote to this global sexual depredation. As a character in Bruce Marshall's book *The World, the Flesh, and Father Smith* says, "the young man who rings the bell at the brothel is unconsciously looking for God."[4]

This is strangely good news. The world's fascination with pornography shows us how hungry people are for love and meaning which can only be found in Christ. As my friend Christopher West likes to point out, if we saw a man eating out of a dumpster, we wouldn't yell at him. We would offer him healthy food that truly satisfies.

The world is sexually sick, with infections reaching into every Christian church. If we hope to help those in need, we need to better understand how pornography has taken a good gift of God and turned it against us.

Separation between God and Man

In his *History of the Christian Church, Volume 1*, nineteenth-century scholar Phillip Schaff explains:

> Idolatry or spiritual whoredom is almost inseparable from bodily pollution. In the case of Solomon polytheism and polygamy went hand in hand. Hence the author of the Apocalypse also closely connects the eating of meat offered to idols with fornication, and denounces them together. Paul had to struggle against this laxity in the Corinthian congregation and condemns all carnal uncleanness as a violation and profanation of the temple of God.[5]

Indeed, we see a similar pattern throughout the Scriptures. Sexual immorality does not just coexist with idolatry. It is idolatry as Paul explains in Romans 1: "They exchanged the truth about God for a lie, and worshiped and served created things rather than the Creator ..."

With pornography, the idolatry is two-fold. First, the user becomes devoted to the sexual images and videos that entrance her.[6] Pioneering

---

[4] Glenn Stanton, "FactChecker: C.S. Lewis and G.K. Chesterton Quotes, thegospelcoalition.org, https://www.thegospelcoalition.org/article/factchecker-c-s-lewis-and-g-k-chesterton-quotes/ (accessed July 22, 2022).

[5] Philip Schaff, *History of the Christian Church, Volume 1* (Hendrickson Publishers, 2002), 348.

[6] Some may be surprised of my use of the female pronoun here and elsewhere. Research amply demonstrates that pornography use is growing among women,

psychologist Patrick Carnes developed an addiction model that also reveals a certain ritualism to porn use.

First, a person feels a prompt, such as a sexual ad or even something sexually innocuous, such as hunger, boredom, or loneliness. This prompt leads to a time of preoccupation where the user plans when and how to view pornography. There may be actual rituals involved, such as waiting until roommates have gone to bed or fantasizing beforehand. Finally, there is the actual viewing, which can be seen as a form of worship involving devotion and ecstatic release. This is followed by post-porn pain, often manifesting as shame. Unhealed shame is simply waiting for a new prompt to trigger another turn of the addictive cycle.

The second element of idolatry reflects a worship of the self. *My needs and desires trump everything else in life.* I develop a sense of entitlement that is only strengthened by the ease at which it can be satisfied. Untethered from moral codes that might restrict my needs, I can now do what I want, to whom I want, when I want.

Unfortunately, this entitlement mentality isn't confined to merely viewing pornography, as research (and countless broken hearts) attests. Untempered sexuality is responsible for many of the great evils in the world. The Christian sexual ethics of the New Testament and the moral law of the Old have undoubtedly done much to restrain sexual appetites throughout the millennia, but there is much more to God's sexual restrictions than simply curbing abuse.

Paul compares the intimacy of a husband and wife to that of Christ's love for the Church. The love of God is self-giving, nurturing, patient, faithful, total, and free, all hallmarks of a healthy marriage as well. We are meant to enjoy the intimate embrace of self-giving love and receptivity and all that proceeds from such a union.

So important is this earthly symbol of divine love, that God chose to weave it through the whole fabric of Scripture. The Bible opens with the marriage of Adam and Eve and closes with the wedding feast of the Lamb and the Bride. The prophets often compared God's love to that of a jealous husband. Israel is the bride, the Church is the bride, we are the bride. Christ alone is the groom, simultaneously initiating a loving relationship with us and making it possible for us to receive and return that love.

The New Testament writers also knew that sexual integrity is a proclamation that there is much more to life than chasing after sex, food, or power. We are called to be set apart from the world so that one of the

---

especially younger women and girls. I believe the Church makes a fatal mistake by considering pornography to be a "man's problem."

primary symbols of God's love can actually be seen and understood by those around us.

Our call to sexual wholeness is as radical today as it was in the promiscuous Roman culture into which the Church was born. As pastor Matthew Reuger makes clear in *Sexual Morality in a Christless World*, the Christian sexual witness not only challenges the secular social order; it threatens to topple it.[7] The secular world opposes Christian sexual morality for this very reason.

While there is extraordinary power in the true sign of God's love, the countersign has a power of its own. By distorting the meaning of male, female, and sexual intimacy, pornography poises a dire threat to the health and continuing function of the *ecclesia* by attacking the cradle of faith: the family.

Division between men and women

According to research I cited earlier, 57 percent of young adults (18-23) and 37 percent of teens (13-17) view porn monthly or even more frequently, compared with only 29 percent of all adults aged 25 and older.[8] This means that those most susceptible to the harmful impact of pornography are also the ones most avidly consuming it. This is leading to dire consequences globally.

A 2006 report found a long list of pornography's negative influences that directly impact relational health and family formation. These include but are not limited to:

- Diminished trust in intimate partners;
- Abandoning the goal of sexual exclusivity with a partner;
- Perceiving promiscuity as a normal state of interaction;
- Perceiving sexual inactivity as constituting a health risk;
- Developing cynical attitudes about love;
- Believing superior sexual satisfaction is attainable without having affection for one's partner;
- Believing marriage is sexually confining; and

---

[7] Matthew Rueger, *Sexual Morality in a Christless World* (Concordia Publishing House, 2016).
[8] *The Porn Phenomenon*, A Barna Report produced in partnership with Josh McDowell Ministry (2016), p. 31.

- Believing that raising children and having a family is as an unattractive prospect.[9]

Pornography is the antithesis of love. This diabolical scheme not only disrupts loving relationships; it prevents many from occurring at all. Who wants the confinement of marriage and the anchor of children, when he can make love to as many different women each night as he wants?

The other side of the breakdown is just as heartbreaking. Many young women are faced with the impossible choice of dating or marrying a porn-addicted (or, at least influenced) man or remaining single, possibly for life. Professor Gail Dines has been sounding the warning about this for years. In 2010 she wrote:

> Porn has become so violent and degrading that we ignore it at our peril. We are now bringing up a generation of boys on cruel, violent porn and given that images shape the way people think and behave, this is going to have a profound effect on their sexuality and on the culture as a whole.[10]

In the twelve years since this was published, we've seen the once pornographic fringe enter the mainstream of intimate relationships. Young women find themselves in a thoroughly pornographic dating culture, where they are not only expected to be okay with their boyfriend's porn use; they are often forced to watch and act it out as well. One of the saddest stories I've ever read and which I'll only paint in the broadest strokes here involved British schoolgirls who are now permanently incontinent because their pornified boyfriends reenacted on them the violent sex they were viewing.

Although we find this shocking, we shouldn't. As researcher Judith Reisman has said many times, today's kids are doing exactly what they are supposed to be doing: imitating the adult culture around them. The world of adult pornography, which has now socialized several generations of kids, is cruel in ways most non-porn users would disbelieve.

In 2007, a university research team analyzed every scene in 50 of the previous year's highest grossing pornography films and found that:

> 88.2 percent contained physical aggression, principally spanking, gagging, and slapping, while 48.7 percent of scenes contained verbal aggression,

---

[9] Jill C. Manning, *Sexual Addiction & Compulsivity*, 13:131–165, 2006.
[10] Gail Dines, "How porn is warping a generation of men," NYPost.com, July 11, 2010, https://nypost.com/2010/07/11/how-porn-is-warping-a-generation-of-men/, (accessed 07/22/2022).

primarily name-calling. Perpetrators of aggression were usually male, whereas targets of aggression were overwhelmingly female. Targets most often showed pleasure or responded neutrally to the aggression.[11]

Pope John Paul II wrote that the opposite of love is not hate, but lust, the using of another for one's own pleasure.[12] Today's pornography is marked by both. It is a violent attack on women and a tragic sabotage of the servant love and leadership to which men are called. We're not only naked with shame, but fear and loathing, as well.

The Disintegration of the Self

Augustine described our corrupt nature with the Latin phrase *incurvatus in se*, which means to be curved in on oneself. This is a helpful term for understanding why people get trapped in pornography and can't seem to get out.

The late Dr. Victor Cline, a clinical psychologist at the University of Utah and a sexual addiction specialist described a four-stage progression that he observed in almost all of the porn users he had treated: addiction, escalation, desensitization, and acting out.[13]

More recent brain research illuminates the chemical process behind this addictive progression. When people become sexually aroused, a flood of neurochemicals is released throughout the brain and body. These include dopamine, serotonin, oxytocin, and norepinephrine, among others. This process is an important element of God's ordered creation. Released during sexual intimacy, they bond spouses to one another, create feelings of intimacy and sexual exclusivity, and leave spouses feeling relaxed and euphoric.

These same neurochemicals are released when a person views pornography, often in superabundance. The brain is literally flooded with a powerful neuro-cocktail that provides a high, similar to that produced by drugs. However, our neural networks weren't designed to receive a never-ending tsunami of pleasure chemicals, so the brain begins shutting down neural receptors in an attempt to restore balance. As the brain shuts down,

---

[11] Ana J Bridges, Robert Wosnitzer, Erica Scharrer, Chyng Sun, Rachael Liberman, "Aggression and Sexual Behavior in Best-Selling Pornography Videos: A Content Analysis Update," *Violence Against Women*, 2010 Oct, 16(10):1065-85.

[12] John Paul II, *Man and Woman He Created Them: A Theology of the Body* (Pauline Books 2006).

[13] Victor B. Cline, "Pornography and Sexual Addictions," *Christian Counseling Today* 4, no.4 (1996), 58.

the addict no longer feels the same high and must work ever harder to stimulate a similar neurochemical release. This process leads many into addiction and to seeking out more deviant pornography or acting out in real life what they've conditioned themselves to in pornography. Simply put, a person can become addicted to his own neurochemicals.

In his book *The Brain That Changes Itself*, Dr. Norman Doidge found that although pornography can appease our sexual appetites for a time, sexual satisfaction is managed by a separate pleasure center in the brain. This is pornography's big secret.[14] The pleasure one receives from pornography can never satisfy. Pornography users are desperately trying to drink from a dry well.

The Church needs to understand this well. I've spoken to many women and men who have shared their porn struggles with church leaders and been told to repent and read the Bible more. These are important elements of healing, but such advice fails to account for the literal brain changes and neurochemical addictions that make stopping so difficult. There are also layers upon layers of deeper spiritual, emotional, and intellectual pain that drive the acting out behavior. To expect a person to change without healing these deeper wounds is callous and cruel.

Become the Body

I've worked on pornography-related issues for two decades and during that time have seen most churches do little or nothing to address this growing threat. There are myriad reasons for this, but all involve fear, insufficient training, naiveté, or a combination of all three.

Jesus didn't shy away from sexual topics, but addressed them with openness, conviction, and grace. In John 8, the Pharisees brought to Jesus a woman caught in adultery. They wanted him to condemn her, but Jesus gave them a powerful lesson instead. I'm not talking about showing grace to others or the realness of Christ's forgiveness, but something just as important.

When Jesus invited those without sin to throw the first stone, they walked away one by one until none remained. They came with judgement and left in isolation. None of them realized the profound gift Jesus had tried to show them: the power and beauty of a sinful community. If sin is "to be curved in upon oneself," then freedom from sin means to become bent back outward for the work of loving God and others.

---

[14] Daniel Weiss and Josh Glaser, *Treading Boldly Through a Pornography World: A Field Guide for Parents* (Salem Books, 2021), 141.

This can't happen in isolation, and is unlikely to happen in a rigid atmosphere that emphasizes behavioral perfection, as Dietrich Bonhoeffer wrote:

> The pious fellowship permits no one to be a sinner. So everyone must conceal his sin from himself and from the fellowship. We dare not be sinners. Many Christians are unthinkably horrified when a real sinner is suddenly discovered among the righteous. So we remain alone with our sin, living in lies and hypocrisy. The fact is that we *are* sinners![15]

It's a hard thing for people to hear, but every last one of us is a sexual sinner: the pastor, the pastor's wife, the young child confused about her identity, the old man who visited a brothel while in the military, the loving wife who slept around as a teenager, the happily married father of four who had an affair. These wounds live in every church, many of which remained hidden, unforgiven, and unhealed. We *know* this is true and still we hide.

Christian leaders need to understand that when we minimize or ignore the devastating impact of pornography and other sexual brokenness, we are keeping people locked in trauma and away from newness of life in Christ. It is Satan's tactic to keep sin hidden and sinners isolated; it should never be the church's choice to do so.

In his 2015 TED Talk, journalist Johann Hari shared that the opposite of addiction is not sobriety, but community.[16] Any renewal of the Christian sexual ethic needs to recognize and build upon the solidarity we all share in our brokenness. But this won't happen without compassionate intentionality. Christian leaders need to go where people are hiding in their sins. Again, Jesus shows us the way. When Jesus met the woman at the well in John 4, he was actually visiting her hiding place. Rather than getting water in the cool of the day, she was out at midday, presumably to avoid the town gossips. She had five husbands and was living with a new man. Lovingly, Jesus helped her to understand that he himself is the only bridegroom that will satisfy her heart.

It's not hard to go where sexual sinners are hiding. We encounter them in our weekly worship. This is where the body regularly comes together and is the first and most important place for us to normalize the sexual fallenness of the world and its impact on every human heart. Believers and visitors alike need to regularly hear and believe that God does not shy away

---

[15] Dietrich Bonhoeffer, *Life Together* (San Francisco: Harper, 1954), 110.
[16] Johann Hari, "Everything you think you know about addiction is wrong," TEDGlobalLondon, https://www.ted.com/talks/johann_hari_everything_you_think_you_know_about_addiction_is_wrong, (accessed 07/22/2022).

from our misery, but is drawn all the way into it. On the cross, Jesus not only bore our sins away; he suffered with us in the very moments of our sinning. The Good News that we proclaim is that Jesus already knows us, loves us in our sin, and openly welcomes us into the freedom he purchased with his body and blood.

By normalizing the *fact* of our sinfulness, the reality of God's forgiving and healing love, and that *this* church is a place for people to receive it, we are also creating a culture in which the presence of Christ is proclaimed, received, and shared with others freely. In a community such as this, people begin to feel safe enough to come out of the shadows and allow the love of Christ to heal the great divisions of the Fall. Men and women will find that they no longer need to hide from God, but can rush toward him, empowered by the grace he has given them. Husbands and wives, dating couples and divorcees, can humbly seek forgiveness and restoration. God's living water seeks to cleanse us at the core of our being, flowing into our wounded emotions, distorted thinking, and finally into our sinful actions. As we are healed from the inside out, we can begin to lean into the goodness of sexuality for which we were created.

In this life, we can never experience the original unity and purity of the Garden, but through Christ, we can still grow into the deeply satisfying community for which we were created. And, as we enjoy the freedom of knowing others and being known by them without fear, we might also follow the footsteps of that sinful Samaritan woman at the well, who became that town's chief evangelist. Many there believed in Jesus because she proclaimed, "Come, see a man who told me everything I ever did. Could this be the Messiah?"

Abortion in the United States after June 24, 2022

Leah Farish, United States

Christians worldwide may be hearing confusing news about abortion in the United States after the US Supreme Court decision on June 24, 2022, *Dobbs v. Jackson Women's Health*.[1]

As a civil rights attorney and previous adoption lawyer, I can summarize this consequential ruling. Then I will suggest some ways forward for Christians, both in the U.S. and elsewhere.

Before 1973, most people in the U.S. assumed that the legal status of abortion was a matter for the country's fifty states, because the U.S. Constitution leaves issues concerning family relationships, most criminal laws, health, and morality regulations to those states. But then the U.S. Supreme Court, in *Roe v. Wade*, struck down a state law that banned most abortions, saying that there was a privacy right to abortion implied in various parts of the national (federal) Constitution. The Court said that the mother had the primary right to choose abortion in her first trimester, and that as the baby approached viability, the state's interest in having children be born weighed heavier in the balance, till at nine months the choice to abort could only be exercised in extreme cases.

In 1992, the Court modified that opinion in *Planned Parenthood v. Casey*, holding that abortion was still a woman's right, but that the legal test in evaluating state laws would be whether the law was an "undue burden" on the woman's right. That was a vague test and spawned many more lawsuits, causing the Supreme (federal) Court to have to grapple with numerous restrictions that streamed in from states around the country.

In June of 2022, the Court reversed those two cases with its ruling in *Dobbs v. Jackson Women's Health*. The new decision held that *Roe* and *Casey* had set out from a false premise: that the Supreme Court could decide about abortion. Instead, the majority (6-3) said, this question is one for the fifty states.

Justice Alito, writing for the majority, said nothing about the value of the unborn or the evil of discarding an innocent life. The opinion only speaks of the importance of giving this momentous issue to the democratic

---

[1] 597 U.S. ___ (2022). https://www.supremecourt.gov/opinions/21pdf/19-1392_6j37.pdf.

process because it is a healthcare decision reserved to the fifty states under the U.S. Constitution, a document that is silent on abortion.

The justices said that if any claimed right is not mentioned by name in the Constitution, it must be "deeply rooted in American history and tradition". The Court reasoned that since *Roe* and *Casey*'s "right" to abortion had no such grounding, the right to abort will have to be found in state laws.For the first time, women (and men) can vote on abortion without being second-guessed by the unelected justices in Washington, D.C.; there is no federal Constitutional right to abortion.

Dobbs is a somewhat Solomonic decision, foregoing the power to decide and giving it to the people. And just like Solomon's ruling, it carries with it a danger of death, injustice, and misinterpretation. While pro-life people rejoice that the Supreme Court will not be the arbiter of whether babies can live or die, American Christians now face fifty different forums in which to debate. Abortion will now be a question decided by voters. While the Supreme Court commendably relinquished its *power* to decide, it also missed an opportunity for *influence*, as it wrote the decision with scrupulously neutral language. And it opened the door to allowing some states to pass laws even more ghastly than were allowed under Supreme Court precedent. Moreover, since as many as 60% of all abortions in the U.S. are not surgical but performed by drugs sent through the mail, it still remains for Christians to reach pregnant women with offers of help, understanding, and affirmation of the value of the life in their womb.

Still unknown are the reactions from the executive branch of American government, which leads the military (Will abortions be allowed on military bases in states that prohibit it? Will the President's State Department advocate for abortion overseas? Will the U.S. Postal Service mail abortifacient pills into states that outlaw them?) and the legislative branch (Will Congress fund travel for abortion out of states that forbid it? Will they try to enact laws that protect those who engage in the procedure? Will they fund abortions overseas?)

Two things must be noted about the dissent in the *Dobbs* case. First, while that opinion from three justices features much useful information and passionate advocacy, there is much that is unfair. It exaggerates the effect and distorts the motives of the justices who wrote the majority and concurring opinions, and it refuses in all of its 66 pages to ever acknowledge the interest of a state or nation in having babies be born alive.[2] Without further referencing the slang terms it uses, suffice to say

---

[2] *Dobbs*, 38 Noted with concern in Alito opinion (Page numbers start over with every different justice who writes). Exaggeration abounds: See [emphasis ours] p. 2

that civil rights law is all about balancing competing, worthy interests; intemperate language and ignoring of one side of the debate is exhausting, divisive, and unhelpful.

We are left to find another way, and this way must always be the way of love. The voiceless party in the litigation, the unborn child, is still vulnerable in the U.S. and elsewhere to the whims of mothers, families who pressure them, cultures who promote sexual irresponsibility (45% of the pregnancies in the U.S. are unplanned[3]), and politicians who fail to provide for needy mothers and children. Our view is that however small, inconvenient, quiet, and helpless a baby is, he or she is made in the image of God and is precious. As Thomas K. Johnson has pointed out, the Judeo-Christian view of human dignity is "personalist": that our worth is a gift from God, *not* "functionalist", that is, based on worth that comes from our self-awareness, or capacity to act or confer material benefits on society.[4]

Communicating this key concept of "personalist" worth and the hope for women who are facing unwanted pregnancies is a matter of education and persuasion. Just as most of our cultures have evolved from shunning children born outside wedlock, or allowing smoking in public places, or permitting the beating of animals that don't obey, the conscience of a vocal group can reshape a wrong-headed majority and change laws, culture, and school curriculum. Avoiding unplanned pregnancy, cultivating devoted fathers, and promoting adoption are emphases our churches should embrace.

This education process will not be easy. A recent study of American women's views on adoption revealed the following numbers:

> [Their] primary sources of information include: family (41%), medical professionals (34%) and friends/peers (25%), followed by counselors/psycho-

---

Dissent, The majority opinion "says that from the very moment of fertilization, a woman has *no rights* to speak of," portraying "a government controlling *all private choices*" (p. 7), "depriv[ing] a woman of *all choice*" (p. 24), "overriding *all rights* of the pregnant woman" (p. 8), that "*no factual developments have undermined Roe and Casey*" (p. 38), and that "to the majority 'balance' is a dirty word, as moderation is a foreign concept" (p. 12), the "Court has *wrenched this choice from women* and given it to the States" (p. 52), and "The majority has overruled Roe and Casey *for one and only one reason*: because it has always despised them, and now it has the votes to discard them" (p. 33).

[3] Dobbs dissent. P. 49.
[4] Thomas K. Johnson, "Is Human Dignity Earned or Is Human Dignity a Gift?" World of Theology, 2021, 34. https://www.academia.edu/45429707/Is_Human_Dignity_Earned_or_Is_Human_Dignity_a_Gift.

logists (20%), no one (20%), and Planned Parenthood (17%). Church and religious leaders ranked seventh on the list at only 12%.

As for how much weight different influences carry in their decision-making on whether to raise, adopt, or abort their child, religious beliefs and convictions were the fifth-most important factor among all women surveyed (15%) and somewhat surprisingly, third among self-identified Christians.[5]

Evangelicals must become trusted, relevant voices in the global abortion discussion. We are at our best when we take two steps:

1. Touch the conscience with Scripture to foster a culture that appreciates the birth of babies. My chapter on the Sixth Commandment in *The Decalogue Project* details many useful passages, but one of them poignantly celebrates that God 'did not kill me before I came from the womb, making my pregnant mother's womb my grave forever.'[6] Verses like this and Psalm 139:13-16 that are written in first person are especially effective in warming cold hearts.
2. Serve women facing an unwanted pregnancy. Meet practical needs and advocate for governments to protect innocent life.

Each step is important as we walk forward from the historic *Dobbs* decision.

Psalm 139:13-16 (NET)

Certainly, you made my mind and heart;
you wove me together in my mother's womb.
I will give you thanks because your deeds are awesome and amazing.
You knew me thoroughly;
my bones were not hidden from you, when I was made in secret
and sewed together in the depths of the earth.
Your eyes saw me when I was inside the womb.
All the days ordained for me were recorded in your scroll
before one of them came into existence.

---

[5] George Barna, "Adoption and Its Competitors" (Arizona Christian University: Opt Institute, 2022). https://assets.website-files.com/6233b9dee4e10c08418d3e8d/628d006165dae498e0e928e4_Adoption%20%26%20Its%20Competitors.pdf.

[6] Jeremiah 20:17, New English Translation.

Homosexuality and the Commandments

The Editors

For several centuries Christians have regarded homosexual practice as contrary to God's will in a manner that is similar to the way in which many other sins are contrary to the moral will of God. The primary basis for this conviction has been the inclusion of homosexual actions in biblical lists of sins which believers must avoid. In recent years, as many countries have decriminalized homosexuality and allowed homosexual marriage, there have been numerous attempts to reinterpret the relevant biblical texts. These new interpretations are sometimes called "revisionist" interpretations, and this entire effort is sometimes called "a new hermeneutic." Though it is difficult to summarize the several revisionist interpretations of scripture, many such attempted reinterpretations claim the Bible only rejects abusive homosexuality, which was commonly tolerated in parts of antiquity, and does not reject some modern forms of homosexual practice that include consent and marriage.

The editors of this volume recognize that it is possible for our churches to misinterpret scripture, but, we believe, most of the current revisionist interpretations of scripture regarding homosexuality are misinterpretations that can lead to destructive results in the lives of individuals and our churches. It is beyond the scope of this book to address all the relevant questions, but one of the regional organizations of the church in which we (William S. Barker and Thomas K. Johnson) are ordained ministers has developed a lengthy and careful study. We would refer pastors and scholars to the text cited below in the footnote.[1] We would also ask readers to consider the following Biblical texts carefully. Please note that, though we quote Leviticus 20, we believe that the Old Testament rules for criminal punishment were intended for a particular time and place in history. Quotations are from the ESV.

---

[1] *Homosexuality And the Gospel Of Grace: Faithfulness To The Lord's Calling In An Age Of Sexual Autonomy*, Missouri Presbytery, Presbyterian Church in America, October 17, 2017; https://drive.google.com/file/d/1iBLGL_2YhsIcI9_kZCBxLZHSYXWhFeLQ/view.

Leviticus 18:19-23

You shall not lie sexually with your neighbor's wife and so make yourself unclean with her. You shall not give any of your children to offer them to Molech, and so profane the name of your God: I am the Lord. You shall not lie with a male as with a woman; it is an abomination. And you shall not lie with any animal and so make yourself unclean with it, neither shall any woman give herself to an animal to lie with it: it is perversion.

Leviticus 20:10-13

If a man commits adultery with the wife of his neighbor, both the adulterer and the adulteress shall surely be put to death. If a man lies with his father's wife, he has uncovered his father's nakedness; both of them shall surely be put to death; their blood is upon them. If a man lies with his daughter-in-law, both of them shall surely be put to death; they have committed perversion; their blood is upon them. If a man lies with a male as with a woman, both of them have committed an abomination; they shall surely be put to death; their blood is upon them.

Romans 1:24-27

Therefore God gave them up in the lusts of their hearts to impurity, to the dishonoring of their bodies among themselves, because they exchanged the truth about God for a lie and worshiped and served the creature rather than the Creator, who is blessed forever! Amen. For this reason God gave them up to dishonorable passions. For their women exchanged natural relations for those that are contrary to nature; and the men likewise gave up natural relations with women and were consumed with passion for one another, men committing shameless acts with men and receiving in themselves the due penalty for their error.

I Corinthians 6:9-11

Or do you not know that the unrighteous will not inherit the kingdom of God? Do not be deceived: neither the sexually immoral, nor idolaters, nor adulterers, nor men who practice homosexuality, nor thieves, nor the greedy, nor drunkards, nor revilers, nor swindlers will inherit the kingdom of God. And such were some of you. But you were washed, you were sanctified, you were justified in the name of the Lord Jesus Christ and by the Spirit of our God.

I Timothy 1:8-11

> Now we know that the law is good, if one uses it lawfully, understanding this, that the law is not laid down for the just but for the lawless and disobedient, for the ungodly and sinners, for the unholy and profane, for those who strike their fathers and mothers, for murderers, the sexually immoral, men who practice homosexuality, enslavers, liars, perjurers, and whatever else is contrary to sound doctrine, in accordance with the gospel of the glory of the blessed God with which I have been entrusted.

Scripture Index

Genesis
1 205
1:1-2 30
1:1-2:3 ...116, 117, 122
1:3 205
1:20-21 30
1:26 .... 83, 203, 231
1:26-28 95
1:26-2:2 122
1:27 .... 145, 151
1:27-28 30
2:2 ..115, 116, 122, 124
2:2-3 .... 113, 114
2:2-3 116
2:4 117
2:4-3:24 117
2:15 196
2:17 55
2:27 122
3 32
4:1 151
4:1-10 167
4:10 145
6:5 225
7:17 100
8:21 225
9:6 .... 54, 181
13:10-13 229
15:6 .... 58, 59
16:7-13 83
21:16 100
21:17-18 83
22:11-18 83
26:5 .... 54, 58
31 205
31:11-13 83
32:25 148
40:13 100
45:8 135

Exodus
3:6-8 82
4 35
4:15a 35
4:10 35
4:15-16 35
4:10b 35
4:15b 35
4:16b 35
6:30 35
7:1-2 35
7:2 35
7:14 134
8:19 41
9:29 14
10:1 134
12:14-20 117
14:13 53
16:30 127
16:34 42
16:26ff 54
17:8-16 56
17:14 40
19 .... 20, 40, 75
19-24 41
19:4 76
19:13 76
19:16 76
19:16-25 114
20 54
20:1-17 .... 41, 50, 87
20:2 .... 9, 53, 77, 88
20:3 46
20:4 46
20:4-6 88
20:7 .... 47, 99
20:8-11 .... 47, 115
20:9 123
20:10 115
20:11 115
20:12 .... 47, 133, 142
20:13 .... 47, 66
20:14 47
20:15 .... 47, 151, 191
20:16 .... 47, 205
20:17 .... 47, 219
20:19 76
20:20 19
20:22 40
20:22-23 76
20:11b 115, 116
21:2 117
21:16 192
21:17 136
21:18 209
21:22-25 147
21:33-34 67
22:1-2 65
22:2-3 67
23:8 48
23:10-11 117
24:1-8 .... 40, 42
24:4 40
24:12 41
25:16 42
25:21 42
25:31 148
27:21 42
30:6 42
30:26 42
30:36 42
31:12-14 55
31:16-17 120
31:18 .... 41, 114, 132
32:1 90
32:16 41
32:8b 89
33:3 57
34:1 114
34:6 37
34:6-7 100
34:10 42
34:27 .... 40, 41, 42
34:28 .... 41, 42
37:17 148
39:30 40
40:20-21 114
40:21 42

Leviticus
1:2-3 48
4-5 56
5:1 213
9:11-13 73

16:30 56	4:16 91	**Joshua**
16:31 118	4:19 91	2:6 67
17:11 150	4:24 91	5:10 118
18:4 51	4:40 18	5:13-15 83
18:5 .... 55, 57	5 50	7 198
18:19-23 252	5:1-33 11	
19:3 134	5:4-5 .... 40, 114	**Judges**
19:11-13 191	5:6 .... 53, 178	5:7 135
19:12 102	5:6-12 87	
19:13 .... 72, 73	5:12-15 115	**1. Samuel**
19:16 209	5:14 118	9:25 67
19:18 .... 59, 63, 66	5:15 115	15:22 65
19:35-36 72	5:16 133	17:28 209
20:10 58	5:17 167	21:1-6 122
20:10-13 252	5:21 .... 219, 220	30:26 209
21:20 119	5:22 .... 41, 114	
23:4-8 117	5:29 18	**2. Samuel**
23:15-22 118	6:4-5 77	11 151
23:22 118	6:4-6 59	12 198
23:24 118	7:8 59	14:14 166
23:32 127	7:9 179	16:22 67
23:33-43 117	7:25 224	
23:35-36 118	9:4-5 56	**1. Kings**
24:3 42	9:10 41	21 198
25:1-7 117	10:1-5 114	21:4 220
25:8 117	12:21 16	21:17-19 199
25:8-55 117	15:1-11 117	22 101
25:8-55 121	15:12-18 117	22:19 149
26:34-5 127	16:9-12 118	
	16:13-17 117	**2. Kings**
Numbers	16:18-18:22 142	2:12 135
5:27 148	16:19 48	4:19-20 101
8:4 148	17:6 205	4:23 118
15:30 56	18:9-12 101	23:21-23 118
15:34 55	19:15 205	
15:32ff 55	21:18-21 136	**1. Chronicles**
17:4 42	22:8 .... 16, 67	7:14 189
17:7 42	23:1 119	23:30-32 117
17:8-10 42	23:24-25 68	30:1-27 118
25:12 120	24:6 68	35:1-19 118
28:9-10 122	24:7 192	36:21 127
28:16-25 117	24:10-11 48	
28:26-31 118	24:14 72	**Ezra**
28:33-36 117	24:14-15 73	6:19-22 118
29:1-6 118	25:4 72	
29:12-39 117	25:13-16 .... 72, 192	**Nehemia**
35 191	27:18 68	1:9 149
	28:58 134	2:10 220
Deuteronomy	30:4 149	8:16 67
4 90	30:11-14 57	9:6 149
4:13 .... 41, 114	31:9-13 117	9:29 55

Scripture Index

10:33 117

Esther
5:13 220

Job
7:3a 100
10:11-12 151
23:12 70
29:8 140
29:15-16 68
Psalm12:2a 100

Psalms
1:1-2 7
9:7-11 119
15:1-3 207
15:3 209
18 58
18:2-3 58
18:20-24 58
18:30 58
18:35 58
18:46 58
19:1 28
19:1-6 31
19:7-11 78
19:10 55
19:8b 177
23:3 99
29:10 119
32:1-2 59
33:10-11 91
47:1-9 119
50:1-2 119
51 .... 58, 65
51:5 147
62:8 180
76:2 119
76:8 119
78:68-69 119
80:1 119
80:14 119
82:3-4 146
89:29 119
93:1-2 119
95:1-7 119
96:10-13 119
97:8-9 119
98:4-6 119
110:1 83

112:9-10 220
119:47 78
119:92-93 64
119:97 20
127:3 151
129:6 67
132:8 .... 116, 119
132:13-14 ...... 119, 120
132:14 .... 116, 119
134:3 119
139:1-3 188
139:13 147
139:13-16 250
139:15-16 147
139:23-24a 188
143:2 55
146:10 119

Proverbs
6:30-31 192
14:5 208
14:25 208
15:16-17 66
15:27 48
16:8 66
16:11 71
17:1 66
17:8 48
20:10 71
20:23 71
31:8-9 213

Ecclesiastes
7:20 .... 55, 225
7:29 32

Isaiah
6:5 32
6:5-8 36
15:3 67
16:3 149
22:1 67
24:20 134
37:27 67
40:8 141
42:4 63
44:2 151
54:10 120
54:13 120
56-66 119
56:1 119

56:1-8 119
56:2 119
56:3-8 119
56:4 119
56:6 119
58:6-7 120
58:7 150
58:13-14 120
60:17c 120
61:1-11 119
61:1-2 121
66:1 .... 116, 119, 120
66:12 120
66:22-24 119
66:23 117

Jeremiah
1:5 147
1:5-9 36
3:1 209
5:2 102
6:10 57
7 65
9:26 57
17:19-27 119
20:17 250
22:13 73
27:9 101
31:33ff 63
36:4 36
45:1 36
48:38 67

Lamentations
3:22-23 180

Ezekiel
11:19-20 63
34:25 120
37:26 120
45:9-12 72
46:1 .... 118, 120
46:4 120
46:12 120

Daniel
4:35 149
9:11a 189
9:5 189
9:19 189
9:17b 189

9:18b 189

Hosea
3:1 209
6:6 ...... 65, 122
12:7 72

Amos
3:7-8 40
8:4-5 72
8:4-6 71
8:4-6 192
8:5 118

Jona
4:2 94

Mica
6:10-11 72

Habakkuk
3:1-19 40

Zephaniah
3:19 149

Zechiariah
8:16 208

Malachi
2:5 120
3:5 101

Wisdom
13:1 31

Matthew
4:17 19
5:17 45
5:17-19 48
5:17-19 60
5:19 124
5:21 172
5:21-22 49
5:21-24 96
5:27-28 49
5:28 ...... 9, 213
5:34 103
6:8-13 111
6:9 47
7:1 209

7:12 ...... 151, 218
7:22-23 102
9:13 65
10:27 67
12 213
12:1 122
12:1-8 121
12:5 122
12:7 65
12:9-14 ...... 121, 123
12:10-12 67
12:12 ...... 123, 124
12:15 213
12:22–23 213
12:24 213
12:34-37 214
15:4 133
18:15 ...... 216, 217
18:15-16 216
18:16 ...... 216, 217
19:6 150
19:8 150
19:16-19 192
19:18-19 46
22:34-40 42
22:37 219
22:37-38 185
22:37-40 ...... 9, 59, 132
22:37-40 204
22:39 ...... 185, 219
23:13 188
24:17 67
28:18-20 7
28:19 84

Mark
1:21-28 121
1:29-31 121
2:4 67
2:23-28 121
2:25-26 124
2:25-28 122
2:27 128
2:28 122
3:1-6 121
3:4 123
3:6 123
7:9-13 137
7:10 133
7:19 63
10:9 150

10:19 72
12:29-31 80
16:2 125

Luke
1:5-6 58
1:41-44 146
4:16 122
4:16-21 121
4:31-37 121
4:38-39 121
5:19 67
6:1-5 121
6:6-11 121
6:7 123
6:9 123
9:51-56 93
9:54 93
10:7 72
10:30-35 167
12:41-48 57
13:10-17 ...... 121, 123
13:15-17 67
13:16 124
14:1-6 121
14:4-6 67
19:1-10 199
52:55-56 93

John
1 203
1:14 ...... 82, 184
1:14,18 188
1:17 79
1:29 33
5:1-18 121
5:17 124
5:18 124
7:14-24 121
8:29 180
9:1-41 121
10:34-35 35
12:1-6 199
14:6 ...... 33, 84, 203
14:15 59
14:23-24 59
15:5 225
15:10 59
20:12 125
20:19 125

Acts
- 7:38 ... 55
- 7:51 ... 57
- 7:53 ... 57
- 10:44-45 ... 211
- 11:26 ... 211
- 13:38-39 ... 61
- 14:15 ... 46
- 17:25-28 ... 31
- 17:29 ... 46
- 20:7 ... 125

Romans
- 1:5 ... 53, 59
- 1:17 ... 79
- 1:18-23 ... 36
- 1:19-20 ... 31
- 1:21 ... 17, 89
- 1:24-27 ... 252
- 1:25 ... 89
- 1:28-32 ... 131
- 1:29 ... 131
- 1:29–30 ... 131
- 1:30 ... 131
- 1:32 ... 62
- 1:20b ... 36
- 1:20b-21 ... 32
- 2:14-15 ... 19
- 2:23 ... 57
- 2:26 ... 57, 62
- 3:9-19 ... 225
- 3:20 ... 18, 50
- 3:25-26 ... 61
- 4:17 ... 147
- 5 ... 55
- 5:12-15 ... 54
- 5:12-21 ... 32
- 5:18 ... 55
- 6 ... 61
- 6:1 ... 61
- 6:14 ... 45
- 6:15 ... 61
- 6:16 ... 61
- 6:17 ... 61
- 7:5 ... 18
- 7:6 ... 45
- 7:7 ... 48
- 7:7-9 ... 219
- 7:7-8 ... 220
- 7:12 ... 55
- 7:14 ... 55
- 7:18-19 ... 225
- 7:22 ... 61
- 7,7-8 ... 224
- 8:1 ... 62
- 8:1-2 ... 61
- 8:3 ... 45, 225
- 8:4 ... 62
- 7,7:9-14 ... 224
- 10:4 ... 79
- 10:6 ... 58
- 11:7 ... 57
- 12:20 ... 46
- 12:21 ... 166
- 13 ... 143, 166
- 13:8-10 ... 47, 63, 193
- 13:8-9 ... 46
- 13:9 ... 47, 220
- 14:5 ... 128
- 14:5-6 ... 125, 126
- 16:26 ... 53, 59

1. Corinthians
- 6:9-11 ... 252
- 6:19 ... 150
- 7:19 ... 63
- 9:9 ... 72
- 10:10 ... 220
- 10:24 ... 227
- 10:31 ... 51
- 12 ... 143
- 12:27 ... 186
- 13:4-5 ... 227
- 13:5 ... 184
- 16:1-2 ... 125, 126
- 16:2 ... 125

2. Corinthians
- 3:7 ... 55
- 3:18 ... 92
- 5:14-21 ... 92
- 5:21 ... 60
- 13:5 ... 94

Galatians
- 1:6 ... 126
- 3:24 ... 79
- 4:4 ... 122
- 4:10 ... 125, 126
- 5:17 ... 225
- 5:22-23 ... 179
- 5:26 ... 220
- 6:1 ... 216, 217
- 6:2 ... 63

Ephesians
- 4:11 ... 102
- 4:15 ... 215
- 4:25 ... 47, 207
- 4:28 ... 47, 193
- 4:30 ... 97
- 5:3-4 ... 227
- 5:21-6:9 ... 143
- 5:22 ... 136
- 6 ... 133
- 6:2 ... 47
- 6:4 ... 135

Philippians
- 2:7-8 ... 122
- 2:8 ... 60
- 2:10-11 ... 103
- 4:7 ... 8

Colossians
- 2:16 ... 121, 126
- 2:16-17 ... 125
- 2:17 ... 121
- 3:5 ... 47, 220, 222

2. Thessalonians
- 3:10-12 ... 196

1. Timothy
- 1:8-11 ... 62, 253
- 1:9-12 ... 193
- 1:10-11 ... 63
- 1:15 ... 200
- 5:17 ... 136
- 5:17-18 ... 66, 73

2. Timothy
- 1:10 ... 60
- 2:19 ... 103
- 3:16 ... 51
- 3:16-17 ... 35

Titus
- 3:8 ... 57

Hebrews
- 1:2 ... 126
- 1:3 ... 231

Reference	Page
2:5-9	126
2:9	231
3:7-4:13	126
4:9	126, 127
5:8-9	60
7:25	95
9:15	61
9:22	60
9:26	126
9:28	126, 127
10:1	60, 121
10:4	60
10:26	62
10:27	56
10:23b	180
12:17	56
13:4	47
13:5	201

James
1:25	63

2:8	63
2:10	178
2:17	57
3:2	225
3:2-13	225
3:9-12	211
3:14,16	220
4:11	207
5:4	72, 73

1. Peter
2:9	76
2:13-14	136
Exodus 19:11	76

2. Peter
1:20	35
1:21	35, 50
2:1-14	222
2:12-13	224

1. John
1:5-7	185
1:8,10	225
3:18-19	186
3:22	186
5:2-3	185
5:3	17

3. John
12	208

Revelation
1:10	129
1:10-11	125
14:12	60
21	203, 204
21:8	47
22	204
22:3-4	231

Contributors

Listed Alphabetically by Surname

Pierre Berthoud served as professor of Old Testament at the Free Reformed Seminary of Aix-en-Provence (now the Faculté Jean Calvin), where he also taught apologetics, from 1975 to 2012. He also served as Doyen (Dean) of the seminary for 19 years, and in 2012 he was appointed President of the Board of the seminary. He has been chairman of Scripture Union Europe, a trustee of the *Parvis des Arts*, and was president of the Fellowship of European Evangelical Theologians from 2008 to 2020.

Glenn N. Davies, Ph.D., D.D., served as Anglican Bishop of North Sydney, Australia, from 2001 to 2013 and then as the 12th Archbishop of Sydney from 2013 until his retirement in March 2021. He chaired EFAC (Evangelical Fellowship in the Anglican Communion) Australia for ten years and has been a board member of the Lausanne Consultation on Evangelization since 2011.

Leah Farish, J.D., a civil rights attorney based in Tulsa, Oklahoma, is host of the Conversation Balloons podcast, which is available on Spotify, Amazon Music, Google Podcasts, Apple Podcasts, and other platforms. She has published books and articles and taught in area colleges in the field of U.S. Constitutional Law for more than 25 years. She also works on humanitarian projects in the Middle East and in North Africa. She is a member of a Presbyterian Church in America (PCA) congregation in Tulsa. Website: https://leahfarish.com/.

Davi Charles Gomes, Ph.D., was installed as International Director of World Reformed Fellowship (WRF) in October 2017. Before transitioning full-time into his role at WRF in the beginning of 2020, he was Chancellor of Mackenzie Presbyterian University in São Paulo, which has a student enrollment of more than 50,000 in six locations in Brazil. A minister of the Presbyterian Church of Brazil, he is president of his denomination's Commission on Inter-Ecclesiastical Relations.

Risimati Hobyane, Ph.D., is Associate Professor of Theology and Director of the School for Ancient Language and Text Studies, North-West University in Potchefstroom, Republic of South Africa. He is an expert in New Testament and Septuagint studies.

Thomas K. Johnson, Ph.D., is Senior Theological Advisor to the World Evangelical Alliance (WEA), which represents and connects over 600 million Christians in 143 countries. He also serves as WEA Special Envoy to the Vatican and as Special Envoy to Engage Humanitarian Islam. He has long been a foremost international Protestant voice on human rights and religious freedom, including numerous publications and consulting with diplomats and religious leaders from around the globe.

Diane Langberg, Ph.D., is Director of a group counseling practice in suburban Philadelphia, Pennsylvania, staffed by Christian psychologists, social workers, and counselors. She is a former member of the World Reformed Fellowship Board of Directors and the former Chair of the Executive Board of the American Association of Christian Counselors. She is Co-Chair of the American Bible Society's Trauma Advisory Council. She is a member of a Presbyterian Church in America (PCA) congregation in Willow Grove, Pennsylvania.

Samuel T. Logan, Jr., Ph.D., currently serves as Associate International Director of the World Reformed Fellowship (WRF), after ten years in the senior position of WRF. His previous positions include Academic Dean, President, and Chancellor of Westminster Theological Seminary (PA). He has served on the Executive Committee of the Association of Theological Schools, and on two occasions, he was a Visiting Fellow at Christ's College, Cambridge.

Kin Yip Louie, Ph.D., serves as Heavenly Blessings Professor of Theological Studies at the China Graduate School of Theology in Hong Kong. He is the author of *The Beauty of the Triune God: The Theological Aesthetics of Jonathan Edwards* (Princeton, 2013). He also serves on the Board of Directors of the World Reformed Fellowship.

Contributors

Fergus MacDonald is a retired minister and former Moderator of the General Assembly of the Free Church of Scotland. He is Chair of the Scottish Evangelical Theological Society. From 1994 to 1998, he was the Executive Chair of the Lausanne Movement and continues as one of the honorary chairmen. He also serves on the Board of Directors of the World Reformed Fellowship.

Andrew T. B. McGowan, Ph.D., is Director of the Rutherford Centre for Reformed Theology and Professor of Theology in the University of Highlands and Islands. He was Principal of the Highland Theological College from its inception in 1994 until 2009. He is President of the Scottish Evangelical Theological Society, and he is a Minister of the Church of Scotland. He is a member of the World Reformed Fellowship Board of Directors and chairs its Theological Commission.

Robert Norris, Ph.D., is a native of Wales. He served as Senior Pastor of Fourth Presbyterian Church (Evangelical Presbyterian Church [EPC]) in Bethesda, Maryland, from 1984 until 2015, at which time he transitioned to the role of Teaching Pastor. Dr. Norris has served as an adjunct professor at Reformed Theological Seminary, teaching courses in theology and church history. He currently serves as Chairman of the Board of Directors of the World Reformed Fellowship.

Thomas Schirrmacher, Archbishop and Prof. Dr. theol., Dr. phil., PhD, DD has been Secretary General of the World Evangelical Alliance, which represents Protestant churches belonging to 143 National Evangelical Alliances with a total of 600 million members, since March 2021. Before that, he was the WEA's Associate Secretary General for Theological Concerns (Theology, Theological Education, Intrafaith and Interfaith Relations, Religious Freedom, Research) and director of the International Institute for Religious Freedom (Bonn, Cape Town, Toronto, Colombo, Brasilia), the world's largest research network involved in supporting religious freedom and opposing the persecution of Christians and other religions or worldviews.

Daniel Weiss is the executive director of the Sexual Integrity Leadership Summit (https://sexualintegrityleaders.com/) which equips, supports, and collaborates with Christian leaders to promote Gospel-centered sexuality in the Church. Daniel has a passion for the sexually broken and the need for pastors, parents, and Christian leaders to respond with courage, compassion, and truth to the sexual challenges of our age. In addition to his professional work, Daniel and his wife strive to create a home of faith, forgiveness, laughter, and love in the Wisconsin countryside where they live with their five children. Daniel's writing is featured at https://www.faithfilled.family/.

John P. Wilson is a minister of the Presbyterian Church of Australia. He has taught practical theology and church history at the Presbyterian Theological College (Victoria). He is now Clerk of Assembly to the Presbyterian Church of Victoria and Deputy Clerk of Assembly to the Presbyterian Church of Australia. He also serves on the Board of Directors of the World Reformed Fellowship.

David Zadok is a former Israeli military officer, and he currently serves as Pastor of Grace and Truth Christian Fellowship in Gedera, Israel. He is also Director of HaGefen Publishing Company in Rishon LeTzion, Israel, and he has written on such subjects as "A Messianic Jewish View on the Israeli Palestinian Conflict."

www.ingramcontent.com/pod-product-compliance
Lightning Source LLC
Chambersburg PA
CBHW050845230426
43667CB00012B/2156